Colloquial
Slovene

The Colloquial Series

The following languages are available in the Colloquial series:

Albanian	Italian
Amharic	Japanese
Arabic (Levantine)	Malay
Arabic of Egypt	Norwegian
Arabic of the Gulf and	Panjabi
Saudi Arabia	Persian
Bulgarian	Polish
Cambodian	Portuguese
Cantonese	Romanian
Chinese	* Russian
Czech	Serbo-Croat
Danish	Slovene
Dutch	Somali
English	* Spanish
Estonian	Spanish of Latin America
French	Swedish
German	Thai
* Greek	Turkish
Gujarati	Ukrainian
Hindi	Vietnamese
Hungarian	Welsh
Indonesian	

Accompanying cassette(s) are available for the above titles.
*Accompanying CDs are also available.

Colloquial
Slovene

A Complete Language Course

Andrea Albretti

London and New York

First published 1995
by Routledge
11 New Fetter Lane, London EC4P 4EE

Simultaneously published in the USA and Canada
by Routledge
29 West 35th Street, New York, NY 10001

© 1995 Andrea Albretti

Typeset in Times Ten by Florencetype Ltd, Stoodleigh, Devon

Printed and bound in England by Clays Ltd, St Ives PLC

Illustrations by Rebecca Moy

British Library Cataloguing in Publication Data
A catalogue record for this book is available from the British Library

Library of Congress Cataloguing in Publication Data
A catalogue record for this book has been requested

ISBN 0–415–08946–8 (book)
ISBN 0–415–08947–6 (cassettes)
ISBN 0–415–08948–4 (book and cassettes course)

Contents

Introduction

The country

Slovenia is one of the youngest and smallest European countries. Its independence dates from 1991. Before that it was the northernmost republic of Yugoslavia.

Geographically, it borders Italy, Austria, Hungary and Croatia. It includes a part of the Alps and also has some 40 kilometres of coastline on the Adriatic; a joke goes that if all the Slovenes went to the seaside at once they could only stand there on one foot. Nevertheless, it is a Mediterranean country and the Slovenes are proud of their sea.

The political, cultural and commercial capital of Slovenia is Ljubljana.

The Slovene language

The Slovene language is spoken by the 2 million people living in the Republic of Slovenia, by Slovene minority groups mainly in Austria, Italy and Hungary, and by emigrants scattered around America, Australia, New Zealand and elsewhere in the world. Slovene belongs to the Indo-European family of languages.

Literacy and general culture reached the Slovenes in the sixteenth century during the period of the Reformation. The first Slovene book was printed in 1551, the first translation of the Bible into Slovene was in 1584, and a book on Slovene grammar followed. Grammatically, Slovene is rather complicated. It is an inflectional language, which means that it has cases and endings added to the words, which you will learn about in this book.

Slovenia is divided into eight regions, each of which has its own dialect. Every Slovene will be happy to tell you how, had he spoken

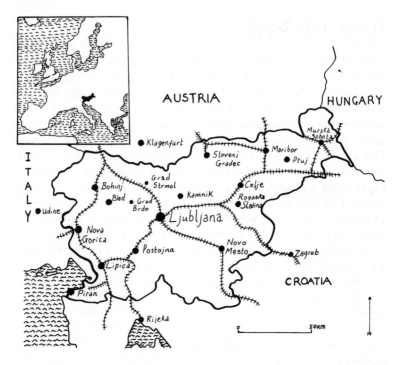

in his dialect, he would not necessarily be understood by a speaker of another dialect. These dialects are spoken at home. At school, every Slovene is soon encouraged to speak standard Slovene in public. The Slovene taught in these lessons is that of 'standard' Slovene, but colloquial in style and vocabulary, and it will be understood by all Slovenes.

About this book

This book is intended for beginners and requires no previous knowledge of the language. It can also be used by students with some knowledge of Slovene to revise or to improve their language skills. By working through the lessons you will be building up words and phrases and learning how they are connected and in which contexts they are used. The language used in the lessons is mostly conversational. As far as possible, the dialogues reflect the kind of language appropriate for the subject of the lesson. By the end of this course you will be able to communicate in most everyday situations.

Using this book

Look at the 'Guide to the alphabet and pronunciation' section first; this will give you some idea of how the language is pronounced. The body of the book consists of thirteen lessons. Each lesson follows the same pattern. You are first given a summary of what you will learn in the lesson. Lessons are divided into two or three parts, each beginning with a *dialogue*, which is the core of the part. The English introduction sets the scene for the dialogue, where, through an everyday situation, you will learn new vocabulary, expressions and grammatical structures, all discussed in *language points*, a section which follows the dialogue. You are always given examples to show you where particular rules apply and where you would use that particular structure. Every part of a lesson is followed by *exercises* where you are given an opportunity to revise and practise what you have learned and to use the language introduced in that part in similar situations. A lesson is completed with the *dialogue for comprehension*, which you should be able to understand.

The answers to the exercises and the translation of the dialogues for comprehension are given in the 'Key to exercises' section at the back of the book.

At the end of the book you are also given a summary of the grammatical points you have learned in the 'Reference grammar' section. You can refer to this section if you need a quick reference on a particular grammar point. Lastly there are 'Slovene–English' and 'English–Slovene' glossaries.

A guide to the alphabet and pronunciation

The alphabet 🔲

The Slovene alphabet (**abeceda**) has twenty-five letters. It differs from the English alphabet in that it has no letters *x*, *y*, *w* and *q*, (you will find them in spellings of foreign names, places, etc.) but the following three letters (known as **šumniki**) are added:

č *ch* as in *chocolate*, *chicken*
š *sh* as in *shop*, *ship*
ž *ge* as in *courgette*, or as the *s* in mea*s*ure

Here are the twenty-five Slovene letters. Each of them is pronounced in the same way as the italicized letters in the English words next to them. The translation of these words into Slovene is given.

a	*a*lphabet	**abeceda**	m	*m*other	**mama**
b	*b*ank	**banka**	n	*n*ature	**narava**
c	piz*z*a	**pica**	o	*o*pera	**opera**
č	*ch*ocolate	**čokolada**	p	*pepp*er	**poper**
d	*d*irector	**direktor**	r	*r*evolution	**revolucija**
e	*e*lectricity	**elektrika**	s	*s*alt	**sol**
f	*f*antasy	**fantazija**	š	*ch*ampagne	**šampanjec**
g	*g*orilla	**gorila**	t	*t*elevision	**televizija**
h	*h*ouse	**hiša**	u	m*oo*n	**luna**
i	*i*nformation	**informacija**	v	*v*illa	**vila**
j	*y*es	**ja**	z	*z*ebra	**zebra**
k	co*ff*ee	**kava**	ž	gara*g*e	**garaža**
l	*l*egend	**legenda**			

A simple guide to pronunciation

This is not a detailed account or an elocution lesson on how particular sounds are pronounced in particular places in Slovene literary language but a basic simple guide which should give you an idea of how the language is pronounced.

The Slovene language is mostly phonetic, which means that it is pronounced as it is written. Each letter has only one specific sound which makes reading and writing easy. It is very important to remember the correct sounds of the letters and once you have done so you will be able to read and write with hardly any mistakes.

Vowels

There are five vowels in Slovene: **a**, **e**, **i**, **o**, **u**. Each syllable contains a vowel. The letter **r** in some Slovene words replaces the vowel when it stands before a consonant, as in **rdeč** (red) or **rjav** (brown), or when it stands between two consonants, as in **Brnik** (the airport in Ljubljana) or in **vrt** (garden). The sound of each vowel is pure and very clear.

Even though stress marks are not placed over the letters, there are rules of stress to be observed in the pronunciation of the Slovene vowels (see below).

Consonants

There are twenty consonants in Slovene. They can be voiced or unvoiced. They are pronounced as they are spelt (refer to the alphabet).

The voiced consonants are: **b**, **d**, **g**, **j**, **l**, **m**, **n**, **r**, **v**, **z**, **ž**.
The unvoiced consonants are: **c**, **č**, **f**, **h**, **k**, **p**, **s**, **š**, **t**.

Look carefully at the letters **č**, **š**, and **ž**. Also note how you pronounce **j** and **h** in Slovene.

Certain letters will at times be grouped with certain other letters and have a slightly different pronunciation. The same happens when they occupy a certain position in the word. For example:

When **l** is at the end of a word or placed after any other consonant than **j** it is pronounced as **w** as in **bel** (white), **popoldan** (popowdan).

V is pronounced as **v** before vowels (**vaja** 'exercise', **voda** 'water'), before the consonants **r** (**vrt** 'garden', **vreme** 'weather') and before vowels within a word (**živeti** 'to live', **zvezek** 'notebook'). When **v** is at the end of the word, after a vowel or before a consonant (except for **r** and **l**) it is pronounced as **w**, as in **prav** (OK), **kovček** (suitcase). When **v** is at the beginning of the word or when it appears between consonants or before two or more consonants it is pronounced as **u** as in **vprašati** (to ask), **vhod** (entrance). The Slovene **r** is pronounced strongly, slightly rolled. It is pronounced as **er** when it stands before another consonant or when it stands between two consonants.

In a few words where they appear, two identical vowels or consonants are pronounced as one long one, as in **priimek** (surname), **oddelek** (department).

You should practise pronouncing these and other sounds throughout the book.

Stress

Stress marks are not marked in Slovene. In most cases only one syllable of the word is stressed, which means that this syllable is pronounced slightly more strongly than other syllables. It isn't possible to predict which syllable the stress will fall on – in words which are formed from the same root the stress is often on a different syllable – so the syllable which is stressed must be memorized. Initially it is best to stress each syllable equally. This way you will soon be able to read long sentences with the correct Slovene pronunciation. Most important is that all sounds, both vowels and consonants, are pronounced clearly, strongly and confidently.

1 Živio, Robert!

Hello, Robert!

In this lesson you will learn about:

- Some forms of greeting and saying farewell
- The personal and some possessive pronouns
- The present tense of 'to be'
- Some masculine and feminine nouns
- Ways of addressing and introducing people
- How to ask and answer some simple questions

Dialogue 1 🔲

Ali si utrujen?

Are you tired?

Robert, an English journalist, has flown to Ljubljana for a year, to work there. An old friend of his, Matej, picks him up at the airport. He goes through customs, collects his suitcase and sees Matej waiting for him

MATEJ: Živio, kako si?
ROBERT: Dobro, hvala. In ti?
MATEJ: Zelo dobro, hvala.
        Ali si utrujen?
ROBERT: Ja, malo.

MATEJ: *Hello, how are you?*
ROBERT: *Well, thank you. And you?*
MATEJ: *Very well, thank you.*
        Are you tired?
ROBERT: *Yes, a little.*

Vocabulary

živio	hello	**zelo**	very
kako si?	how are you?	**ali**	(indicates a question)
dobro	well, fine, good	**si**	are
hvala	thank you	**utrujen**	tired
in	and	**ja**	yes
ti	you	**malo**	a little

Language points

Meeting and greeting people in Slovenia

Slovenes usually introduce themselves by shaking hands and saying their surname and first name in more official situations or only a first name in casual situations.

Greetings

The standard greetings in Slovene are:

up to about 10 a.m.   **Dobro jutro**.   Good morning.

| between 10 a.m. and 6 p.m. | **Dober dan**. | Good day. |
| after 6 p.m. | **Dober večer**. | Good evening. |

You will see later in this lesson why we say *dobro* **jutro** but *dober* **dan**.

Farewells

| at any time of the day | **Na svidenje**. | Goodbye. |
| late at night (also before going to bed) | **Lahko noč**. | Good night. |

Friends usually greet each other with **Živio** (Hello) and **Adijo** (Bye).

Personal pronouns

jaz	(I)	**mi**	(we)
ti	(you)	**vi**	(you)
on	(he)	**oni**	(they)
ona	(she)		
ono	(it)		

Present tense of biti (to be)

In the dialogue Metej asked Robert **Ali si utrujen? Si** (are) is actually one of the forms of the verb **biti** (to be). **Biti** is an irregular verb. You must simply memorize its different forms.

(**jaz**)	**sem**	I am	(**mi**)	**smo**	we are
(**ti**)	**si**	you are	(**vi**)	**ste**	you are
(**on**)	**je**	he is	(**oni**)	**so**	they are
(**ona**)	**je**	she is			
(**ono**)	**je**	it is			

Unless you want to stress them, personal pronouns can be omitted when used as a subject because the ending of the verb indicates the person.

| letališče | airport |

For example:

Smo v Sloveniji. *rather than*
Mi smo v Sloveniji.   We are in Slovenia.

Sem utrujen. *rather than*
Jaz sem utrujen.   I am tired.

So na letališču. *rather than*
Oni so na letališču.   They are at the airport.

In the first few lessons the pronouns will be listed together with their verbs because it is easier to recognize the two together.

How to ask a question

Ali is used to indicate a question. You simply put it in front of the verb. You also reverse the word order, i.e. the verb comes before the personal pronoun. Note that Matej asks Robert: **Ali si utrujen?** (Are you tired?). Here are some more examples:

Jaz sem v Sloveniji.   I am in Slovenia.
Ali sem (jaz) v Sloveniji?   Am I in Slovenia?

On je utrujen.   He is tired.
Ali je (on) utrujen?   Is he tired?

The question word **ali** may, however, be omitted. As in the English translations of the examples below, you can show that you are asking a question by reversing the word order, i.e. putting the verb before the subject. Matej could have asked: **Si utrujen?** (Are you tired?). Some more examples:

Jaz sem v Sloveniji.   I am in Slovenia.
Sem (jaz) v Sloveniji?   Am I in Slovenia?

On je utrujen.   He is tired.
Je (on) utrujen?   Is he tired?

Countries

Here are a few Slovene names for countries:

država	country

Anglija	England	**Italija**	Italy
Slovenija	Slovenia	**Španija**	Spain
Amerika	America	**Francija**	France
Nemčija	Germany	**Rusija**	Russia

How to use v (in)

In Slovene the endings of nouns depend on their function in the sentence. When it is in subject position, for example, the name of the country is **Slovenija**. When it follows a preposition the ending of the noun changes. After the preposition **v** (in) the final **a** becomes **i**. You would, for example, say **v Sloveniji**, or **v Angliji**.

Exercise 1

Re-arrange these utterances to make a conversation:

Zelo sem utrujun.
Živio, kako si?
Zelo dobro, hvala, in ti?

Exercise 2

Greet or say farewell to these people:

1 It is 7 a.m. and you have met a neighbour at the bus stop.
2 It is 4 p.m. and you are leaving work.
3 It is 8 p.m. and you meet three friends in front of the cinema.
4 It is 11:30 p.m. and after having watched a television programme with your host family you are going to bed.
5 It is 2 p.m. and you meet your landlady on your way to work.
6 It is 7 p.m. and you meet someone you know slightly at a party.
7 It is 11 p.m. and you are leaving a friend's house.

Exercise 3

restavracija	restaurant
gostilna	pub

1 You get a surprise phone call from a friend and you are not sure where she is. Ask her if she is: in Italy / in Ljubljana / at the airport / in a restaurant / in a pub.

2 You are trying to trace an old friend, Milan. How would you ask someone if he is: in Germany / in Slovenia / in England / in America / in Spain?

3 You wake up after a nightmare and you have no idea where you are. How would you ask someone if you are at the airport / in Ljubljana / in Slovenia / at home / in a pub?

Exercise 4

Answer the questions using the personal pronouns:

danes	today
doma	at home

1 Ali je Robert utrujen?
  Ja, . . .
2 Ali je Tanja v Angliji?
  Ja, . . .
3 Ali je Sabina v Sloveniji?
  Ja, . . .
4 Ali smo mi danes doma?
  Ja, . . .
5 Ali je Sandra dobro?
  Ja, . . .

Exercise 5

Fill in the blanks in this dialogue:

SANDI: Dobro jutro, Peter. Kako . . . ?
PETER: Zelo . . ., hvala. In . . . ?
SANDI: Dobro, . . . Ali je Marko . . . Sloveniji?
PETER: Ja, Marko . . . v Ljubljani. In Sabina?
SANDI: Sabina je . . . Italiji.

Dialogue 2 ▣

Naprej!

Come in!

While Robert is in Slovenia he makes a social call at the house of Marko Koren. Mrs Koren answers the door

ROBERT:	Dober večer. Jaz sem Robert Brown.
	Je gospod Koren doma?
GOSPA KOREN:	Ja, je doma.
	Danes ni v službi.
MARKO KOREN:	O, dober večer. Kako ste?
ROBERT:	Dobro, hvala. In vi?
MARKO KOREN:	Dobro. Naprej, prosim!
	To je moja žena, Anita.

ROBERT:	*Good evening. I am Robert Brown.*
	Is Mr Koren at home?
MRS KOREN:	*Yes, he is (at home).*
	He is not at work today.
MARKO KOREN:	*Oh, good evening. How are you?*
ROBERT:	*Well, thank you. And you?*
MARKO KOREN:	*I'm fine. Please, come in!*
	This is my wife, Anita.

Vocabulary

obisk	a visit	**prosim**	please
ni	is not	**to je**	this is
v službi	at work	**moja**	my
naprej	come in	**žena**	wife

Language points

Familiar and polite forms of address

Slovene, like many other languages, has both familiar and formal pronouns for addressing people. **Ti** ('you', singular) is the familiar form used with friends, members of the family or children. **Vi** ('you', plural) is the polite form used when talking to people you don't know and in all official contexts.

When you are not sure which form to use it is always safer to use the polite form. People will soon tell you to use the familiar form if they want you to.

Addressing people

You address a man as **gospod** (Mr) and a woman as **gospa** (Mrs). (Note that Robert asks **Je gospod Koren doma?**)

You address an unmarried woman as **gospodična** (Miss). Slovene does not yet have an equivalent for 'Ms'.

When meeting people the usual question, 'How are you?', is **kako ste?** in polite form and **kako si?** in the familiar.

Note that the conversation between Robert and Matej, who are friends, was in the familiar form whilst the conversation between Robert and the people he visits was in the polite form.

Introducing people

When you introduce someone you say, as in English, 'This is ... ' Note that Mr Koren says: **To je moja žena**.

To je Robert.   This is Robert.

You use the expression **me veseli** when you are introduced to somebody. It means 'Nice to meet you'.

The negative form of biti (to be)

With most verbs you make the negative construction simply by putting a negative word before the verb (as we shall see in lesson 3). The verb 'to be', however, is irregular even in its negative form.

(jaz)	nisem	I am not	(mi)	nismo	we are not
(ti)	nisi	you are not	(vi)	niste	you are not
(on)	ni	he is not	(oni)	niso	they are not
(ona)	ni	she is not			
(ono)	ni	it is not			

Note that Mrs Koren says:

On *ni* **v službi.**   He *is not* at work.

Had he been at work she would have said:

On *je* **v službi.**   He *is* at work.

Answering questions which require a 'yes/no' answer

When you answer a question with **ja** (yes) or **ne** (no) you usually answer by repeating the information asked for.

Ali je gospod Koren doma?   Is Mr Koren at home?
Ja, gospod Koren je doma.   Yes, he is (at home).
Ne, gospod Koren ni doma.   No, he isn't (at home).

Masculine, feminine and neuter nouns

You will remember that in the first part of this lesson you learned

Dobro jutro.   Good morning.
Dober dan.   Good day.

Dobro is the neuter form of the adjective; **dober** is the masculine form. We say **dobro jutro** because **jutro** is a neuter noun and **dober dan** because **dan** is a masculine noun. The ending of the adjective always agrees with the ending of the noun.

There are three genders in Slovene: masculine, feminine and neuter. In English what is masculine by nature (man, father, boy) is referred to as 'he' and what is feminine by nature (woman, wife, girl) is referred to as 'she'. This rule, however, *does not* apply in Slovene: for example, **dekle** means 'girl' but it is of neuter gender. You must memorize the gender of the Slovene nouns. When important, the gender of the nouns will be indicated with the following abbreviations: m. (for masculine), f. (for feminine), n. (for neuter).

There are no definite rules for determining the gender. These few clues may be helpful:

1 Nouns ending in **a** are almost always feminine:

restavracija	restaurant	**mama**	mother
gostilna	pub	**gospa**	Mrs
žena	wife		

2 Nouns ending in a consonant are almost always masculine:

dan	day	**mož**	husband
večer	evening	**gospod**	Mr
prijatelj	friend		

3 Nouns ending in **o** or in **e** are almost always neuter:

letališče	airport	**okno**	window
jutro	morning	**delo**	work
dekle	girl		

Possessive pronouns

In Slovene the possessive pronouns (my, your, etc.) have a masculine, a feminine and a neuter form.

Masculine	Feminine	Neuter	
moj	**moja**	**moje**	my, mine
tvoj	**tvoja**	**tvoje**	your, yours
njegov	**njegova**	**njegovo**	his, its
njen	**njena**	**njeno**	her, hers
naš	**naša**	**naše**	our, ours
vaš	**vaša**	**vaše**	your, yours
njihov	**njihova**	**njihovo**	their, theirs

When the possessive pronouns are used as adjectives (as in 'my wife') they must agree with the noun they refer to.

In this lesson you will only practise the pronouns corresponding to 'my' and 'your'.

Exercise 6

Insert the correct form of the verb 'to be':

1 Robert ... malo utrujen.
2 Ali ... gospod Koren doma?

3 Mi ... v službi.
4 Jaz ... danes zelo utrujen.
5 Moja žena ... v Španiji.
6 Jaz ... v Ameriki.

Exercise 7

How would you introduce the following people to someone: your wife, Robert, your friend (male), Mr Koren, your husband.

Exercise 8

Are these statements about you true (T) or false (F)?

	zaseden	busy

1 Danes sem malo utrujen. T F
2 Moja žena je v Nemčiji. T F
3 Jaz sem v Angliji. T F
4 Danes nisem v službi. T F
5 Danes sem zelo zaseden. T F

Exercise 9

Ask if these people are at home: Bojan, Mrs Kobal, Marija, Mr Koren, Mrs Koren.

Exercise 10

Say that these people are not at work: Mr Dolenc, Jana, Samo, your wife, Mrs Koren.

Exercise 11

Choose the answers which fit the two dialogues in the lesson:

1 Ali je Robert v Sloveniji?
   (a) Ja, Robert je v Sloveniji.
   (b) Ne, Robert ni v Sloveniji.
2 Ali je Robert utrujen?
   (a) Ja, Robert je malo utrujen.
   (b) Ne, Robert ni utrujen.

3 Ali je gospod Koren v službi?
  (a) Ja, on je v službi.
  (b) Ne, on ni v službi.
4 Ali je gospa Koren doma?
  (a) Ja, ona je doma.
  (b) Ne, ona ni doma.
5 Ali je gospa Koren v Ameriki?
  (a) Ja, ona je v Ameriki.
  (b) Ne, ona ni v Ameriki.

Exercise 12

Answer these questions about yourself.

zvečer	in the evening

1 Ali si ti v Angliji?
2 Ali je tvoja žena v Sloveniji?
3 Ali si danes utrujen?
4 Ali si v službi?
5 Ali si danes zvečer doma?

Exercise 13

Match the response on the right with the statement or question on the left:

1 Živio, kako si?   (a) Ja, malo.
2 Ali si utrujen?   (b) Hvala.
3 Naprej!   (c) Me veseli.
4 Ali je gospa Koren doma?   (d) Dobro, hvala.
5 To je moja žena, Anita.   (e) Ne, gospa Koren ni doma.

Exercise 14

Are these words masculine, feminine or neuter?

1 gostilna   m.   f.   n.
2 jutro   m.   f.   n.
3 večer   m.   f.   n.
4 mama   m.   f.   n.
5 mož   m.   f.   n.

6 dan   m.   f.   n.
7 letališče   m.   f.   n.

Exercise 15 🔲

Pronunciation exercise. You'll have noticed that two or three consonants often follow one another. All of them have to be pronounced firmly. Let's practise:

Dobro jutro.
Živio, Branko.
On je moj prijatelj.
To je letališče Brnik.
Kako ste? Dobro, hvala.
Lahko noč.

Dialogue for comprehension 🔲

Robert has been invited to supper at the house of Mr Stopar (a friend of his friend, Matej), whom he has met once before. Find out where Robert's girlfriend is

punca	girlfriend	**ampak**	but
tukaj	here	**kako vam gre?**	how is it going?
tudi	also, too	**Brnik**	the airport just outside Ljubljana

GOSPOD STOPAR: Živio, Robert. Kako si?
ROBERT: Dobro, hvala. In ti?
GOSPOD STOPAR: O, jaz danes nisem dobro. Zelo sem utrujen. Naprej, prosim.
ROBERT: Hvala.
GOSPOD STOPAR: Robert, to je moja žena.
ROBERT: Me veseli.
GOSPA STOPAR: Me veseli, Robert.
GOSPOD STOPAR: In to je moj prijatelj, Tomaž Rataj.
TOMAŽ RATAJ: Dober večer, Robert. Kako vam gre? Ali je vaša punca tukaj?
ROBERT: Ne, ona ni tukaj.
TOMAŽ RATAJ: Ali je ona v Ljubljani?

ROBERT:	Ne, ona ni v Sloveniji. Ona je v Angliji. Ali je vaša žena tukaj?
TOMAŽ RATAJ:	Ne, ni. Ona je danes v službi.
ROBERT:	Ali je v Ljubljani?
TOMAŽ RATAJ:	Ja, ona je v službi na letališču Brnik. Jaz sem tudi v službi na letališču Brnik, ampak danes sem doma. Zelo sem utrujen.
ROBERT:	O, danes smo vsi zelo utrujeni!

2 Ali si v sredo doma?

Are you at home on Wednesday?

In this lesson you will learn about:

- Days of the week
- Countries and their inhabitants
- How to make arrangements on the telephone
- The present tense of 'to have' and some common phrases using this verb
- More nouns and adjectives and the way they are used
- How to ask and answer the questions 'who' and 'what' something is

Dialogue 1 ▣

Prosim!

Hello!

Denis has returned from his holidays in Spain. He has promised to show Sabina his photographs. He telephones her to arrange a day

SABINA: Prosim!
DENIS: Živio, Sabina. Denis tukaj. Imam fotografije.
Ali imaš v torek zvečer čas?
SABINA: Ne, žal mi je. V torek nimam časa.
Kaj pa v sredo?
DENIS: Ne, ob sredah imam jaz angleški tečaj.
In v četrtek?
SABINA: Ja, prav. V četrtek sem ves dan doma.
V četrtek zvečer! Se že veselim!
DENIS: Jaz tudi. Adijo!

SABINA: *Hello!*
Denis: *Hello, Sabina. This is Denis. I have the photographs.*
Have you got time on Tuesday evening?
SABINA: *No, I am sorry. I don't have time on Tuesday.*
What about Wednesday?
DENIS: *No, on Wednesdays I have my English course.*
And on Thursday?
SABINA: *Yes, OK. On Thursday I am at home all day.*
On Thursday evening! I am looking forward to it already!
DENIS: *So am I. Bye!*

Vocabulary

imaš	you have	**v sredo**	on Wednesday
v torek	on Tuesday	**prav**	fine, OK, correct
čas	time	**angleški tečaj**	English course
žal mi je	I am sorry	**ves dan**	all day
nimam	I don't have	**v četrtek**	on Thursday
kaj pa?	what about	**veselim se**	I am looking forward to

Note: The word **pa** has various meanings. It is used a lot in Slovene. It can be used as a conjunction word to mean 'and' or it can be used to mean 'about' as in **Kaj pa v sredo?** (What about on Wednesday?).

Language points

Speaking on the telephone

telefon	telephone
trenutek	moment

When you first answer the telephone you say **prosim**. If you are calling, it is polite to say who you are: for example, **Dober dan**, **Marko pri telefonu**, or **Marko tukaj**.

Pri telefonu literally means 'by the telephone'. In this context it simply means 'speaking'. If you don't introduce yourself the person at the other end might ask you: **Kdo je pri telefonu?** (Who is speaking?). If you are calling, for example, Marko's home number you ask: **Ali je Marko doma?** If you are calling him at work you say: **Ali je Marko tam?** In both cases, the person at the other end will probably say: **Samo trenutek!** or **Trenutek prosim!** meaning 'Just a moment!'

It is useful if you understand the names of important telephone numbers usually listed on the telephone or in any telephone box.

Pomembne telefonske številke	*Important telephone numbers*
policija	police
gasilci	fire brigade
prva pomoč	first aid
splošne informacije	general information
pomoč na cesti	car breakdown service
taksi	taxi service
turistične informacije	tourist information

Days of the week

The days of the week are:

ponedeljek	Monday	**petek**	Friday
torek	Tuesday	**sobota**	Saturday
sredo	Wednesday	**nedelja**	Sunday
četrtek	Thursday		

In Slovene the days of the week are spelt with a small letter. With the days of the week, *on* is expressed with the preposition **v**.

Note that when you use **v** the days of the week ending with **a** change their ending to **o**.

v ponedeljek	on Monday	**v petek**	on Friday
v torek	on Tuesday	**v soboto**	on Saturday
v sredo	on Wednesday	**v nedeljo**	on Sunday
v četrtek	on Thursday		

When a certain action takes place on a certain day of each week you use the preposition **ob** to express this.

Days of the week ending in **a** take an **h** ending and the others drop the semi-silent **e** and take an **ih** ending.

If you want to ask the question 'when' you say **kdaj?**

ob ponedeljkih	on Mondays	**ob petkih**	on Fridays
ob torkih	on Tuesdays	**ob sobotah**	on Saturdays
ob sredah	on Wednesdays	**ob nedeljah**	on Sundays
ob četrtkih	on Thursdays		

When you want to say that something is happening on a particular day, like 'this Tuesday', you say **ta torek**.

Present tense of imeti (to have)

In the dialogue Denis asks Sabina: **Ali imaš v torek čas?** He also says: **Ob sredah imam jaz angleški tečaj.** These show forms of the verb 'to have'.

(jaz)	**imam**	I have	**(mi)**	**imamo**	we have
(ti)	**imaš**	you have	**(vi)**	**imate**	you have
(on)	**ima**	he has	**(oni)**	**imajo**	they have
(ona)	**ima**	she has			
(ono)	**ima**	it has			

Negative form of imeti (to have)

Sabina answers: **V torek nimam časa. Nimam** is a negative form of the verb 'to have'.

(jaz)	**nimam**	I don't have	**(mi)**	**nimamo**	we don't have
(ti)	**nimaš**	you don't have	**(vi)**	**nimate**	you don't have
(on)	**nima**	he doesn't have	**(oni)**	**nimajo**	they don't have
(ona)	**nima**	she doesn't have			
(ono)	**nima**	it doesn't have			

Here are a few common expressions using 'to have'. You only need to conjugate 'to have' and you can refer to whoever you like. For example:

smola	bad luck
sreča	luck

Imaš prav.	You are right.
Nimajo prav.	They aren't right. (i.e. 'They are wrong'.)
Imam smolo.	I have bad luck.
Imam srečo.	I am lucky.
Nimam sreče.	I have no luck.

Note: You have seen that Sabina said in the dialogue **nimam časa**. **Sreča**, for example, means 'luck' but you say **imam srečo** or **nimam sreče**. The nouns following 'to have' get different endings and the nouns following a negative form of 'to have' also get different endings. These are case endings and you will see more about them later.

To be at home

Doma means 'at home'. It usually follows 'to be'. Note how Sabina says in the dialogue **V četrtek sem ves dan *doma***. Here are a few more examples, using **doma**:

Ob nedeljah sem zmeraj doma.	I'm always at home on Sundays.
Žal mi je, v torek nisem doma.	I'm sorry, I'm not at home on Tuesday.

Exercise 1

Match the words in the left column to those in the right:

Tuesday	**petek**
on Saturday	**ob nedeljah**
Wednesday	**torek**
on Sundays	**v soboto**
Friday	**ponedeljek**
Monday	**sreda**

Exercise 2

Ask your friend, Miran, if he has time on Tuesday / on Saturday / on Sundays / on Friday / on Mondays.

Exercise 3

Tell your friend that you're sorry but you don't have time on Tuesday / on Fridays / on Sunday / on Saturdays / on Monday.

Exercise 4

1 Say that you are at work on these days: on Monday, on Wednesday, on Friday.
2 Say that your female friend is at home on these days: on Tuesday, on Thursday, on Saturday.

Exercise 5

Write a short summary of the following telephone conversation:

> Sabina doesn't have time on Tuesday. Denis has no luck. Denis doesn't have time on Wednesdays. Sabina has bad luck. Sabina is at home all day on Thursday and Denis also has time on Thursday evening.

Dialogue 2 🔲

Kdo je to?

Who is this?

It is Thursday evening and Denis is at Sabina's house. He is showing her his photographs and answering her questions

SABINA: Kdo je to?
DENIS: To je moj dober prijatelj John. On je Anglež.
In to je njegova punca Clara.
SABINA: Ali je Španka?
DENIS: Ne, Francozinja je.
SABINA: Ona je zelo velika!
DENIS: Imaš prav! Velika je.
SABINA: Kakšna lepa slika! Kje ste tukaj?
DENIS: Tukaj smo v Barceloni.
SABINA: O, Barcelona je lepo mesto. Kaj je ta velika hiša?
DENIS: To je naš hotel.
SABINA: In čigav je ta avto?
DENIS: To je moj novi avto! Tukaj je, v garaži!

SABINA: *Who is this?*
DENIS: *This is a good friend of mine, John. He is English.*
And that is his girlfriend Clara.

SABINA:	*Is she Spanish?*
DENIS:	*No, she is French.*
SABINA:	*She is very tall!*
DENIS:	*You're right! She is tall.*
SABINA:	*What a lovely photo! Where are you here?*
DENIS:	*Here we're in Barcelona.*
SABINA:	*Oh, Barcelona is a beautiful town. What is this big house?*
DENIS:	*This is our hotel.*
SABINA:	*And whose car is this?*
DENIS:	*This is my new car! It's here, in the garage!*

Vocabulary

kdo?	who?	**lepo**	beautiful
Anglež	Englishman	**mesto**	town
punca	girlfriend	**hotel**	hotel
Francozinja	French woman	**čigav?**	whose?
velika	big, tall	**novi**	new
slika	photo	**avto**	car
kje?	where?	**garaža**	garage

Note: **punca** means 'a girl' and **fant** means 'a boy'. These words are used when you want to say that someone is your girlfriend or boyfriend. For example:

Tanja je moja punca.	Tanja is my girlfriend.
Denis je moj fant.	Denis is my boyfriend.

Language points

'A' and 'the'

Slovene has no article: 'photograph' and 'the photograph' both translate as **fotografija**. This becomes more difficult when translating from Slovene into English where the context of the text has to be taken into account.

Adjectival endings

In the dialogue Sabina said **Clara je velika**, because **Clara** is feminine in gender. Had she been describing John she would have said

John je *velik*, because **John** is masculine in gender. **Mesto** (town) is neuter in gender, and for the town Barcelona she'd say **Barcelona je** *veliko* **mesto**.

All Slovene adjectives have three endings, depending on whether they modify a feminine, a masculine or a neuter noun. Using the adjective **velik** (big), for example, you say:

velik hotel	m.
velika hiša	f.
veliko mesto	n.

The stem of the adjective is usually given in the masculine form. Masculine adjectives normally end in a consonant. All adjectives modifying a feminine noun take an **a** ending and the adjectives modifying a neuter noun usually take an **o** ending and occasionally an **e** ending.

The semi-silent **e** usually drops from the masculine form and then the endings **a**, **o**, or **e** are added. This is the case with **dober** (good); you have learned in lesson 1 how you say **dober dan**, **dobro jutro** or **dobra prijateljica**. Sometimes the endings are simply added to the stem, as in **lep hotel**, **lepa hiša**, **lepo mesto**.

Here are the adjectives you have learned by now together with their opposite meanings:

majhen–velik	small–big
dober–slab	good–bad
lahek–težek	easy–difficult, *or* light–heavy
nov–star	new–old
lep–grd	beautiful–ugly

Note: Whenever you use the possessive pronouns as adjectives the same rules apply to them, i.e. they take the endings of the noun they modify:

moj, tvoj, njen prijatelj	my, your, her friend (male)
moja, tvoja, njena prijateljica	my, your, her friend (female)

When the verb 'to be' follows the words 'this' or 'these' you say **to** in Slovene, regardless of number and gender. For example:

To je moj prijatelj.	This is my friend.
To so moji prijatelji.	These are my friends.

When a noun follows the word 'this' then it has to modify the noun in number and gender. For example:

Ta hiša je velika.	This house is big.
To mesto je veliko.	This town is big.

'This' and 'that'

Pronouns stand in place of nouns. In lesson 1 you learned about personal pronouns (I, you, he, etc.) and possessive pronouns (mine, yours, his, etc.). Words like English 'this' and 'that' can function as pronouns ('What is this?') or as adjectives ('This house is beautiful'). They are demonstrative pronouns and in Slovene they have masculine, feminine, neuter and plural forms.

Masculine	Feminine	Neuter	Plural	
ta	**ta**	**to**	**ti**	this/these
tisti	**tista**	**tisto**	**tisti**	that/those
oni	**ona**	**ono**	**oni**	that/those

In Slovene **tisti** points to people or things which are a little bit further away and are dealt with more indirectly; **oni** points to people or things which are very far away in place or time. **Tisti** and **oni** are both translated by 'that' in English.

Čigav/–a/–o? (whose?)

The possessive pronouns answer the question 'whose?', in Slovene **čigav** (m.), **čigava** (f.), **čigavo** (n.). When you use the possessive pronouns as pronouns you use the neuter form. For example:

To je moje.	This is mine.
Ali je to njegovo?	Is this his?
To ni naše.	This is not ours.

Countries and their inhabitants

In Slovene, nouns indicating nationalities have a different form for a male and a female inhabitant of a country and are spelt with a capital letter as in English. Note how Denis explains to Sabina that John is **Anglež** but his girlfriend is **Francozinja**.

Here are the Slovene names for some countries and their inhabitants:

Country	Male inhabitant	Female inhabitant	Plural inhabitants
Anglija	Anglež	Angležinja	Angleži
Slovenija	Slovenec	Slovenka	Slovenci
Amerika	Amerčan	Američanka	Američani
Nemčija	Nemec	Nemka	Nemci
Italija	Italijan	Italijanka	Italijani
Španija	Španec	Španka	Španci
Francija	Francoz	Francozinja	Francozi
Rusija	Rus	Rusinja	Rusi

Adjectives indicating the language are spelt with a small letter. **Jezik** means 'language'; its literal meaning is 'tongue'.

angleški jezik
slovenski jezik
nemški jezik
italijanski jezik

španski jezik
francoski jezik
ruski jezik

Questions kdo (who) and kaj (what)

The question **Kdo je to?** means 'Who is this?' and **Kaj je to?** means 'What is this?'. The answer to both these questions is **To je ...** (This is ...) or **To ni ...** (This is not ...). If you want to ask whether this is someone or something you say **Ali je to ...?** as in English *Is this ...?* The question word **ali** may be omitted and you can just say **Je to ...?** However, it is not wrong to use **ali**. In order to help you understand that a sentence indicates a question, **ali** will always be used in the first few lessons. Here are a few common phrases using these constructions:

važno, pomembno	important	**nemogoče**	impossible
res	true	**vse**	everything
mogoče	possible	**nič**	nothing

Ali je to važno?

Ja, to je važno. *or*
Ne, to ni važno.

Ali je to res?

Ja, to je res. *or*
Ne, to ni res.

Ali je to mogoče?

Ja, to je mogoče. *or*
Ne, to ni mogoče. *or*
To je nemogoče.

Ali je to prav?	Ja, to je prav. *or*
	Ne, to ni prav.
Ali je to vse?	Ja, to je vse.
	Ne, to ni vse.
	To ni nič. (See Double negative below.)

Ali; ali ... ali (or; either ... or)

Ali is, apart from the word which indicates a question, also a conjunction word meaning 'or', as in **Ali je to on ali ne?** (Is this him or not?).

When you want to use the English construction either ... or, you simply say **ali ... ali**, for example:

Ali vse ali nič.	Either everything or nothing.
Ali ti ali on.	Either you or him.
Biti ali ne biti ...	To be or not to be ...

Double negative

Whilst it is wrong in English to use a double negative, you must use it in Slovene. Negative words, such as **nikoli** (never), **nič** (nothing), **nihče** (nobody) require a negative verb. Here are a few common expressions where a double negative is used:

To ni nič.	This is nothing.
On ni nikoli utrujen.	He is never tired.
Nihče ni tukaj.	Nobody is here.

You know this?

You have learned that to form a question in Slovene you need the question word **ali**. As in English, you can also form a question by your voice intonation, as in:

To je vse?	This is all?
On je v Sloveniji?	He is in Slovenia?

More about nouns

You have seen by now that the endings of Slovene nouns change. There are six cases, each of them having a particular function and, as you have seen, three genders – masculine, feminine and neuter.

Slovene nouns are divided into four groups, known as declensions. They are as follows:

First declension

Into this group come nouns of feminine gender that end in **a**, for example:

hiša	house	**prijateljica**	female friend
garaža	garage	**sreča**	luck

Second declension

Into this group come nouns of feminine gender ending in a consonant, for example:

cerkev	church	**luč**	light

Third declension

Into this group come nouns of masculine gender, for example:

hotel	hotel	**telefon**	telephone
avto	car		

Fourth declension

Into this group come nouns of neuter gender ending in **o** or **e**, for example:

jabolko	apple	**vreme**	weather
mesto	town		

Knowing about this will be useful to you later when we look into the way in which Slovene cases work.

The nominative case

The subject of a sentence is the noun or pronoun which governs its verb. You can find the subject of a sentence by putting the questions **Kdo?** or **Kaj?** ('who?' or 'what') in front of the verb. In the sentence **To je moj prijatelj John**, **John** is the subject because 'John' answers the question 'Who is this?'. In the sentence **To je naš hotel**,

hotel is the subject because it answers the question 'What is this?'. Whenever you get the answer to the question 'who?' or 'what?' you get the noun in the nominative case. You will find all the nouns listed in the vocabulary in the nominative case even though you might have found them in the passage with a different ending. This is because of their function: in that particular sentence they were in a different case.

Exercise 6

You are telling a friend about some men you met at a party. Following the example below, tell your friend what you found rather amusing:

Marko/Slovenec
Marko je Slovenec ampak njegova punca ni Slovenka.

1 Patrice/Francoz
2 Vittorio/Italijan
3 Martin/Anglež
4 Jaroslav/Rus
5 Pedro/Španec

Exercise 7

You are at a bus stop waiting for your friend. You are talking to some women when your friend arrives. Introduce them to him and tell him where they are from, following the example below:

Katja/Slovene
To je Katja. Ona je Slovenka.

1 Lynda/English
2 Pamela/American
3 Gusti/German
4 Maria/Spanish
5 Laura/Italian

Exercise 8

A colleague from work telephones you because he'd like to meet you. Fill in your part of the dialogue as suggested:

You: *The telephone is ringing, answer it!*

YOUR COLLEAGUE:	Živio, Marko tukaj. Ali imaš jutri zvečer čas?
YOU:	*Say that you're sorry, but you don't have time tomorrow evening.*
YOUR COLLEAGUE:	Kaj pa v četrtek zvečer?
YOU:	*Say that is fine. You are at home all day on Thursday.*
YOUR COLLEAGUE:	Moja prijateljica je tukaj v Sloveniji.
YOU:	*Ask if she is English.*
YOUR COLLEAGUE:	Ne, Italijanka je.

Exercise 9

Ask the people below if they are at home on the following days in the evening

1 Darko/Tuesday
2 Lara/Thursday
3 Peter/Monday
4 Darja/Saturday
5 Nataša/Friday

Exercise 10

Whilst waiting in front of a telephone box you have overheard this conversation. Fill in the correct forms of 'to be' and 'to have':

Ali ... v četrtek čas?
Ne, v četrtek ... časa. V četrtek ... v službi. Ampak v petek
... čas.
Imaš srečo! Jaz ... v petek ves dan doma. Moja punca ... v
Ljubljani. Ona ... Angležinja.

Exercise 11

Answer these questions as suggested!

1 Ali ima Tim prav ali ne?
  Ja, ...
2 Ali ima ona srečo?
  Ne, ...
3 Ali imaš danes zvečer čas?
  Ne, ...
4 Ali je to res ali ne?

Ja, . . .
5 Ali je to prav ali ne?
   Ne, . . .
6. Ali je to važno?
   Ja, . . .

Exercise 12 📼

1 A friend who is going on holiday for three months wants you to join him. Say to him: *This is impossible!*
2 Someone says to you: 'Did you know that Slovenia was bigger than England?' Say: *This is not true!*
3 A friend tells you that he is going to go abroad next week and does not have a passport. Say to him: *But this is very important!*
4 He also tells you how he knows some people who forgot their passports and were let through the border anyway. Say: *This isn't right!*
5 Your friend, after a long argument with you, eventually says to you *You're right!*

Exercise 13

Match the adjectives on the left in their correct ending with the nouns on the right and say what they mean:

majhen/-hna/-o   avto
dober/-bra/-o   jutro
lep/-a/-o   hiša
velik/-a/-o   mesto
težek/-žka/-o   lekcija
slab/-a/-o   vreme

Exercise 14

Put the twenty words below into five groups so that they will be connected by meaning

Španka	Rusija	Francozinja	Slovenka
Slovenec	prva pomoč	četrtek	Američan
sreda	gasilci	Francoz	sobota
policija	ponedeljek	Nemka	pomoč na cesti
Nemčija	Anglež	Francija	Anglija

Exercise 15 [image]

Pronunciation exercise. (a) Although the Slovene names for many countries are very similar to the English names, they are pronounced differently. Let's pronounce these countries in the following sentences:

Velika Britanija	Great Britain
sosed	neighbour (male)

Robert je iz Velike Britanije.
Anglija je lepa država.
Slovenija je zelo majhna država.
V Nemčiji in v Avstriji govorijo nemški jezik.
Francija, Španija in Italija so zahodno-evropske države.
Njegov sosed gre v petek v Rusijo.

(b) The sentences you read out were all positive statements. You have learned that you can ask questions by intonation alone. Read out the sentences again imagining they had a question mark after them.

Dialogue for comprehension [image]

Denis telephones Matej at work to arrange to meet him. Matej, however, is busy these days. See what he is doing

prijeten	pleasant	**popoldne**	in the afternoon
dopust	holiday	**imeti v planu**	to have planned
odličen	superb	**pridite na večerjo**	come and have supper
pride	(she) comes	**gremo na izlet**	let's go for a trip
teden	week	**nogometni trening**	football training
dežuje	it's raining	**lahko**	can, could

TAJNICA: Prosim?
DENIS: Dober dan, Denis Golob pri telefonu. Ali je Matej Novak tam?
TAJNICA: Samo trenutek, prosim.
MATEJ: Prosim?
DENIS: Živio Matej, Denis tukaj.

MATEJ:	O, si že doma, kako si?
DENIS:	Odlično. In kako si ti?
MATEJ:	Zelo sem zaposlen. V službi imam veliko dela in Robert je tukaj v Sloveniji.
DENIS:	Kdo je Robert?
MATEJ:	Robert je moj prijatelj iz Anglije. Njegova mama je Slovenka. In konec tedna pride še njegova punca, Jane.
DENIS:	O, ta Anglež nima sreče. Vreme je zelo slabo.
MATEJ:	Imaš prav. Že ves teden dežuje.
DENIS:	Kdaj pride Jane?
MATEJ:	V četrtek popoldne.
DENIS:	Ali je Angležinja?
MATEJ:	Ja, Angležinja je.
DENIS:	Ali imaš za v petek zvečer kaj v planu?
MATEJ:	Ne še.
DENIS:	Moja prijateljica Sabina pride k meni. Ona govori zelo dobro angleško. Pridite na večerjo!
MATEJ:	O, hvala. Ali imaš ti v soboto čas. Jaz imam novi avto in v soboto gremo lahko kam na izlet.
DENIS:	Ampak Matej, ali nimaš ti ob sobotah nogometni trening?
MATEJ:	Ja, ampak to ni tako pomembno.

3 Ura je tri

It is three o'clock

In this lesson you will learn about:

- Words and expressions about transport
- How to ask what time it is and how to tell the time
- Some adjectives describing physical state and emotions
- The Slovene cardinal and ordinal numbers
- The months of the year
- The professions
- How to express a possibility
- How to conjugate verbs in the present tense

Dialogue 1 ▣

Oprostite . . .

Excuse me . . .

Robert's girlfriend Jane, who is also half-Slovene, is travelling to Ljubljana to visit him. Her watch says that the time of arrival has passed and she is anxious not to miss her station. As the train is approaching a town she addresses the passenger sitting next to her

JANE: Oprostite, ali smo že v Ljubljani?
POTNIK: Ne še, še deset minut. Vlak ima zamudo.
JANE: Ura je že tri. Pozni smo.

JANE: *Excuse me, are we in Ljubljana yet?*
PASSENGER: *Not yet, another ten minutes. The train is late.*
JANE: *It is already three o'clock. We're late.*

Vocabulary

oprostite	excuse me	**ura**	time, watch, clock
minuta	minute	**že**	already
vlak	train	**pozni smo**	we are late
zamudo	delay		

Language points

Excuse me . . .

Whenever you want to approach somebody with a question, draw attention or apologise, you say **oprostite** when you are speaking in polite form or **oprosti** when you are speaking in familiar form. It means both 'excuse me' and 'I am sorry'.

When you say that a train, a bus or a plane is late you use the expression **imeti zamudo**. It literally means 'to have a delay'.

avtobus	bus
letalo	plane
ladja	ship

For example:

Avtobus ima vsak dan zamudo.	The bus is late every day.
Letalo ima danes zamudo.	The plane is late today.
Vlak nima nikoli zamude.	The train is never late.

When you want to say that you are going somewhere by car, by plane, etc., you express this with the preposition **z**, which means 'with'. In other words, in Slovene, you say that you go somewhere 'with a car', 'with a plane'. When you use **z**, nouns take a different ending because **z** indicates the instrumental case, about which you will see more in lesson 13. Here are a few expressions using the preposition **z** with words for transport:

z železnico	by rail	**z letalom**	by plane
z vlakom	by train	**z ladjo**	by ship
z avtom	by car		

When you say that a person is late you use the expression **biti pozen** (to be late). For example:

Robert, ti si zmeraj pozen.	Robert, you are always late.
Jana ni nikoli pozna.	Jane is never late.
Oprosti, danes smo pozni.	I'm sorry, we are late today.

When you say that someone is on time you use the expression **biti točen** (to be on time). For example:

Jaz nisem nikoli točen.	I am never punctual.
Ona je zmeraj točna.	She is always on time.
Mi smo danes točni.	We are on time today.

Notice how the adjectives **pozen** and **točen** change their endings depending on who is speaking, i.e. if a man is speaking he says **pozen sem**, if a woman is speaking she says **pozna sem**. In lesson 1 Robert tells Matej that he is a little tired (**malo utrujen**). A woman would have said **malo utrujena**. Here are some more adjectives describing physical states and emotions. As in English, you use these adjectives with 'to be', which you conjugate to indicate whom you are referring to.

biti lačen	to be hungry	**biti zadovoljen**	to be satisfied
biti žejen	to be thirsty	**biti razočaran**	to be disappointed
biti zaspan	to be sleepy	**biti prepričan**	to be sure
biti prehlajen	to have a cold	**biti jezen**	to be angry

Another ten minutes!

The passenger said to Jane **Še 10** *minut*. **Minuta** means 'minute' but with the numbers from 5 onwards the **a** ending drops and you say **5, 10, 15 minut**. The same rule applies to **ura** (hour). You would say **Na vlaku smo že 6 ur**.

Is this place free?

When you are about to take a seat somewhere and you want to check that it is free you say:

Ali je tukaj prosto?	Is this place free?

The answer is likely to be:

Ja, prosto je.	Yes it is free.
Ne, zasedeno je.	No, it is taken.

Numerals in Slovene

Cardinal	Ordinal
	These are used as adjectives and change their ending depending on the gender of the noun they modify
0 **nič**	
1 **eden** (when used on its own)	
1 **en** (m.), **ena** (f.) **eno** (n.) (when used with a noun)	**prvi/-a/-o**
2 **dva** (m.), **dve** (f.), **dve** (n.)	**drugi/-a/-o**
3 **trije** (m.), **tri** (f.), **tri** (n.)	**tretji/-a/-o**
4 **štirje** (m.), **štiri** (f.), **štiri** (n.)	**četrti/-a/-o**
5 **pet**	**peti/-a/-o**
6 **šest**	**šesti/-a/-o**
7 **sedem**	**sedmi/-a/-o**
8 **osem**	**osmi/-a/-o**
9 **devet**	**deveti/-a/-o**
10 **deset**	**deseti/-a/-o**
11 **enajst**	**enajsti/-a/-o**
12 **dvanajst**	**dvanajsti/-a/-o**
13 **trinajst**	**trinajsti/-a/-o**
14 **štirinajst**	**štirinajsti/-a/-o**
15 **petnajst**	**petnajsti/-a/-o**
16 **šestnajst**	**šestnajsti/-a/-o**
17 **sedemnajst**	**sedemnajsti/-a/-o**
18 **osemnajst**	**osemnajsti/-a/-o**
19 **devetnajst**	**devetnajsti/-a/-o**
20 **dvajset**	**dvajseti/-a/-o**
30 **trideset**	**trideseti/-a/-o**
40 **štirideset**	**štirideseti/-a/-o**
50 **petdeset**	**petdeseti/-a/-o**
60 **šestdeset**	**šestdeseti/-a/-o**
70 **sedemdeset**	**sedemdeseti/-a/-o**
80 **osemdeset**	**osemdeseti/-a/-o**
90 **devetdeset**	**devetdeseti/-a/-o**
21 **enaindvajset**	**enaindvajseti/-a/-o**
22 **dvaindvajset**	**dvaindvajseti/-a/-o**
23 **triindvajset**	**triindvajseti/-a/-o**
24 **štiriindvajset**	**štiriindvajseti/-a/-o**

25	petindvajset	petindvajseti/-a/-o
26	šestindvajset	šestindvajseti/-a/-o
27	sedemindvajset	sedemindvajseti/-a/-o
28	osemindvajset	osemindvajseti/-a/-o
29	devetindvajset	devetindvajseti/-a/-o
100	sto	stoti/-a/-o
200	dvesto	dvestoti/-a/-o
300	tristo	tristoti/-a/-o
400	štiristo	štiristoti/-a/-o
500	petsto	petstoti/-a/-o
600	šeststo	šeststoti/-a/-o
700	sedemsto	sedemstoti/-a/-o
800	osemsto	osemstoti/-a/-o
900	devetsto	devetstoti/-a/-o
1 000	tisoč	tisoči/-a/-o
2 000	dva tisoč	
3 000	tri tisoč	
4 526	štiri tisoč petsto šestindvajset	

Note that in Slovene numbers expressed by two words in English are said back to front, e.g. 'twenty-four' is **štiriindvajset**. Ordinal numbers have a full stop after them (e.g. **1.**). They are used as adjectives and have to agree with the noun. Since the months are masculine in gender you say **peti november**. You say, however, **peta lekcija**, because the noun 'lesson' is feminine. Cardinal numbers from 5 onwards don't have different forms for different genders.

The months of the year

januar	**januarja**	in January
februar	**februarja**	in February
marec	**marca**	in March
april	**aprila**	in April
maj	**maja**	in May
junij	**junija**	in June
julij	**julija**	in July
avgust	**avgusta**	in August
september	**septembra**	in September
oktober	**oktobra**	in October
november	**novembra**	in November
december	**decembra**	in December

In Slovene the months of the year are not spelt with a capital letter.

When you want to say that something is happening in a particular month you *do not translate the preposition 'in'*. You simply say, for example, **junija**, and this means 'in June'.

All the months of the year are masculine in gender.

The date

The question 'What date is it today?' is **Katerega smo danes?** You can say **Danes je ...** or **Danes smo ...** For the time being it is better if you use the first example (i.e. **Danes je ...**) where the numbers don't have any endings.

The dates are written in the following manner in Slovene:

4. 5. 1873   4 May 1873

This would be read out as:

četrti peti tisoč osemsto triinsedemdeset

28. 12. 1995   28 December 1995
osemindvajseti dvanajsti tisoč devetsto petindevetdeset

Useful expressions of time

vedno, **zmeraj**	always	**včasih**	sometimes
nikoli	never	**redko**	rarely
po navadi, **navadno**	usually		

telefonska številka	telephone number

Telephone numbers

The telephone numbers in Slovenia consist of five, six or seven figures. When you give someone a telephone number you read it out as follows:

25 438	petindvajset štiristo osemintrideset
475 834	štiristo petinsedemdeset osemsto štiriintrideset
132 712	sto dvaintrideset sedemsto dvanajst

You can also read out the numbers individually.

Exercise 1

Select the two possible responses you could give to someone who asks you the following questions:

1 Oprostite, ali smo že v Ljubljani?
   (a) Ja, to je Ljubljana.
   (b) Ne še, še deset minut.
   (c) Ura je točno tri.
2 Ali ima avtobus zamudo?
   (a) Vlak je danes pozen.
   (b) Ja, avtobus ima danes zamudo.
   (c) Ne, avtobus nima zamude.
3 Ali si žejen?
   (a) Ja, prehlajen sem.
   (b) Ne, nisem žejen.
   (c) Ja, žejen in lačen sem.
4 Ali je Tanja zadovoljna?
   (a) Ne, ona ni nikoli zadovoljna.
   (b) Ja, zelo je zadovoljna.
   (c) Ja, Tanja je danes lačna.
5 Ali je tukaj prosto?
   (a) Ja, to je London.
   (b) Ne, tukaj ni prosto.
   (c) Ja, prosto je.

Exercise 2

Tell your friend who is visiting you in your country that the bus / the train / the plane is sometimes late.

Exercise 3 ▫▫

You are in Slovenia and take weekend trips. The bus seems to be always late on Fridays. Approach the man sitting next to you and ask him:

Ask: 1 *Excuse me, is the bus always late on Fridays?*
      Ne, ne vedno. Včasih.
Say: 2 *It is already 10 o'clock. We're very late!*
      Še pet minut in smo tukaj.
Say: 3 *Thank you.*
      Ali ste Slovenec?
Say: 4 *No, I'm English.*

Exercise 4

Tell a colleague at work that your telephone number is 274 837 / 253 857 / 247 294 / 184 926 / 264 057.

Exercise 5

Say what the date today is:

1 5 November 1996
2 27 June 1994
3 31 December 1973
4 12 May 1845
5 23 October 1873

Dialogue 2 🔘

Oprostite še enkrat . . .

Excuse me once again . . .

Jane has been sitting on the train for another hour. She is thinking about Robert waiting for her and is getting rather impatient. She once more addresses the man sitting in her carriage

JANE:	Oprostite še enkrat, gospod, koliko je ura?
(SO)POTNIK:	Ura je tri in petindvajset minut.
JANE:	Moja ura je že štiri.
	Mogoče prehiteva?
(SO)POTNIK:	Mogoče moja ura zaostaja. Samo trenutek . . .
	(he asks a woman who is just passing by)
	Oprostite, gospa, koliko je ura?
POTNICA:	Moja ura je točno štiri.

JANE:	*Excuse me once more, sir, what is the time?*
(CO)PASSENGER:	*It is 3:25.*
JANE:	*My watch says four already.*
	Maybe it is fast.
(CO)PASSENGER:	*Maybe my watch is slow. Just a minute . . .*
	(he asks a woman who is just passing by).
	Excuse me, madam, what time is it?
PASSENGER:	*My watch says exactly four o'clock.*

Vocabulary

še enkrat	once more	**prehiteva**	is fast
ura	time, watch, clock	**zaostaja**	is slow, literally 'late'
sedaj	now	**točno**	exactly

Language points

Telling the time

The word **ura** means 'watch' and 'clock'. It also means 'time' in the expression **Koliko je ura?** The abstract word for 'time' in Slovene is **čas**, as you have seen in **Imam čas** (I have time) or **Nimam časa** (I don't have time).

In everyday speech the twelve-hour clock is used. In official time, e.g. in timetables, on radio and television, in programme schedules, etc. the twenty-four-hour clock is used. For the time being it may be easier for you to use the twenty-four-hour clock. Note that the word 'clock' at the end of the English sentence is not translated into Slovene as in **Ura je točno štiri** (It is exactly four (o'clock)).

15:10	Ura je petnajst in deset minut.
14:30	Ura je štirinajst in trideset minut.

Fractions and sums

ena polovica or **pol**	one half or half
ena četrtina or **četrt**	one quarter or quarter
tri četrtine or **tri četrt**	three quarters
ena tretjina	one third
ena petina	one fifth

$3 + 4 = 7$	tri plus štiri je sedem
$9 - 4 = 5$	devet minus štiri je pet
$2 \times 4 = 8$	dva krat štiri je osem

Possibly

When you want to express a possibility of something (which in English you do with words like 'perhaps, maybe, possibly, probably'), you use the words **mogoče** or **morda** in Slovene.

How much, how many, how many times?

The question **koliko?** has several meanings in Slovene. It can mean:

koliko?	how much?
Koliko **je 5+3?**	*What* is 5+3?
Koliko **ljudi je tukaj?**	*How many* people are here?
Koliko **je ura?**	*What* is the time?

The question **kolikokrat?** means 'how many times?', 'how often?'. When you want to ask someone how many times a day, a week, a year they do something you need the preposition **na** (on). For example:

Kolikokrat na dan?	How many times a day?
teden?	week?
mesec?	month?
leto?	year?

As an answer to this question you will get:

enkrat	once
dvakrat	twice
trikrat	three times
štirikrat	four times
petkrat	five times
and so on	

You can form the rest of these numbers by adding **krat** to the cardinal numbers. You may like to use other adverbs like:

nobenkrat (nikoli)	never
malokrat	rarely
večkrat *or* **velikokrat**	often

Plural of nouns

The Slovene plural of nouns is not formed as in English by adding 's' to the singular form but rather more irregularly. The nouns of each gender take particular endings when they are used in the plural form. You will see more about this in lesson 9.

Here is the word for 'a man', 'a person': **človek**. This word has an irregular plural **ljudje** (men, people).

Exercise 6

Tell a man who stopped you on the street and asked you the time that the time is: 15:50, 16:10, 22:30, 12:15, 18:45.

Exercise 7

Križanka (crossword puzzle)

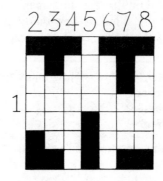

1 bus
2 train
3 car
4 plane
5 year
6 Saturday
7 watch
8 month

Exercise 8

Koliko je?

1 šestnajst plus triindvajset
2 štiriintrideset minus osem
3 štiriinštirideset plus triindvajset
4 štiriinsedemdeset minus dvanajst
5 osem krat štiri

Dialogue 3 📼

Vidim, da berete angleški časopis

I see you are reading an English newspaper

Robert, the English journalist, goes to the café where he has arranged to meet Jane and sits down at a table on the terrace. A Slovene professor addresses him and they enter into conversation

PROFESSOR: Oprostite, ali ste Anglež? Vidim, da berete angleški časopis.
ROBERT: Ja, Anglež sem. Ampak moja mama je Slovenka.
PROFESSOR: Ah, zato govorite slovensko.
ROBERT: Ja, malo govorim. Ampak slovenščina je zelo težka.
PROFESSOR: Ja, vem. Ali ste v Ljubljani na dopustu?
ROBERT: Ne, po poklicu sem novinar in pišem reportažo o Sloveniji.
PROFESSOR: O, zanimivo.
ROBERT: In kaj ste vi po poklicu?
PROFESSOR: Jaz sem profesor na univerzi. Učim tuje jezike: angleščino in italijanščino. Moja hčerka je prevajalka. Če potrbujete pomoč ... moja telefonska številka je 061 354 768.
ROBERT: Najlepša hvala.

PROFESSOR: *Excuse me, are you English?*
I see you're reading an English newspaper.
ROBERT: *Yes, I'm English. But my mother is Slovene.*
PROFESSOR: *Ah, that is why you speak Slovene.*
ROBERT: *Yes, I speak a little, but Slovene is very difficult.*
PROFESSOR: *Yes, I know.*
Are you on holiday in Slovenia?
ROBERT: *No, I am a journalist and I am writing a report on Slovenia.*
PROFESSOR: *Oh, interesting.*
ROBERT: *And what do you do for a living?*
PROFESSOR: *I am a lecturer at a University. I teach foreign languages: English and Italian. My daughter is an interpreter. If you need any help ... my telephone number is 061 354 768.*
ROBERT: *Thank you very much.*

Vocabulary

videti	to see	**učiti**	to teach
da	that	**hčerka**	daughter
govoriti	to speak	**prevajalka**	interpreter
na dopustu	on holiday	**potrebovati**	to need
biti po poklicu	to have an occupation (literally 'to be in an occupation')	**pisati**	to write
		pomoč	help
		zanimivo	interesting
reportaža	report	**telefonska**	telephone
o	about	**številka**	number

Language points

Slovene verbs

Most of the Slovene infinitives end in **ti** and some in **či**. It is important to memorize the infinitive (you will see later on that some verbs are always followed by an infinitive). Some verbs have a regular present stem (they drop the **ti** ending and the corresponding ending of a person is added). However, this is not always the case. The present stem sometimes differs beyond recognition from the infinitive. In lessons and in the glossary at the end of the book, you will be given the first person singular form and from there you will be able to add the appropriate endings. Here are three basic patterns of verbs in the present stem:

delati	to work
pisati	to write
govoriti	to speak

		delati	*pisati*	*govoriti*	
1	jaz	dela*m*	piše*m*	govori*m*	
2	ti	dela*š*	piše*š*	govori*š*	
3	ona on ono	dela	piše	govori	(no ending, only stem)
1	mi	dela*mo*	piše*mo*	govori*mo*	
2	vi	dela*te*	piše*te*	govori*te*	
3	oni	dela*jo*	piše*jo*	govori*jo*	

It will be helpful if you memorize the endings:

1	**m**	**mo**
2	**š**	**te**
3	no ending, only stem	**jo**

The verb **iti** 'to go' is irregular and is conjugated like this:

1	**grem**	**gremo**
2	**greš**	**greste**
3	**gre**	**grejo**

The verb **priti** 'to come' is irregular in the same way and it is conjugated like this:

1	**pridem**	**pridemo**
2	**prideš**	**pridete**
3	**pride**	**pridejo**

Note that **delati** can mean 'to work' or 'to do'. For example:

Kaj delaš danes popoldne?	What are you doing this afternoon?
Nič ne delam. Imam čas.	I am doing nothing. I am free.
Kje delate?	Where do you work?
Trenutno ne delam.	I am not working at the moment.

The verb **vedeti** 'to know' is also slightly irregular. It is conjugated as follows:

1	**vem**	**vemo**
2	**veš**	**veste**
3	**ve**	**vedo**

The Slovene present tense covers the English present simple and present continuous tense, i.e. there is no present continuous tense in Slovene. For example, **govorim** can mean 'I speak' or 'I am speaking'. If you are using the present continuous tense in English you must not translate the auxiliary words of this tense into Slovene; not only does this sound wrong in Slovene but it really does not make sense.

To make a verb negative you simply put **ne** in front of it. For example:

(Mi)	**Ne delamo**.	We don't work.
(Jaz)	**Ne vem**.	I don't know.
(Oni)	**Ne pišejo**.	They don't write.

As you have already learned with 'to be' and 'to have', you put the question word **ali** in front of the verb to make a question. This goes for all Slovene verbs. For example:

letos	this year

Ali delaš danes ves dan?   Are you working all day today?
Ali greš letos na dopust?   Are you going on holiday this year?

Note: There is a phrase **iti na dopust** meaning 'to go on holiday'.

Personal pronouns

Since every verb has its ending which clearly indicates the person, the personal pronouns in Slovene are usually omitted. Note the sentences in the dialogue:

Ali ste Anglež?   Are you English?
Vidim, da berete ...   I see you are reading ...

However, you use the personal pronouns when you want to stress them, as in sentences:

In kaj ste *vi* po poklicu?   And what do *you* do for a living?

Robert could have asked the professor:

Ali ste tudi *vi* Anglež?   Are *you* also English?

Da (that)

Da (that) is probably the most frequently used conjunction in Slovene. It introduces a subordinate clause and every subordinate clause in Slovene is always preceded by a comma. Note how the professor says to Robert: **Vidim, da berete angleški časopis ...**

Speaking a language 🔲

In lesson 2 you learnt that **jezik** means language and that you say, for example, **slovenski jezik**. **Angleški** and **slovenski** are both adjectives; they derive from the countries **Anglija** and **Slovenija**. Many Slovene adjectives end in **-ski** or **-ški**; most countries and towns form their adjectives with these suffixes. When you want to say that you speak a language you say:

Govorim	slovensko	I speak	Slovene
	angleško		English
	nemško		German
	italijansko		Italian
	špansko		Spanish
	francosko		French
	rusko		Russian

The language one speaks is not spelt with a capital letter in Slovene.

Occupations

You will have noticed in lesson 2 that there is a different form for a male and for a female inhabitant of a country. The same applies to occupations. The original noun is in the male form and the female form usually takes the endings **ka**, **inja** or, most commonly, **ica**. Here are a few examples:

Male	*Female*	
novinar	**novinarka**	journalist
študent	**študentka**	student
prevajalec	**prevajalka**	interpreter
frizer	**frizerka**	barber/hairdresser
igralec	**igralka**	actor/actress
prodajalec	**prodajalka**	shop assistant
	gospodinja	housewife
učitelj	**učiteljica**	teacher
natakar	**natakarica**	waiter/waitress
zdravnik	**zdravnica**	doctor
profesor	**profesorica**	lecturer
tajnik	**tajnica**	secretary
pisatelj	**pisateljica**	writer

The word **poklic** means 'profession'. You use the phrase **biti po poklicu** when you ask someone what their profession is, what they do for a living, or when you want to tell them about yourself. For example:

Kaj si po poklicu?	What is your profession?
Jaz sem po poklicu zdravnik.	I'm a doctor.
Kaj ste po poklicu?	What do you do for a living?

Exercise 9

You are in Slovenia on a train. A man comes into your carriage and starts to talk to you. Answer his questions:

A MAN: Dober dan.
YOU: 1 *Return his greeting.*
A MAN: Ali je tukaj prosto?
YOU: 2 *Say that it is.*
A MAN: Ali ste Slovenec?
YOU: 3 *Say no, you're English.*
A MAN: Ali razumete slovensko?
YOU: 4 *Tell him that you understand a little. Ask him if he understands English. You see that he has an English newspaper.*
A MAN: Ja, malo razumem. Ampak to ni moj časopis. Moja žena je prevajalka in bere angleške časopise.
YOU: 5 *Say how interesting. Ask if she has a lot of work?*
A MAN: Včasih ja, včasih ne. Trenutno je zelo zaposlena.
YOU: 6 *Say that if she needs some help . . . your telephone number in Slovenia is 061 576 824.*

Exercise 10

You are at a party talking to Miran about what you do. Fill in your part of the conversation:

MIRAN: Kaj ste po poklicu?
YOU: 1 *Say that you are a student.*
MIRAN: Kaj študirate?
YOU: 2 *Say that you are studying the Slovene language.*
MIRAN: Oh, zanimivo. Moja hčerka je tudi študentka.
YOU: 3 *Ask what she studies?*
MIRAN: Ona študira angleščino.
YOU: 4 *Ask where she studies?*
MIRAN: V Ljubljani. In kje vi študirate?
YOU: 5 *Say in England.*

Exercise 11

Choose the correct alternative in italics for the people below:

1 Greta Garbo je *igralec/igralka.*
2 Moj prijatelj je *novinar/novinarka.*

3 Njegova prijateljica je *pisatelj/pisateljica*.
4 Marija Rajter je *frizer/frizerka*.
5 Jaz sem *študent/študentka*.

Exercise 12

(a) Tell your friend that your father is not a teacher / a professor / a doctor / a journalist / a student.
(b) Ask your friend if his mother is a student / an interpreter / a journalist / a housewife / a secretary.

Exercise 13

You are at a party and have just met a man who introduced himself to you with the following words:

Jaz sem Patrice. Francoz sem. Govorim francosko in razumem tudi že malo slovensko.

Introduce the people below to Patrice by making up similar sentences:

1 John/English
2 Pauline/American
3 Maria/Spanish
4 Laura/Italian
5 Angela/English
6 Darja/Slovene

Exercise 14

Unscramble the following groups of letters and form words and expressions.

lefonteska vilšteka
sočapis
likoko ej rua
retutnke asom ropims
lipokcu op ems tudšent
iv lia est lovSence

Exercise 15 🔳

Pronunciation exercise. You have a job in Slovenia and you have to get in touch with these people. Read them out.

Janez Vogrin
Darko in Sandra Pokeržnik
Irena Maček
Matic Fras
Majda Čegovnik
Danijela Zupančič
Sonja in Ivan Kobal

Dialogue for comprehension 🔳

Jane has finally got to the café where Robert is waiting for her. She is very late but this doesn't matter to Robert since he is very pleased to see her anyway. Find out how long Robert has been in Slovenia and how he is coping with the Slovene language!

dobro izgledaš	you look well	**ni mi dolg čas**	I'm not bored
nič za to	it doesn't matter	**biti prost**	to be free
nikoli več	never again		

ROBERT: Jane, živio, kako si? Dobro izgledaš.
JANE: Oprosti, pozna sem. Ura je že šest.
ROBERT: Nič za to. Ali si utrujena?
JANE: Ja, zelo. Nikoli več ne pridem z vlakom. Ali že dolgo čakaš?
ROBERT: Ja, od treh. Ampak ni mi dolg čas. Tukaj poznam že nekaj ljudi.
JANE: Ali velikokrat prideš sem?
ROBERT: Ja, dva, trikrat na teden. Po navadi popoldne. Včasih imam tukaj kosilo. Ali si lačna?
JANE: Ne, samo žejna sem. In zaspana. Že tri mesece si tukaj. Ali govoriš že dobro slovesko?
ROBERT: Kar gre. Včasih imam probleme. Ampak tukaj veliko ljudi govori angleško.
JANE: Vedno pišeš, da imaš veliko dela.
ROBERT: Ja, zmeraj sem zelo zaposlen. Ampak danes zvečer sem prost!

4 Zakaj se smejiš? Zato, ker sem dobre volje!

Why are you smiling? Because I'm in a good mood!

In this lesson you will learn about:

- How to use and understand reflexive verbs
- How to ask for and give directions
- How to express ability and inability
- Words and expressions about the post office
- Verbs which are followed by an infinitive
- How to construct indirect questions
- The Slovene word **prosim** (please)
- How to give a command or advice to someone

Dialogue 1

Kam greš?

Where are you going?

Matej was going to call at Robert's place. On the way there he met Robert in front of his hotel, dashing somewhere, looking rather worried

MATEJ: O, živio Robert. Kam greš?
ROBERT: V knjigarno. Moram si kupiti slovenski slovar in eno knjigo.
MATEJ: Ali se učiš slovensko?
ROBERT: Ja, hodim na tečaj. Ne smej se!
MATEJ: Ali prideš v soboto zvečer na zabavo?
ROBERT: Ne vem še. Ne morem se odločiti.

Matej: Zakaj ne?
Robert: Zato, ker imam trenutno veliko dela. In malo sem prehlajen. Ne počutim se zelo dobro. Že ves teden sem slabe volje.
Matej: Ali ti lahko kako pomagam? Oglasi se zvečer, če imaš čas.

Matej: *Oh, hello Robert. Where are you going?*
Robert: *To the bookshop. I must buy myself a Slovene dictionary and a book.*
Matej: *Are you learning Slovene?*
Robert: *Yes, I am attending a course. Don't laugh!*
Matej: *Are you coming to the party on Saturday evening?*
Robert: *I don't know yet. I can't decide.*
Matej: *Why not?*
Robert: *Because I have a lot of work to do at the moment. And I have flu. I'm not feeling very well. I've been in a bad mood the whole week.*
Matej: *Can I help you somehow? Come by in the evening if you have time.*

Vocabulary

kam?	where to?	**odločiti se**	to decide
knjigarna	bookshop	**zakaj?**	why?
kupiti si	to buy oneself	**zato ker**	because
slovar	dictionary	**trenutno**	at the moment
knjiga	book	**biti prehlajen**	to have flu
učiti se	to learn	**počutiti se**	to feel
hoditi	to attend	**pomagati**	to help
smejati se	to laugh, to smile	**oglasiti se**	to go by someone's house
zabava	party	**če**	if

Language points

Why?/Because

As in English, the question **zakaj?** (why) is usually followed by **zato ker** (because). For example:

Zakaj se smejiš?   *Why* are you smiling?
Zato ker sem dobre volje. *Because* I'm in a good mood.

In the dialogue Matej asks Robert **Zakaj ne?** (Why not?). This phrase is also usually followed by **zato ker** (because) plus the explanation.

To be in a good/bad mood

To say that you are in a good or in a bad mood you need the expression **biti dobre volje** (to be in a good mood) or **biti slabe volje** (to be in a bad mood). You conjugate the verb 'to be' to say this for the person you want. For example:

Robert ni dobre volje.	Robert is not in a good mood.
Ali je Matej dobre volje?	Is Matej in a good mood?
Jaz sem danes slabe volje.	I am in a bad mood today.
Ali si ti vedno slabe volje?	Are you always in a bad mood?

Hoditi

The verb **hoditi** means 'to go' or 'to walk'. When you regularly go somewhere it means 'to attend'. Notice how Robert explains: **Hodim na tečaj**.

The uses of the present tense

As in English the present tense can be used with future meaning. Note how Matej asks Robert: **Ali prideš v soboto zvečer na zabavo?** Sentences like this one are expressed with the present continuous tense in English and since there is no present continuous tense in Slovene you use the simple present tense. Neither is there a present perfect tense in Slovene, and sentences like 'I've already been living here for a year' are expressed with the present simple tense, e.g. **Tukaj živim že eno leto** ('I have already been living here for a year', literally I am living. . .').

Reflexive verbs

Very many Slovene verbs are reflexive. You recognize them by the reflexive pronouns **se** or sometimes **si**. They are conjugated like all other verbs but are preceded or followed by **se** or **si**. For example:

odločiti se	to decide
kupiti si	to buy oneself

jaz se odločim	jaz si kupim
ti se odločiš	ti si kupiš
on ⎫	on ⎫
ona ⎬ se odloči	ona ⎬ si kupi
ono ⎭	ono ⎭
mi se odločimo	mi si kupimo
vi se odločite	vi si kupite
oni se odločijo	oni si kupijo

In the negative form **ne** is placed between **se** or **si** and the verb, and when the question is formed **ali** is followed first by **se** or **si** and then the verb. For example:

Jaz se veselim.   I am looking forward to it.
Ali se ti veseliš?   Are you looking forward to it?

Sometimes a verb which is reflexive can have an entirely different meaning from the one it has when it is not reflexive. The verb **učiti** means 'to teach', but the reflexive **učiti se** means 'to learn', 'to study'.

The verb **igrati** means 'to play' and must always be followed by an object. For example: **Barbara igra klavir** (Barbara is playing the piano). When it is reflexive it means 'to play', as in **Boris se igra** (Boris is playing).

Questions you may want to ask people about themselves or answer in order to introduce yourself

> **predstaviti se**   to introduce oneself

The verb **pisati** means 'to write' but when you're asking or giving someone's surname you say **pisati se**:

Kako se pišete? (polite form)
Kako se pišeš? (familiar form)

The expression means 'What is your surname?' Its literal meaning is 'What do you write yourself as?' The answer is:

Pišem se ... (your surname)

When you're saying what someone is called you use **imenovati se**. You'd ask:

Kako se imenujete? (polite form)

Kako se imenuješ? (familiar form)

The answer is:

Imenujem se ... (your name and surname)

A more commonly used question to ask someone's name is:

Kako vam je ime? (polite form)
Kako ti je ime? (familiar form)

The expression means 'What is your name?' The answer is:

Ime mi je ... (your name)

The question

Koliko ste stari? (polite form)
Koliko si star? (familiar form)

means 'How old are you?' The answer is:

Star (stara) sem ... 12, 24, 35 let.

The question 'Where do you live?' is:

Kje stanujete? (polite form)
Kje stanuješ? (familiar form)

Address

naslov	address, title
ulica	street
cesta	road

The word **naslov** means 'address' and 'title', as in 'the title of the book'. Note that Slovenes write the number of the street *after* the name of the street, as in **Slovenska cesta 43**. The abbreviation for **ulica** is **ul.**, for example **Ljubljanska ul. 6**

The expression of ability and inability: 'can' and 'cannot'

In Slovene you express ability with the adverb **lahko**, which never changes. With it you need the verb in the form of the person you are referring to, for example:

Jaz ti lahko pomagam.	I can help you.
Ali lahko grem peš?	Can I go on foot?
Kje lahko kupim slovenski slovar?	Where can I buy a dictionary?

Lahko is used only in the positive form. When you want to express inability you use the verb **moči**. In the dialogue Robert says **Ne morem se odločiti** (I cannot decide). **Moči** is irregular and is always followed by an infinitive. These are the forms of **moči** in the negative:

jaz ne morem	mi ne moremo
ti ne moreš	vi ne morete
on	
ona } ne more	oni ne morejo
ono	

Some examples:

Mi se ne moremo odločiti.	We cannot decide.
Jaz ne morem priti danes zvečer.	I cannot come tonight.
Ona ne more iti v Slovenijo.	She cannot go to Slovenia.

Infinitives are those parts of a verb which do not indicate a person. In English they are preceded by 'to', e.g. 'to work, to write', and in Slovene they usually end in **ti**, e.g. **delati**, **pisati**. As in English, there are verbs in Slovene which are always followed by an infinitive:

hoteti (hočem)	to want
smeti (smem)	to be allowed
začeti (začnem)	to start, to begin
želeti (želim)	to wish, to desire
nameravati (nameravam)	to intend
morati (moram)	must

Note: You have learned that the verbs **biti** and **imeti** form their negative as one word, as in **Danes nisem doma** or **Nimamo sreče**. The verb **hoteti** also forms its negative as one word. Here are the forms of **hoteti** in the negative:

1	nočem	nočemo
2	nočeš	nočete
3	noče	nočejo

All the other Slovene verbs form their negative by putting **ne** in front of them.

Exercise 1

Change these sentences so that they become negative statements and keep in mind that negative words require a negative verb.

1 Robert se zmeraj uči slovensko.
2 Danes smo vsi doma.
3 Jaz se vedno počutim dobro.
4 Moj prijatelj se zmeraj smeji.
5 Sabina vedno vse ve.

Exercise 2

You are in a bookshop wanting to buy a dictionary but they don't have it at the moment. The shop-assistant tells you that it is on order and that they will receive it soon. He is willing to contact you as soon as it arrives. He asks for the following information. Can you fill in your part of the dialogue?

TRGOVEC: Kako vam je ime?
YOU: 1 (*Tell him*).
TRGOVEC: In kako se pišete?
YOU: 2 (*Tell him*).
TRGOVEC: Kje stanujete?
YOU: 3 (*Say in Ljubljana, this is my address*).
TRGOVEC: Ali imate telefon?
YOU: 4 *Yes, my telephone number is 061 375 354.*
TRGOVEC: Ali ste prvič v Sloveniji?
YOU: 5 *No, for the third time.*
TRGOVEC: Ali ste na dopustu?
you: 6 *No, I work here.*
TRGOVEC: In učite se slovensko?
YOU: 7 *Yes, it always helps if you speak the language.*
TRGOVEC: Ja, seveda.

Exercise 3

Write down the opposite meaning of the adjectives listed here together with the nouns.

1 dobre volje
2 nov slovar
3 težek jezik
4 velika knjigarna
5 lepo mesto

Exercise 4

Ask questions as suggested which will give you the following sentences as an answer:

1 Robert ima trikrat na teden slovenski tečaj.
   ASK: *How many times a week has Robert got his Slovene course?*
2 Jane je njegova punca.
   ASK: *Who is Jane?*
3 Ura je točno pet.
   ASK: *What time is it?*
4 To je moja knjiga.
   ASK: *Whose book is this?*
5 Knjigarna je v centru.
   ASK: *Excuse me, where is the bookshop?*

Exercise 5

Križanka

(a) Robert remembers that he still has to go somewhere after he's been to the bookshop. Fill in the Slovene words across and you will see where he has to go:

1 five
2 town
3 house
4 car
5 dictionary

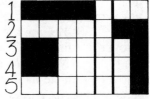

(b) He has to post a letter. Fill in the words down and you will get the Slovene word for a letter across

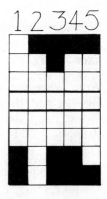

1 Mr
2 male teacher
3 eight
4 help
5 please

Dialogue 2 ▄▄

Oprostite, kje je pošta?

Excuse me, where is the post office?

Robert has got lost on his way to the bookshop which has been recommended to him. He asks a pedestrian if he could help him

ROBERT: Oprostite, ali mi lahko poveste, kje je ta knjigarna?
                    Mladinska Knjiga
                    Slovenska Cesta 29
                    61 000 Ljubljana

PEŠEC: Na žalost ne vem. Tam na vogalu stoji policaj. On sigurno ve.

ROBERT: Oprostite, ali veste kje je ta knjigarna?

POLICIST: O, ni blizu. Ampak tukaj pred hotelom je avtobusna postaja. Avtobus številka 3 pelje tja. Je že tukaj! Pohitite!

ROBERT: Hvala.

ROBERT: *Excuse me, can you tell me where this bookshop is?*
                    Mladinska Knjiga
                    Slovenska Cesta 29
                    61 000 Ljubljana

PASSER-BY: *Unfortunately I don't know. There at the corner is a policeman. He certainly knows.*

ROBERT: *Excuse me, do you know where this bookshop is?*

POLICEMAN: *Oh, it isn't close by. But here in front of the hotel is a bus stop. The number 3 bus goes there. It is here already! Hurry!*

ROBERT: *Thank you.*

Robert found the bookshop and bought his dictionary and now he has to buy a stamp for the letter he has to post. He asks where the post office is

ROBERT: Oprostite, kje je pošta?

PEŠEC: Tukaj za vogalom je poštni nabiralnik.

ROBERT: Moram iti na pošto. Kupiti moram znamko.

PEŠEC: Ali vidite tisti semafor in prehod za pešce? Tam zavijte na levo in pojdite približno sto metrov na ravnost pa ste tam.

ROBERT:	Ali grem lahko peš?
PEŠEC:	Ja, seveda.

ROBERT:	*Excuse me, where is the post office?*
PASSER-BY:	*Around the corner is a letter-box.*
ROBERT:	*I must go to the post office. I must buy a stamp.*
PASSER-BY:	*Do you see the traffic lights and the zebra crossing? Turn left there and go approximately 100 metres straight on and you're there.*
ROBERT:	*Can I walk?*
PASSER-BY:	*Yes, of course.*

Vocabulary

vogal	corner	**poštni nabiralnik**	letter-box
stati (stojim)	to stand	**znamka**	stamp
policist	policeman	**semafor**	traffic light
sigurno	certainly, definitely	**prehod za pešce**	zebra crossing
blizu	close by	**zaviti (zavijem)**	to turn
pohiteti (pohitim)	to hurry	**približno**	approximately
pošta	post office		

Language points

Asking for and giving directions

When you are lost or when you are looking for something, you need to ask for directions. You approach somebody with one of the following phrases:

Oprostite, kje je ...?	Excuse me, where is ... ?
Oprostite, ali mi lahko poveste ...?	Excuse me, can you tell me ... ?
Oprostite, ali veste ...?	Excuse me, do you know ... ?

The person's reply will probably be:

na levo	on the left	**na ravnost**	straight on
na desno	on the right	**ne vem**	I don't know

You will also need the prepositions:

pred	in front of	**na vogalu**	at the corner
za	behind	**za vogalom**	round the corner

and adverbs

blizu	close by
daleč	far away

Note: When you are given a distance it will be in metres and kilometres.

Indirect questions

Unlike in English, there is no reversal in the word order in Slovene when you ask an indirect question. For example:

Kje je pošta?	Where is the post office?
Ali veste, kje je pošta?	Do you know where the post office is?
Ali mi lahko poveste, kje je avtobusna postaja.	Can you tell me where the bus stop is?

To go on foot

'To go somewhere on foot' is expressed in Slovene with the verb **iti** and the adverb **peš**. For example:

Robert gre peš v knjigarno.	Robert walks to the bookshop.
Jaz ne grem nikoli nikamor peš.	I never walk anywhere.
Mi gremo peš v mesto.	We walk to town.

Ta/tisti

The Slovene language has no article. However, when you want to stress something you can use the demonstrative pronouns to express this. Notice how Robert asks **Kje je *ta* knjigarna?**, meaning 'Where is *this particular* bookshop?' as opposed to any bookshop. Another example is in dialogue 2, where the policeman says **Ali vidite *tisti* semafor?** (Do you see *that* traffic light?), referring to a particular traffic light.

Smile! Be happy!

The verb **smejati se** means 'to laugh (at)' or 'to smile' and is conjugated like this:

1 jaz se smejim   mi se smejimo
2 ti se smejiš   vi se smejite
3 on se smeji   oni se smejijo

The imperative

You will have noticed that Matej says to Robert in the dialogue: **Ne smej se!** In this sentence **smej** is the imperative form of the verb **smejati se**.

The imperative is a verbal form which is used when we command, ask someone to do something, or advise. In Slovene the imperative is formed from the present tense of the verb in the following way:

---

1 *Verbs of the -a conjugation (**delati**)*
You drop the **m** from the first person singular and add:

for the familiar form, **j**   **delaj!**
for the plural or polite form, **jte**   **delajte!**
for 'we' as in 'Let us . . .', **jmo**   **delajmo!**

2 *Verbs of the -e conjugation (**pisati**)*
You drop the **em** ending from the first person singular and add:

for the familiar form, **i**   **piši!**
for the plural and polite form, **ite**   **pišite!**
for the 'we' form, **imo**   **pišimo!**

3 *Verbs of the -i conjugation (**govoriti**)*
You drop the 'm' from the first person singular and add:

for the familiar form, nothing   **govori!**
for the plural and polite form, **ite**   **govorite!**
for the 'we' form, **imo**   **govorimo!**

Note how the policeman said to Robert **Pohitite!** The verb **pohiteti** falls into the third group above. You drop the **m** from **pohitim** and add **ite** in order to get **pohitite**. He addressed Robert in the polite form. Had he addressed him in a familiar form he would have said **pohiti!**

The pedestrian said to Robert **Pojdite ...** This is the imperative form of **iti**, which, together with a few other commonly used verbs, is irregular:

	Familiar form	Polite form	'We' form
biti	bodi	bodite	bodimo
iti	pojdi	pojdite	pojdimo
imeti	imej	imejte	imejmo
pogledati	poglej	poglejte	poglejmo
vedeti	vedi	vedite	vedimo
smejati se	smej se	smejte se	smejmo se

Note: What is called the 'we' form is translated into English with 'Let's ...'.

In the first dialogue in this lesson you will have noticed Robert saying to Matej **Ne smej se!** To make any of the commands negative you put **ne** in front of the imperative.

Here are few commonly used expressions in the imperative form:

Familiar	Polite	
Oprosti!	**Oprostite!**	Excuse me!
Pohiti!	**Pohitite!**	Hurry up!
Pridi sem!	**Pridite sem!**	Come here!
Počakaj!	**Počakajte!**	Wait!
Pazi se!	**Pazite se!**	Be careful!
Ne skrbi!	**Ne skrbite!**	Don't worry!
Vozi previdno!	**Vozite previdno!**	Drive carefully!
Bodi tiho!	**Bodite tiho!**	Be quiet!
Ne jezi se!	**Ne jezite se!**	Don't be angry!
Verjemi mi!	**Verjemite mi!**	Believe me!

Exercise 6

letos	this year
v kino	to the cinema
zgodaj	early

(a) Ask your friend if he:

1 intends to go away for a holiday this year.
2 wants to come to the cinema this evening.
3 must start work early tomorrow morning.

(b) Tell him that you:

1 can help him.
2 cannot decide at the moment.
3 cannot go to the party on Friday evening.

Exercise 7

(a) Answer the questions you've been asked as suggested:

1 Zakaj se smejiš?
   SAY: *Because I'm in a good mood.*
2 Zakaj si moraš kupiti slovenski slovar?
   SAY: *Because I'm learning Slovene.*
3 Zakaj si vsak dan pozen?
   SAY: *Because my bus is late every day.*

(b) Ask questions as suggested so that you will get the following answers:

1 ASK: *Why are you in a bad mood?*
   Zato, ker imam zelo veliko dela.
2 ASK: *Why are you going to the post office?*
   Zato, ker moram poslati priporočeno pismo.
3 ASK: *Why are you going on foot?*
   Zato, ker ni daleč.

Exercise 8

Ask questions so that you get these answers:

1 Ne, tukaj ne smeš kaditi.
2 Ne, hvala. Danes ne morem iti v kino.
3 Ne, žal mi je. Danes zvečer ne morem priti.
4 Ne, v kiosku ne moreš kupiti slovarja.
5 Ne, ne morete iti peš.

Exercise 9 🔲

1 Your friend is telling you about something terrible that has happened to him. Say to him: *Don't worry!*
2 You're going out and your friend is not ready yet. Say to him: *Hurry up!*
3 You're on a crowded bus and you step on someone's foot. Say to them: *I'm sorry!*
4 You're on a trip with your friend and you have just seen something you'd like her to see too. Shout out to her: *Come here!*
5 You're telling her how you saw a similar thing somewhere else but she is looking at you rather suspiciously. Say to her: *Believe me!*
6 She is fed up listening to you and is walking away. *Ask her to wait!*

Exercise 10 🔲

You are on a trip abroad and lose your way frequently. How would you ask a stranger on the street:

1 Excuse me, where is the hotel Slon?
2 Excuse me, can you tell me where the post office is?
3 Is there a bus stop close by?
4 Is the bus usually on time?
5 Do you know what time it is?

Dialogue 3 🔲

Izvolite!

Here you are!

Robert has got to the post office and is being served

PRODAJALEC: Prosim?
ROBERT: Eno znamko za pismo, prosim.
PRODAJALEC: Za Slovenijo ali za tujino?
ROBERT: Za tujino. In te tri razglednice, prosim.
PRODAJALEC: Izvolite!
ROBERT: Hvala.

Robert has done what he had planned to do and thinks to himself:
        In sedaj grem lahko domov.

ASSISTANT:	*How may I help you?*
ROBERT:	*A stamp for a letter, please.*
ASSISTANT:	*For Slovenia or for abroad?*
ROBERT:	*For abroad. And these three postcards, please.*
ASSISTANT:	*Here you are.*
ROBERT:	*Thank you.*

Robert has done what he had planned to do and thinks to himself:
        And now I can go home.

Vocabulary

znamka	stamp	**izvolite**	here you are
pismo	letter	**domov**	home
razglednica	postcard		

Language points

About the post office

If you want to send an air-mail letter you will have to ask for **letalsko pismo**. To send something by registered post you need to send it **priporočeno**. You can put ordinary letters (**navadna pisma**) and postcards (**razglednice**) into a letter-box **poštni nabiralnik**. The postman (**poštar**) will bring the post to your home. Should you need a telephone number you look it up in a telephone directory (**telefonski imenik**). You can telephone from the post office at a much cheaper rate than from a hotel or from a telephone box (**telefonska govorilnica**). You can buy postcards, stamps, newspapers, cigarettes and other small items at a **kiosk**.

Please

Prosim means 'please'. You use this word where you would in English, but also in some additional ways.

1 When someone thanks you, reply **Prosim** or **Ni za kaj** which corresponds to 'Not at all' in English.

2 When you first answer the telephone, as you have seen in lesson 2, you say **Prosim** which corresponds to 'Hello' in English.

3 When you haven't heard what someone has said and you'd like them to repeat it, you say **Prosim?** which corresponds to 'I beg your pardon?' or 'Sorry?' in English.

4 In shops or at any similar place when someone is about to serve you they will probably say **Prosim** when they first address you, corresponding to 'How may I help you?' in English.

Here you are

A shop assistant, a waiter or whoever might give you something will probably say **Izvolite** when addressing you in a polite form or **Izvoli** when addressing you in a familiar form. The word means 'Here you are'.

To go home

In lesson 2 you learnt about the adverb **doma** which means 'at home'. The adverb **domov** means '(to) home' and like **doma** never changes. Note how Robert thinks to himself: **Sedaj grem lahko domov**.

The noun **dom** means 'one's home'. In other words, Slovene has three words for the English word 'home'. Look at the following examples showing how they are used:

To je moj dom.	This is my home.
Ali greš domov?	Are you going home? (i.e 'to your home')
Žal mi je, danes nisem doma.	I'm sorry, I'm not at home today.

Exercise 11

trgovina	shop

Explain to the person who has asked you for directions that:

1 The hotel is not far away. You can go on foot.
2 The shop is close by. Here, behind the hotel.
3 The bus stop is not very far away. One hundred metres straight on.
4 You are sorry but you don't know where the postbox is.
5 They can buy stamps in a kiosk.

Exercise 12

Re-arrange the words of the dialogue below so that they will make
sense. Clue: start with the word which has a capital letter.

kje je pošta Oprostite, ali veste
na levo ulica Prva
zaprta Tista je pošta
želite kupiti Ali znamke
in Ja, razglednice
za Tukaj vogalom kiosk je. lahko Tam znamke kupite
grem lahko Ali peš
ni Ja, daleč. minut Pet peš

Exercise 13 📼

How would you find out:

1 where the post office is?
2 where the letter-box is?
3 where the telephone box is?
4 where you could buy stamps?
5 where you could make a telephone call?

Exercise 14

Which word among the five in each of the following lines would
be odd in this particular group and why?

1 novinar, frizer, četrtek, pisatelj, učitelj
2 Angležinja, Slovenka, Američan, Italjanka, Nemka
3 govorim, delam, prideš, grem, vidim
4 ponedeljek, prevajalec, sreda, nedelja, torek
5 lep, star, nov, grd, velika

Exercise 15 📼

Pronunciation exercise. Notice that the Slovene **r** is always
pronounced as a consonant and is never absent or semi-pronounced
as it often is in English. It is pronounced strongly, slightly rolled.

Grem v trgovino.
Ne govorim rusko.
V torek in v sredo zvečer sem doma.

Oprostite, ali mi lahko poveste, kje je poštni nabiralnik?
Moj prijatelj Robert pride v četrtek.

Dialogue for comprehension 🔲

*On his way back home Robert has been stopped by someone who
is lost and Robert helps him. What nationality does the man turn
out to be and what does he do in Slovenia?*

v tisto smer	in that direction
čez vikend	over the weekend
službeno	on business

GOSPOD: Oprostite, ali veste mogoče, kje je hotel Lev?
ROBERT: Ja, vem. Jaz tam blizu stanujem. V enem drugem hotelu.
GOSPOD: Ali je daleč?
ROBERT: Hmm ... Ali ste peš?
GOSPOD: Ja. Ampak lahko se peljem z avtobusom.
ROBERT: Jaz grem v tisto smer. Lahko pridete z mano. Dvajset
minut hoje je.
GOSPOD: O, hvala. Moram rezervirati sobe v hotelu. Čez vikend
dobim obisk.
ROBERT: Ali ste turist?
GOSPOD: Ne, službeno sem tukaj za eno leto. Učim angleščino na
univerzi.
ROBERT: Ali ste Anglež?
GOSPOD: Ne, Američan sem.
ROBERT: O, potem se lahko pogovarjava po angleško!

5 Nič ne skrbi!

Don't worry!

Dialogue 1

Greva na kavo!

Let's go for a coffee!

Ann and Nick Moore, friends of a Slovene couple, Tomaž and Barbara Rataj, have gone to Slovenia to visit them. It is their first day and they have a lot to do. In spite of that, Ann suggests that they should have a cup of coffee somewhere

ANN:	Nick, greva na kavo!
NICK:	Nimava časa, pozna sva. Morava iti še na banko in zamenjati denar.
ANN:	Nisva pozna. Banka je odprta od osmih do šestih. Ura je šele pet. Ali imaš tukaj potni list?
NICK:	Ne, nimam. Imam pa vozniško dovoljenje in osebno izkaznico.
ANN:	Ne vem, če so to tukaj uradni dokumenti. Ampak nič ne skrbi! Jaz imam potni list! Popijva tukaj eno kavo.

NICK: Ali pride natakarica sem, ali greva midva tja?
NATAKARICA: Sem že tukaj!

ANN: *Nick, let's go for a coffee.*
NICK: *We haven't got time. We're late. We still have to go to the bank and change some money.*
ANN: *We aren't late. The bank is open from eight to six. It is only five o'clock now. Do you have your passport on you?*
NICK: *No, I haven't. But I have my driving licence and my ID.*
ANN: *I don't know if these are official documents here. But don't worry! I have my passport. Let's have a coffee here.*
NICK: *Does the waitress come here or do we go there?*
WAITRESS: *I'm already here!*

Vocabulary

kava	coffee	**potni list**	passport
banka	bank	**vozniško dovoljenje**	driving licence
zamenjati	to change	**osebna izkaznica**	identity card (ID)
denar	money	**uradni dokumenti**	official documents

Language points

Dual form

In this dialogue you will have noticed the verb forms **greva**, **nimava**, **sva**, **morava**, **nisva**, **popijva**. These are all dual forms of the verbs.

The dual form is an ancient Slavic form which has been lost in most languages but is still in use in Slovene. All Slovene nouns, verbs and pronouns have, in addition to singular and plural, the *dual form*, which is used when one talks about two things or two people. This increases the number of Slovene grammatical forms enormously. For example:

Ti in jaz **sva v Sloveniji.**   *You and I* are in Slovenia.
Midva **sva v Sloveniji.**   *We* are in Slovenia.

In English you say 'we' when you mean two people but in Slovene you say **midva** (we two). You use the plural when you talk about two people or two things in English but you need to use the dual form in Slovene. In other words, Slovene has:

singular form (one person or one thing);
dual form (two people or two things);
plural form (more than two people or things).

You must recognize the dual form because it is used all the time in Slovene.

Generally you can get by by using the plural when you mean two people or two things. Sometimes when referring to two people you cannot avoid using the dual form. For example:

Midva (i.e. 'we two') **sva poročena.**	*We* are married.
Onadva (i.e. 'they two') **sta dvojčka.**	*Marko and Denis* are twins.
Vidva sta dobra prijatelja.	*You two* are good friends.

In addition to this there is a feminine dual form (when talking of two females) and feminine plural form (when talking of more than two females):

Onidve (i.e. 'they two') **sta doma.**	*Marta and Sabina* are at home.

Let's conjugate the verbs 'to be', 'to have' and 'to go' in dual form:

	biti	*imeti*	*iti*
midva (we two)	**sva**	**imava**	**grava**
vidva (you two)	**sta**	**imata**	**gresta**
onadva (they two)	**sta**	**imata**	**gresta**

The endings of the verbs in dual form are:

midva	-va
vidva	-ta
onadva	-ta

The possessive pronouns in the dual form are:

Masculine	*Feminine*	*Neuter*	
najin	**najina**	**najino**	yours and mine, our(s) (two)
vajin	**vajina**	**vajino**	yours and his or hers, your(s) (two)
njun	**njuna**	**njuno**	his and hers, their(s) (two)

For example:

sin	son	
hčerka	daughter	

Rudi je najin sin.   Rudi is our son.
Martina je njuna hčerka.   Martina is their (two) daughter.
Ali je to vajin avto?   Is this your (two) car?

Here/there

There are two words in Slovene for each of the English words,
'here' and 'there'. Look at these sentences:

Jaz sem *tukaj.*   I am *here.*
Ali prideš tudi ti *sem?*   Are you coming *here* too?

Simona je *tam.*   Simona is *there.*
Tudi jaz grem *tja.*   I am going *there* too.

When something is being placed here or there you use the words
tukaj or **tam**. Whenever there is a movement involved, e.g. whenever someone or something is coming or going here or there, you
use the words **sem** or **tja**.

Do not confuse the meaning of **sem** 'here' with the verb 'to be'
as in **Jaz sem** (I am). You will be able to see the difference from
the context.

Open/closed

The word **odprto** means 'open' and the word **zaprto** means 'closed'.
They come from the verbs **odpreti** (to open), and **zapreti** (to close).
For example:

Vsako jutro odprem okno.   I open the window every morning.
Vedno pozabim zapreti vrata. I always forget to close the door.

One usually sees these verbs in the imperative form as in:

Odpri okno!   Open the window!
Zapri vrata!   Close the door!

In most official places you will see the sign:

Odprto od .... do ...   Open from ... until ...

At what time? (At 1, 2, 3 o'clock)

The question **ob kateri uri?** means 'at what time?', however, most people will simply use **kdaj?** meaning 'when?'. When you answer this question you need the following endings, using the twelve-hour clock:

1	enih	5	petih	9	devetih
2	dveh	6	šestih	10	desetih
3	treh	7	sedmih	11	enajstih
4	štirih	8	osmih	12	dvanajstih

These endings are also used with prepositions:

od	from
do	until
ob	at
okoli	around, at about

For example:

V službi sem od devetih do petih. Kosilo imam včasih ob dvanájstih in včasih ob enih. Po navadi pridem domov okoli šestih.

I'm at work from nine to five. I have lunch sometimes at twelve and sometimes at one. I usually come home at about six.

When you want to enquire when the first (**prvi**) or the last (**zadnji**) train, bus or plane leaves for a town, city or country these places will have the accusative ending, for example:

Ob kateri uri pelje prvi vlak v (za) Ljubljano?	At what time does the first train to Ljubljana leave?
Ob kateri uri pelje zadnji avtobus v (za) Maribor?	At what time does the last bus to Maribor leave?

You will have noticed the preposition **za** (for). As in English, you can say 'for', as in 'At what time does the first train for Ljubljana leave?'

About the bank

The word you will need most when having anything to do with a bank is 'money' (**denar**). You may not have cash (**gotovina**) but a cheque (**ček**) or a travellers' cheque (**potovalni ček**). If you are dealing with cheques you will need a cheque book (**čekovna knjižica**). At the bank you can deposit money (**vložiti denar**) or withdraw money (**dvigniti denar**). You may have a credit card (**kreditna kartica**) which you use at a cash point (**bančni avtomat**) and for which you have your personal number (**osebna številka**). To do any of this you will need an official document (**uradni dokument**). In Slovenia an identity form (**osebna izkaznica**) is usually an official document; foreigners are mostly requested to present their passport (**potni list**).

You can change your money in banks, in larger hotels, in *bureaux de change* and in some travel agencies. Travellers' cheques, Eurocheques and major credit cards are accepted in most places. Here are a few adjectives you may like to use when you want to describe people:

bogat	rich	**pošten**	honest
reven	poor	**skromen**	modest

Exercise 1

Insert the words for 'here' and 'there' in these sentences:

1 Moja prijateljica je ... (*here*).
2 Jaz grem ... tomorrow. (*there*)
3 Prosim, pridi ... (*here*)
4 Nihče ni ... (*there*)
5 Mislim, da so vsi ... (*here*)

Exercise 2

Change the verbs in bold in this conversation so that the conversation will be in the polite form of address:

stanovati	to live

Ali **govoriš** slovensko?
Ja, študiram slovenščino. Ali **si ti** Slovenec?
Ne, nisem. Moja mama je Slovenka. V Sloveniji sem na dopustu. Pridem vsako leto.
Kje **stanuješ**?
V Ljubljani v centru. In **ti**?
Tudi jaz stanujem v centru. Ali **imaš** telefon?
Ja, moja telefonska številka je 671 468. Kako **ti** je ime?
Ime mi je Renata. Pišem se Javornik. In kako je **tebi** ime?
Ali **imaš** telefon?

Exercise 3

You are on holiday in Slovenia with a friend. Tell a Slovene person you have met what you two do in England.

1 We work from nine to five.
2 We usually have lunch at 1 o'clock.
3 On Saturdays and on Sundays we are not at work.
4 We come home at about 7 o'clock.
5 We go on holiday every year in August.

Exercise 4

Ask at the station when the first train for the following town leaves. The first one has been done for you.

Mesto	Čas
1 London	06.00
2 Ljubljana	07.00
3 Pariz	08.00
4 Amsterdam	05.00
5 Ženeva	09.00
6 Praga	04.00

1 Prvi vlak v London pelje ob šestih zjutraj.

Exercise 5

Suppose you work at the tourist information office. Tell the person who asked you that the last bus to the places in exercise 4 leaves at the times given. The first example has been done for you

1 Zadnji avtobus v London pelje ob šestih zvečer.

Dialogue 2 🔲

Čaj z mlekom?

Tea with milk?

Ann and Nick are sitting in the café and talking about how different people like their tea and coffee

ANN: Jaz imam zelo rada čaj z mlekom, ampak tukaj pijem čaj z limono. Vsi čudno gledajo, če naročim čaj z mlekom.

NICK: Moj sodelavec ima rad čaj z medom. Baje je zelo dober. Ali vprašam natakarico, če ga imajo?

ANN: Ne, raje bi čaj z limono.

NICK: Jaz imam pa najraje črno kavo. Ampak mislim, da je kava v Sloveniji zelo močna. Tukaj pijem belo kavo.

ANN: Slovenci so navajeni, piti močno kavo. Vsi jo imajo radi.

ANN: *I very much like tea with milk but here I drink lemon tea. Everybody looks at me if I order tea with milk.*

NICK: *A colleague of mine drinks tea with honey. It is supposedly very good. Shall I ask if they have it?*

ANN: *No, I'd prefer lemon tea.*

NICK: *I like coffee best. But I think that the coffee in Slovenia is very strong. I drink white coffee here.*

ANN: *The Slovenes are used to drinking strong coffee. They all like it.*

Vocabulary

kavarna	café	**med**	honey
čaj	tea	**baje**	supposedly
mleko	milk	**misliti**	to think
limona	lemon	**močen**	strong
čudno	strangely	**biti navajen**	to be used to
naročiti	to order	**piti**	to drink
sodelavec	colleague		

Note: The expression **biti navajen** 'to be used to' is followed by an infinitive in Slovene. Note how Ann says **Slovenci so navajeni, piti močno kavo**.

The verbs **piti** (to drink), **peti** (to sing), **poslati** 'to send' fall into a category of verbs with **-je** stem. They are conjugated like this:

	piti	*peti*	*poslati*
1	pijem	pojem	pošljem
2	piješ	poješ	pošlješ
3	pije	poje	pošlje
1	pijemo	pojemo	pošljemo
2	pijete	pojete	pošljete
3	pijejo	pojejo	pošljejo

Would you like a drink?

Places where you have a drink are **kavarna** (café), or **bife** (buffet), where you usually just stand by the bar. You can have a snack in a café but for a meal you go to **restavracija** (a restaurant). The English preposition 'for', as in 'to go for' a drink, is translated as **na**. Note how Barbara says to Tomaž **Greva *na* kavo!** A waiter will probably say to you **Želite, prosim?**, or just **Prosim?**, both meaning 'What would you like?' Here are a few drinks you may like to order:

malo pivo	a small beer
veliko pivo	a large beer
kozarec belega vina	a glass of white wine
kozarec rdečega vina	a glass of red wine
sok	juice

To like something

You express 'to like (something)' with the verb **imeti** plus **rad** (m.), **rada** (f.), **rado** (n.) and **radi** (pl.). For example:

Melita ima rada čaj.	Melita likes tea.
Janez ima rad kavo.	Janez likes coffee.
Slovenci imajo radi močno kavo.	Slovenes like strong coffee.

The noun of whatever you like will be in the accusative case because you can ask yourself the question 'Whom/what do I like?'

The use of the accusative case

In lesson 2 you learnt about the nominative case, which is used for the subject of a sentence or as a predicate nominative in a sentence (e.g. 'a teacher' in the sentence 'Jana is a teacher'). The accusative case is used as a direct object and as the object of some prepositions. Let us first see how it is used as a direct object.

Črna kava je zelo dobra.   *Black coffee* is very good.

In this sentence 'black coffee' is the subject; it governs the verb, i.e. it tells you what is very good.

Jaz imam rad *črno kavo.***   I like *black coffee.*

In this sentence 'black coffee' is the object; it receives the action of the verb, i.e. it tells you what I like.

The object of a sentence is in the accusative case and in Slovene it has a different ending from the subject. The endings are as follows:

First declension
Feminine nouns ending in **a** change their ending to **o**. For example:

Tanja je *moja prijateljica.*   Tanja is my friend.
Vsak dan vidim *mojo*   I see my friend every day.
   prijateljico.

Second declension
Feminine nouns ending in a consonant stay the same but the adjective which has the ending **a** in the nominative changes the ending to **o**. For example:

To je *velika cerkev.*   This is a big church.
Ali vidiš tisto *veliko cerkev*?   Do you see that big church?

All adjectives modifying nouns of the first and second declensions have an **o** ending.

Third declension
Masculine nouns denoting non-living objects and their adjectives stay the same. For example:

V garaži stoji moj *novi avto.* My new car is in the garage.
                            (Literally 'In the garage
                            stands my new car').
Kupiti si moram *nov avto.*   I must buy myself a new car.

Masculine nouns denoting living objects take the ending **a** in the accusative case. For example:

Marko je moj *dober prijatelj.*   Marko is a good friend of mine.
                            (Literally 'Marko is my good
                            friend')
Imam *dobrega prijatelja.*   I have a good friend.

Note: Adjectives modifying non-living objects do not have any ending in the accusative case; they remain as in the nominative case. Adjectives modifying living objects have the ending **ega** as in **dobrega**.

Fourth declension
Neuter nouns stay the same. For example:

London je *veliko mesto.*   London is a big city.
Grem v *mesto.*   I'm going to town.

Most adjectives modifying neuter nouns take an **o** ending. Very few adjectives take an **e** ending.

Personal pronouns in the accusative case

Singular

jaz	**mene**	*or*	**me**	me
ti	**tebe**	*or*	**te**	you
on	**njega**	*or*	**ga**	him
ona	**njo**	*or*	**jo**	her
ono	**njega**	*or*	**ga**	it

Dual

midva	**naju**			us two
vidva	**vaju**			you two
onadva	**njiju**	*or*	**ju**	them two

Plural

mi	**nas**			us
vi	**vas**			you
oni	**njih**	*or*	**jih**	them

The long form of the personal pronouns (**mene**, **tebe**, etc.) is usually used for emphasis and after prepositions. Short forms are used much more often.

The question you can ask yourself in order to have a noun in the accusative case in an answer is **koga?** for people or **kaj?** for things.

The prepositions used with the accusative case are **v**, **na**, **po**, and **za**.

When you want to translate the pronoun 'it' you must keep in mind that the Slovene nouns distinguish three genders, whereas in English, 'it' is always neuter. Look at the following examples:

Tomaž išče dežnik. Kdo ga išče?
Tomaž is looking for an umbrella. Who is looking for it?

Because **dežnik** is masculine in gender you need to use the masculine pronoun in the accusative case (**ga**) to express 'it'.

Kje je hrana za psa? Dal sem jo v hladilnik.
Where is the food for the dog? I put it in the fridge.

Because **hrana** is feminine in gender you need to use the feminine pronoun in the accusative case (**jo**) to express 'it'.

Colours

To ask what colour something is you say **Kakšne barve je ...?** As a response you will get the colours:

bel/-a/-o	white	**moder/-a/-o**	blue
črn/-a/-o	black	**rjav/-a/-o**	brown
rdeč/-a/-e	red	**siv/-a/-o**	grey
zelen/-a/-o	green	**rumen/-a/-o**	yellow

All colours are adjectives; therefore they take the ending of the noun they modify in a particular case. For example:

Črna kava je dobra. Black coffee is good.
Nick ima rad črno kavo ampak Nick likes black coffee but in
v Sloveniji pije belo kavo. Slovenia he drinks white coffee.

The neuter form of the adjectives has an **e** ending at times rather than the usual **o** ending. This occurs when the masculine which is the stem form of the adjective ends in the following consonants: **c**, **č**, **j**, **š**, **ž**. This applies to all adjectives.

Exercise 6

Choose the correct answer:

1 Kaj ima rada Ann?
   (a) Čaj z limono.
   (b) Čaj z mlekom.
   (c) Čaj z medom.
2 Kaj ima najraje Nick?
   (a) Belo kavo.
   (b) Črno kavo.
   (c) Močno kavo.

3 Kaj imate vi najraje?
  (a) Čaj z limono..
  (b) Čaj z mlekom.
  (c) Belo kavo.
  (d) Črno kavo.

Exercise 7

Fill in the suggested personal pronouns in the accusative case:

1 Ali ... pogosto vidiš? (*them two*)
2 Ne poznajo ... (*us*)
3 On ... ima rad. (*her*)
4 Ona ... ima rada. (*him*)
5 Vidim ... vsak dan. (*them*)

Exercise 8

Say that:

1 This book is dark blue.
2 Her dictionary is red.
3 This hotel is grey.
4 His new car is light brown.
5 My old driving licence is purple.

Exercise 9

Križanka

1 milk
2 tea
3 coffee
4 Wednesday
5 money
6 lemon
7 bank
8 café

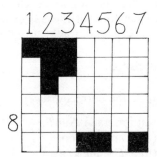

Exercise 10

How would you write yourself these notes in your diary:

1 I must go to the bank on Wednesday and change some money.
2 I am going to Italy in August.
3 I have a meeting in Ljubljana on Thursday.
4 I must ask at what time the last train to Milan leaves.
5 My secretary is in Germany in December.

Dialogue 3 ▭

Ali igraš tenis?

Do you play tennis?

After having had their coffee Nick and Ann talk about what they will do during their stay

ANN: Nick, ali veš, kje je v Ljubljani odprti bazen? Jaz zelo rada plavam.
NICK: Ne, ne vem. Vprašati moraš Barbaro. Lahko jo tudi vprašaš, kje je teniško igrišče.
ANN: Tomaž igra tenis. On mora vedeti. Ampak sedaj smo sredi poletja in je zelo vroče.
NICK: Ali misliš, da igra tenis pozimi, ko sneži?
ANN: Ne bodi nesramen!
       O, poglej to lepo zgradbo. 'G L E D A L I Š Č E'. Kaj to pomeni? Kje imava slovar?
NICK: Ti ga imaš v torbi.
ANN: Ja, seveda. Gledališče pomeni teater. Poglej, Barbara in Tomaž naju že čakata. Ali ju vidiš?

ANN: *Nick, do you know where there is an open-air swimming pool in Ljubljana? I very much like swimming.*
NICK: *No, I don't know. You must ask Barbara. You can also ask her where the tennis court is.*
ANN: *Tomaž plays tennis. He must know. But we're in the middle of the summer now and it is very hot.*
NICK: *Do you think he plays tennis in the winter when it snows?*
ANN: *Don't be rude!*
       Oh, look at that beautiful building. 'G L E D A L I Š Č E'. What does it mean? Where do we have our dictionary?
NICK: *You have it in your bag.*
ANN: *Yes, of course. Gledališče means theatre. Look, Barbara and Tomaž are already waiting for us. Do you see them?*

Vocabulary

odprti bazen	open-air pool	**zima**	winter
plavati	to swim	**sneži**	it snows
vprašati	to ask	**gledališče**	theatre
sredi	in the middle of	**nesramen**	rude
poletje	summer	**torba**	bag

Language points

To like to do something

You express 'to like to do something' with the correct personal ending of **rad** plus the verb with the correct personal ending, for example, **rad** (m.), **rada** (f.), **radi** (pl.):

Ann *rada pije* čaj.	Ann likes drinking coffee.
Nick *rad pije* kavo.	Nick likes drinking coffee.
Slovenci *radi pijejo* močno kavo.	The Slovenes like drinking strong coffee.
Ann *rada plava*.	Ann likes swimming.
Nick *rad igra* tenis.	Nick likes playing tennis.

About sport

You express someone's involvement with sport with the expression
ukvarjati se s športom. For example:

Ann se ukvarja s športom.	Ann plays a lot of sport.
	or Ann is into sport.
Jaz se ne ukvarjam s športom.	I'm not sporty.
	or I'm not a sportsman.
Ali se ti ukvarjaš s športom?	Are you a sportsman?
	or Are you into sport?
	or Do you play a lot of sport?

Common sports in Slovenia are:

tenis	tennis	**badminton**	badminton
namizni tenis	table tennis	**hokej**	hockey
nogomet	football	**gimnastika**	gymnastics
rokomet	volleyball	**drsanje**	ice-skating
košarka	basketball	**smučanje**	skiing

To say that you play a particular sport you use the verb **igrati**. You
would, for example say:

Tomaž igra tenis, rokomet, nogomet ...

However, at times you express your involvement with a particular
sport with the verb form of the sport, for example:

plavati	to swim
jahati	to ride
smučati	to ski

You can swim in:

odprti bazen	open-air pool
zaprti bazen	covered pool

Other recreational facilities are:

športni park	sports park
športno igrišče	playground
rekreacijski center	leisure centre
trim steza	running track
drsališče	skating rink

You may want to talk to Slovenes about cricket (**kriket**), golf (**golf**),
or rugby (**ragby**) but they are unlikely to know much about them.

Seasons

pomlad	spring	**jesen**	autumn/fall
poletje	summer	**zima**	winter

When you want to say that something is going on in a particular season you express this as follows:

spomladi	in spring	**v jeseni**	in autumn/fall
poleti	in summer	**pozimi**	in winter

The adjectives for the seasons are:

pomladni, spomladni, pomladanski
poletni
jesenski
zimski

What does it mean?

When you want to ask someone what a particular word means you say: **Kaj to pomeni?** or **Kaj pomeni ... ?**

You may want to know how you say a particular thing. You ask:

Kako se reče ...?   How do you say ...?

More about the accusative case

In the dialogue you have seen how the personal pronouns in the accusative case are used, as in:

misliti na	to think of

Jaz *ga* imam v torbi.
Ali *ju* vidiš?

There are a few expressions where you need to use the personal pronoun in the accusative case.

Ona misli na njega.	She thinks of him.
Mi mislimo na vas.	We think of you.

skrbeti	to worry
motiti	to disturb

You use these verbs like this:

Kaj te skrbi?	What worries you?
Nič me ne skrbi?	Nothing worries me.
Ali te to moti?	Does this disturb you?
Njega moti, mene ne.	It disturbs him, not me.

You will have noticed that the names **Tomaž** and **Barbara** have endings. Where possible, first names, surnames, towns and countries follow the same rules as all other nouns. You will see more about this later on.

Exercise 11

sestra	sister

Tell your friend that:

1 The English like to play football.
2 Ann likes swimming.
3 Tomaž likes playing tennis.
4 You like playing badminton.
5 Your sister likes to ski.

Exercise 12

Test yourself! Kako se reče:

1 a stamp for a letter
2 a passport
3 an umbrella
4 a playground
5 autumn/fall

Exercise 13

Tell the person who had asked you what these words mean:

1 uradni dokument
2 osebna izkaznica

3 razglednica
4 vozniško dovoljenje
5 cerkev

Exercise 14

Choose adjectives you think are suitable for the following nouns.
Bear in mind that they have to suit the noun grammatically and
in meaning. Some adjectives are given below for you, but if you
can think of any others do use them:

1 film
2 vreme
3 delo
4 jezik
5 kava
6 prijateljica

majhen, dober, lahek, nov, lep, velik, slab, težek, star, grd, bogat,
reven, pomemben.

Exercise 15 ▭▭

Pronunciation exercise. You have come across the three letters
which do not exist in English: **č, š, ž.** Let's pronounce some words
in which you have seen them:

letališče	študent
četrtek	učitelj
dežuje	črn avto
hiša	poštni nabiralnik
garaža	športno igrišče

Dialogue for comprehension ▭▭

*Tomaž and Barbara have taken Nick and Ann for a coffee. Barbara
goes to the bar to give their order and Tomaž and Nick start talking
about sport. Find out what their plan for tomorrow is*

dolgočasen	boring

BARBARA:	Natakarica, ali lahko naročim, prosim?
NATAKARICA:	Ja, seveda. Kaj želite?
BARBARA:	Eno belo kavo, eno črno kavo, en sok in en čaj z limono.
NICK:	Tomaž, ali greš pogosto v rekreacijski center?
TOMAŽ:	Ja, pozimi grem pogosto tja. Sedaj spomladi sem več zunaj. Nick, ali ti igraš kriket? Jaz ne vem ničesar o tej igri.
NICK:	Jaz ne igram kriket, ampak veliko mojih prijateljev igra to igro.
TOMAŽ:	Ne morem razumeti. ... Meni se zdi tako dolgočasna ...
NICK:	Če malo premisliš, tenis je tudi dolgočasna igra.
TOMAŽ:	O, ne ... če želiš, greva lahko jutri igrat tenis.
NICK:	Ja, Barbara in Ann pa gresta lahko plavat.

6 Kaj iščeš?

What are you looking for?

In this lesson you will learn about:

- The dative and the locative case
- More words and expressions about traffic
- Words and expressions describing weather
- More ways of expressing what you like
- How to express 'to go' and 'to be' somewhere

Dialogue 1 🎧

Mudi se nama!

We're in a hurry!

Tomaž and Barbara are leaving their house for their one-week holiday in England. They are getting their last few things ready

BARBARA: Kaj iščeš?

TOMAŽ: Iščem dežnik. V Angliji dežuje. In mrzlo je. Kje je moj plašč?

BARBARA: V dnevni sobi na stolu. Dežnik je v kopalnici. Tvoj ključ je na mizi v kuhinji. Avto moraš še zapeljati v garažo.

TOMAŽ: Avto je že v garaži.

BARBARA: Sosedi moram napisati sporočilo. Hrana za psa je v hladilniku.

TOMAŽ: Psu je treba dati še vodo.

BARBARA: Ja. V hiši je vse v redu. Samo radio moram še ugasniti in greva. Mudi se nama! Ali si pripravljen?

BARBARA: *What are you looking for?*

Tomaž: *I'm looking for my umbrella. It rains in England. And it is cold. Where is my coat?*

Barbara: *In the living room on the chair. Your umbrella is in the bathroom. And your key is on the table in the kitchen. You have to put the car in the garage.*

Tomaž: *The car is already in the garage.*

Barbara: *I must write a message for the neighbour. The food for the dog is in the fridge.*

Tomaž: *We must still give some water to the dog.*

Barbara: *Yes. I think everything is fine in the house. I only need to switch off the radio and we're off! We're in a hurry! Are you ready?*

Vocabulary

iskati (iščem)	to look for	**sosed/soseda**	neighbour
dežnik	umbrella		(male/female)
dežuje	it rains	**napisati (napišem)**	to write
mrzlo je	it's cold	**sporočilo**	message
plašč	coat	**hrana**	food
dnevna soba	living room	**pes**	dog
stol	chair	**hladilnik**	fridge
kopalnica	bathroom	**voda**	water
ključ	key	**red**	order
kuhinja	kitchen	**radio**	radio
zapeljati	to put, to drive	**biti pripravljen**	to be ready
(zapeljem)	to run		

Language points

You know the verb **pisati**, which means 'to write'. In this dialogue you have come across the verb **napisati**, which also means 'to write'. Some Slovene verbs have prefixes at times and this marginally changes the meaning; but we will look into this more thoroughly later on.

To go somewhere and to be somewhere

In lesson 1 you saw that the preposition **v** means 'in' as in **v Sloveniji**. **V** can also mean 'to' when you use it with the so-called verbs of movement. You would, for example, say:

Grem *v Slovenijo.*   I am going *to Slovenia.*

but

Sem *v Sloveniji.*   I am *in Slovenia.*

The difference between these two sentences is caused by the verb and is indicated by the ending of the noun.

The question 'where?' has two meanings in Slovene:

1 **kje?**, meaning where something is placed;
2 **kam?**, meaning where something is going to.

Whenever something is in motion you need the accusative case to express this, e.g. **Grem v Anglijo**.

živeti	to live

When something is stationary you need the locative case to express this, i.e. **Živim v Angliji**. You will see more about the locative case in lesson 12.

To say that you are going somewhere you use the verb **iti** 'to go'. In English the usual preposition is 'to' but in Slovene there are the prepositions **k**, **po**, **na**, **v**, all covering the English preposition 'to'. Look at the following sentences:

---

zdravnik	doctor
kruh	bread
mleko	milk
sestanek	meeting

Grem v gledališče	I'm going to the theatre
v trgovino	the shop
k zdravniku	the doctor's
k prijatelju,	see my (male) friend,
k prijateljici	(female) friend
na pošto	the post office
na sestanek	the meeting
po kruh in mleko	get some bread and milk
po časopis	get the newspaper

Note: The preposition **po** is used when you are going somewhere in order to get something, as in 'I'm going to get some milk and bread' or 'I'm going to get the paper'.

When you say that you are *in* these places the nouns will have different endings, i.e. the endings of the locative case. You will say:

Sem v gledališču	I am in a/the theatre
v trgovini	in a/the shop
pri zdravniku	at the doctor's
pri prijatelju,	at my (male) friend's
pri prijateljici	(female) friend's
na pošti	at the post office
na sestanku	at the meeting

In the singular, the endings of the locative and the dative case are the same. We will first study the dative case.

The use of the dative case

The dative case is most often used for an indirect object; this tells you to whom or for whom something is done. In English the prepositions 'to' and 'for' indicate an indirect object; in Slovene you simply need to put the correct ending on the noun and you do not translate the prepositions. The endings in the dative case are as follows.
The nouns of first and second declensions take the ending **i**. For example:

Ona je moja *soseda*.	She is my neighbour.
Moji *sosedi* pišem sporočilo.	I'm writing a message to my neighbour.

The nouns of third and fourth declensions take the ending **u**. For example:

On je moj *sosed*.	He is my neighbour.
Mojemu *sosedu* pišem sporočilo.	I'm writing a message to my neighbour.

Adjectives also have these endings.

Personal pronouns in the dative case

jaz	meni	*or*	mi	to me
ti	tebi	*or*	ti	to you
on	njemu	*or*	mu	to him
ona	njej	*or*	ji	to her
ono	njemu	*or*	mu	to it

midva	nama			to the two of us
vidva	vama			to the two of you
onadva	njima	*or*	jima	to the two of them

mi	nam			to us
vi	vam			to you
oni	njim	*or*	jim	to them

The question you can ask in order to have a noun in the dative case as an answer is **komu?** (to whom?) for people, **čemu?** (to what?) for things.

Some commonly used verbs which require the dative case are:

dati	to give
pomagati	to help
pokazati	to show
povedati	to tell
pisati	to write to someone
zahvaliti se	to thank oneself
oprostiti	to excuse
svetovati	to advise, to suggest, to recommend

The prepositions used with the dative case are: **k/h** (to), **kljub** (in spite of), **proti** (to, towards, against). **K** is used when you want to say 'to whom' or to whose place you are going, for example:

Grem k prijatelju, k Tanji, h gospodu Korenu ...
I am going to see a friend (male), Tanja, Mr Koren ...

You use **h** when a noun after the preposition begins with **k** or **g**. **K** and **h** mean exactly the same.

Kakšen/-a/-o?

The question **kakšen?** means 'what, what kind of, what is it like?', as in **Kakšen avto imaš?** (What car do you have?)

You also use this question when you ask about the weather, for example:

Kakšno je danes vreme?	What's the weather like today?
Kakšno je vreme v Angliji, v Sloveniji?	What's the weather like in England, in Slovenia?

Everyday expressions about the weather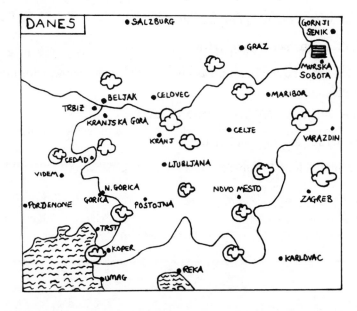

mrzlo je	it is cold
toplo je	it is warm
vroče je	it is hot
soparno je	it is humid
sonce sije	the sun is shining
sončno je	it is sunny
vetrovno je	it is windy
dežuje	it is raining
sneži	it is snowing

Danes je lepo/slabo vreme.	The weather is nice/bad today.
Zelo mrzlo/vroče je.	It's cold/hot.

You use the personal pronoun in the dative or in the accusative case in order to describe how you feel, for example:

Zebe me.	I'm cold.
Vroče mu je.	He's hot.
Ali te zebe ali ti je vroče?	Are you cold or hot?

Temperatura

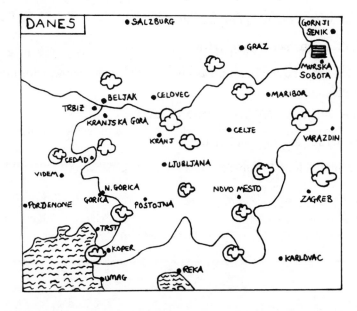

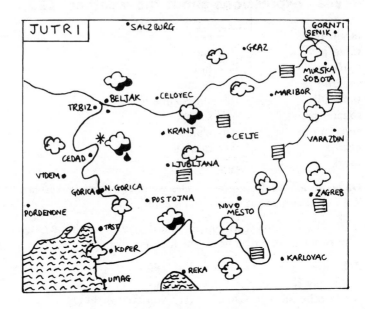

The temperature in Slovenia is given in degrees celsius as follows:

25°C petindvajset stopinj celzija

In the winter the temperature might be

–5°C minus pet stopinj celzija

Notice how the temperature is given in the table below, with the heading

TEMPERATURE AROUND EUROPE

yesterday at 8a.m. and 2p.m.

Also notice how European cities are spelt in Slovene.

```
TEMPERATURE
PO EVROPI

včeraj ob 8. in ob 14. uri

HELSINKI ..............     -3/-2
STOCKHOLM.......          -4/0
MOSKVA.............       -17/-10
BERLIN .................     -1/4
VARŠAVA...........          0/3
LONDON ............         -4/7
AMSTERDAM.......            0/8
BRUSELJ..............        -1/8
PARIZ .....................   -1/9
DUNAJ ................        0/6
ZÜRICH .. ...........        -2/5
ŽENEVA...............         4/9
RIM......................     7/15
MILAN ................        3/7
BEOGRAD ..........           -1/9
BARCELONA......             7/17
ISTAMBUL............         7/14
MADRID.............          3/16
LIZBONA.............        11/20
ATENE.................      11/18
BUCAREST...........         2/13
MALTA.................      16/20
PRAGA................        -3/3
```

To be in a hurry

To say that someone is in a hurry in Slovene you use the expression **mudi se** plus the personal pronoun of the person in question in the dative case. For example:

Mudi se mi.   I am in a hurry.
Ali se ti mudi?   Are you in a hurry?
Danes se nam ne mudi.   We're not in a hurry today.

Note how Barbara said to Tomaž **Mudi se nama** meaning 'We two are in a hurry'.

The verb **hiteti** means 'to hurry', 'to rush', and you can ask someone:

Kam hitiš?   Where are you hurrying?
Zakaj tako hitiš?   Why are you hurrying?

They will give you as an answer:

Hitim, mudi se mi!   I'm rushing, I'm in a hurry!

Vklopiti/izklopiti, prižgati/ugasniti

The verbs **vklopiti** and **prižgati** 'to switch on' and **izklopiti** and **ugasniti** 'to switch off' are conjugated like all other verbs and are used as in English. For example:

Ali lahko vkolopim radio?	May I switch on the radio?
Zakaj ne ugasneš televizor?	Why don't you switch off the TV?
Temno je že. Prižgimo luč.	It's dark. Let's switch on the light.

Še/že/šele

You know all of these words:

še	still, yet
že	already, yet, before
šele	only, not later than, not until

Since they all have various possibilities in meaning and since they are used a lot in Slovene, here are a few sentences using these words for you to try to get your ear tuned to the way you can use them:

Ali še nisi gotov?	Aren't you ready yet?
Ne poznam ga še.	I don't know him yet.
Ali se je še spomniš?	Do you still remember her?
Ura je šele osem in sem že utrujen.	It is only 8 o'clock and I'm already tired.

Exercise 1

Answer the questions referring to the dialogue:

1 Kaj išče Tomaž?
2 Kje je njegov plašč?
3 Kje je njegov dežnik?
4 Kje je njegov ključ?
5 Kje je hrana za psa?

Exercise 2

Ask the people below if they are going to the places indicated, as in the example given. Use the familiar form of address:

Marko/work

Marko, ali greš v službo?

1 Monika/post office
2 Petra/bank
3 Oto/a meeting
4 Nadja/to see a male friend
5 Sebastjan/the doctor
6 Anja/the shop
7 Sergej/to get a paper

Exercise 3 💾

A friend is visiting you for a weekend. You are going out to the theatre one evening and before leaving the house you have this conversation. Fill in your part.

ključ od avta   car key

YOU: 1 *Ask your friend what he is looking for.*

YOUR FRIEND: Iščem moj plašč.

YOU: 2 *Tell him that you think his coat is in the living room.*

YOUR FRIEND: Ali veš, kakšno je danes vreme?

YOU: 3 *Say that it is cold. Tell him that the temperature is minus 2 degrees celsius and that it's windy.*

YOUR FRIEND: Ali greva z avtom?

YOU: 4 *Say yes. Ask him if he knows where the car key is.*

YOUR FRIEND: V kuhinji na mizi.

YOU: 5 *Ask if he is ready. Tell him that you (two) are in a hurry. Tell him that it is already 7 o'clock.*

Exercise 4

Insert the words **še**, **že** or **šele**.

1 Ali si ... gotov?
2 Ne, nisem ... gotov.
3 Sporočilo moram ... napisati prijatelju.
4 Vsi smo ... pripravljeni, ti si pa ... v kopalnici.
5 Ne mudi se nam. Ura je ... tri.

Exercise 5

nekaj	something

1 Ask your friend:
   Can you help me tomorrow afternoon?
2 Telephone your friend and say to him:
   Can I come to your place this evening. I must tell you something.
3 You're telling your friend about something terrible that happened to you. Ask him:
   Can you suggest what I should do?
4 You visited a friend who told you what an expensive coat she had bought. Say to her:
   Show me your new coat!
5 You are in a café with your friend and you would like to order another drink. Ask him:
   Are you in a hurry?

Dialogue 2 ▭

Srečno pot!

Have a good trip!

Tomaž and Barbara are at the bus stop. They're waiting for the number 5 bus, which goes to the airport. They are already late and Tomaž hails a taxi

BARBARA: Tomaž, že pol ure čakava na avtobus in še ga ni. Ustavi ta taksi!

(Tomaž hails a taxi and the taxi draws up.)

TAKSIST: Kam želita iti?

TOMAŽ: Na letališče, prosim.

TAKSIST: Vstopita!

BARBARA: Danes je promet zelo gost. Zdi se mi, da gredo vsi iz mesta.

TAKSIST: Ja, petek je in ob petkih je po navadi tako. In kam vidva potujeta?

BARBARA: V Anglijo.

TAKSIST: Ali gresta na službeno potovanje?

BARBARA: Ne, na obisk. Prijatelje imava tam.
TAKSIST: Moj prijatelj vozi tovornjak in pelje pogosto v Anglijo. Pravi, da mu tam ni všeč.
BARBARA: Vsak ima svoj okus. Nama je v Angliji zelo všeč.
TAKSIST: Ja, seveda gospa. Prav imate. Kako dolgo ostaneta?
BARBARA: Deset dni.
(They get to the airport.)
TAKSIST: Prijeten dopust! In srečno pot!

BARBARA: *Tomaž, we've already been waiting for the bus for half an hour and it hasn't come. Stop this taxi!*
(Tomaž hails the taxi and the taxi draws up.)
TAXI-DRIVER: *Where do you want to go?*
TOMAŽ: *To the airport, please.*
TAXI-DRIVER: *Get in!*
BARBARA: *The traffic today is terrible. It seems to me that everyone is going out of town.*
TAXI-DRIVER: *Yes, it is Friday and on Fridays it is usually like this. And where are you two going?*
BARBARA: *To England.*
TAXI-DRIVER: *Are you going for a business trip?*
BARBARA: *No, for a visit. We have friends there.*
TAXI-DRIVER: *A friend of mine drives a lorry and he often goes to England. He says he doesn't like it there.*

BARBARA: *Everyone has their own tastes. We like it very much in England.*
TAXI-DRIVER: *Yes, of course madam. You're right. How long are you staying?*
BARBARA: *Ten days.*
(They get to the airport.)
TAXI-DRIVER: *Have a pleasant holiday! And have a good trip!*

Vocabulary

čakati	to wait	**službeno potovanje**	business trip
ustaviti	to stop	**tovornjak**	lorry
vstopiti	to enter	**biti všeč**	to like
gost	heavy	**okus**	taste
zdi se	it seems	**ostati**	to stay
potovati	to travel		

Language points

To like something 🔲🔲

In lesson 4 you learnt that you express 'to like something' with the verb **imeti** plus **rad/-a/-o/-i** and 'to like to do something' with **rad/-a/-o/-i** *plus the verb with the correct personal ending*. There is an expression **všeč mi je** which literally means 'it is pleasing to me'. You use this expression with the personal pronoun of the person you are referring to in the dative case. Note how Barbara says in the dialogue: **Nama je všeč Anglija**. In the dialogue between Petra and Alenka you can see a few more examples using this expression:

PETRA:	**Ali ti je všeč Boštjan?**	Do you like Boštjan?
ALENKA:	**Ne, Boštjan mi ni všeč.**	No, I don't like Boštjan.
PETRA:	**Tebi ni nihče všeč.**	You don't like anybody.
ALENKA:	**To ni res. Všeč mi je Boris.**	This is not true. I like Boris.
PETRA:	**Nimaš sreče. Njemu je všeč Tina.**	You're not lucky. He likes Tina.

It seems to me . . .

The verb **zdeti se** means 'to seem', 'to appear'. You use this reflexive verb with the personal pronoun of the person you are referring to in the dative case in order to express what seems or appears to someone. Note how Barbara says in the dialogue: **Zdi se mi, da gredo danes vsi iz mesta.** Here are a few more examples:

> **Ali se ti ne zdi, da je danes promet zelo gost.**
> Doesn't it seem to you that the traffic is very heavy today?

> **Zdi se mi, da je zelo mrzlo.**   It seem to me that it is very cold.

Traffic

Avtobus, vlak, letalo are all **javni promet** (public transport). If you drive a car you need **vozniško dovoljenje** (a driving licence). When you do something wrong on the road you will have to **plačati kazen** (pay a fine). For the public transport you need **vozovnico** (a ticket). You can get **enosmerno vozovnico** (a one-way ticket) or **povratno karto** (a return ticket).

On the road you will also find:

kolo	bicycle	**vozniki**	drivers
kolesar	a bicyclist	**tovornjak**	lorry
motorist	a motorcyclist	**pešec**	pedestrian

More about the imperative

In lesson 4 you learnt about the imperative. Note how Barbara says to Tomaž *Ustavi* **ta taksi**. The taxi-driver says to them **Vstopita!** This is the dual form of the imperative, which you form as following:

1 *Verbs of the -a conjugation*
   You drop the **m** from the first person singular and add **jta**:
   delati – delam – *delajta!*
2 *Verbs of the -e conjugation*
   You drop the **em** from the first person singular and add **ita**:
   pisati – pišem – *pišita!*
3 *Verbs of the -i conjugation*
   You drop the **m** from the first person singular and add **ta**:
   govoriti – govorim – *govorita!*

On most signs in Slovenia you will see a command expressed with the adjective **prepovedano** which means 'prohibited', for example:

Kaditi prepovedano!	No smoking
Parkijanje prepovedano!	No parking
Vstop prepovedan!	No entry

When you want to stop somebody from doing something, particularly people you know well, you use the imperative form of the verb **nehati** 'to stop' plus the infinitive, for example:

Nehaj govoriti!	Stop talking!
Nehajta se smejati!	(You two) stop laughing!
Nehajte kaditi!	Stop (you pl.) smoking!
Nehajmo se prepirati!	Let's stop arguing!

Wish me a good trip

There are a few phrases which you may like to use in order to wish someone certain things. You have noticed the taxi-driver saying **Srečno pot!**. This is what you say to someone who is going away; it literally means 'Have a safe drive'. He also said to Barbara and Tomaž **Prijeten dopust!**, which means 'Have a good holiday'. Another word for a holiday is **počitnice** (pl.). This is used particularly for school holidays.

   Prijeten means 'pleasant', and you can wish all sorts of things to people using this adjective, for example:

Prijeten večer!	Have a good evening!
Prijetne počitnice!	Have a good holiday!
Prijeten konec tedna!	Have a good weekend!

Vstopiti/Izstopiti

The verb **vstopiti** means 'to enter' and the verb **izstopiti** means 'to exit', 'to get out'. From these verbs come the nouns **vstop** 'entrance' and **izstop** 'exit'.

   The word for an entrance fee in Slovene is **vstopnina**.

Exercise 6

Answer these questions:

1 Kje sta Tomaž in Barbara?
2 Kam pelje avtobus številka 5?

3 Zakaj je promet zelo gost?
4 Ali gresta Tomaž in Barbara v Anglijo na službeno potovanje?
5 Kaj jima zaželi taksist?

Exercise 7

(a) Say that you are waiting for a bus / the train / your female friend.
(b) Say that Matic is waiting for his girlfriend / Sonja / the plane.

Exercise 8

Your secretary in on holiday for a week and you have to manage by yourself. You have no one to remind you of things and you write yourself these notes in your diary. Write them in Slovene:

1 On Tuesday I must go to the doctor.
2 I must go to get the paper tomorrow morning.
3 Silva must go to the post office in the afternoon.
4 I am going to visit a friend this evening.
5 I must get some milk and bread on Saturday.

Exercise 9

You are in a café chatting to a friend and among other things you say the following. Can you say it in Slovene?

1 This glass is empty.
2 In the south it is usually warm.
3 This street is narrow.
4 My neighbour Larisa is very friendly.
5 London is a big city.

Exercise 10

Suppose the table below is from today's newspaper. Study the table and make up sentences like the one which has been done for you.

1 London   rain   7°C
2 Pariz   warm   17°C
3 Berlin   rain   12°C
4 Moskva   cold   –22°C
5 Lizbona   sunny   19°C
6 Rim   hot   28°C

1 V Londonu danes dežuje. Temperatura je sedem stopinj celzija.

Dialogue 3 ▣

Lepo jo pozdravi!

Give her my regards!

Tomaž and Barbara are now in England and have been invited to Nick and Ann's house for tea

TOMAŽ: O, to je ena malenkost za vaju.
ANN: Najlepša hvala. Samo trenutek, rože moram postaviti v vazo.
NICK: Ali sta prvič v Angliji?
TOMAŽ: Ne, jaz sem drugič, Barbara pa že tretjič. Oba zelo rada potujeva.
ANN: Jutri zvečer vaju nameravam peljati na koncert, v soboto pa lahko gremo na razstavo v narodni muzej.
BARBARA: O, lepo. Mimogrede, ali se spomniš Tatjane? Lepo te pozdravlja!
ANN: Hvala enako. Kaj lahko ponudim? Kavo? Čaj? Kje je Nick?
BARBARA: Pogovarja se s Tomažem.

TOMAŽ: *Oh, this is a little something for you.*
ANN: *Thank you very much. Just a moment, I must put these flowers in the vase.*
NICK: *Is this your first time in England?*
TOMAŽ: *No, I am here for the second time and Barbara for the third. We both like travelling very much.*
ANN: *I intend to take you to a concert tomorrow evening and on Saturday we can go to see an exhibition in a national museum.*
BARBARA: *Oh, how interesting. By the way, do you remember Tatjana? She sends you her regards.*
ANN: *Give her my regards too. What can I offer you? Coffee? Tea? Where is Nick?*
BARBARA: *He is talking to Tomaž.*

Vocabulary

malenkost	a small thing	**razstava**	exhibition
rože	flowers	**narodni muzej**	national museum
postaviti	to put	**mimogrede**	by the way
vaza	vase	**spomniti se**	to remember
potovati	to travel	**ponuditi**	to offer
nameravati	to intend	**pogovarjati se**	to converse

Language points

For the first time

To say that something is taking place for the first, the second, etc., time you need the masculine form of the ordinal numbers and the ending **č**, as in:

prvič	for the first time
drugič	for the second time
tretjič	for the third time
četrtič	for the fourth time
petič	for the fifth time
šestič ...	for the sixth time ...
zadnjič	for the last time

Note how Nick asks in the dialogue: **Ali sta prvič v Angliji** and Tomaž replies **jaz sem drugič Barbara pa že tretjič**.

Peljati/peljati se, voziti/voziti se

These two verbs are more examples of verbs which are used differently when they are reflexive, for example:

Ta avotobus pelje na letališče.	This bus goes to the airport.
Peljati te moram v gledališče.	I must take you to the theatre.
Ali voziš?	Are you driving?
Ta avtobus vozi tudi ob nedeljah.	This bus also runs on Sundays.
Peljem se v mesto.	I am going to the town.
Nikoli se ne peljem z avtom.	I never go by car.
Zelo rada se vozi z avtobusom.	She likes travelling by bus very much.

Čakati

When you say that you are waiting for somebody you normally don't need any preposition, but put the name of the person in the accusative case. For example:

Čakam Mateja.	I'm waiting for Matej.
Čakam Marijo.	I'm waiting for Marija.
Ali me čakaš?	Are you waiting for me?
Marija te čaka.	Marija is waiting for you.

When you are waiting somewhere or for something you usually need the preposition **na**, for example:

Čakamo na prehodu za pešce. We're waiting at the zebra crossing.
Čakata na avtobus, ne na vlak. They (two) are waiting for the bus, not for the train.

The expression **komaj čakam** means 'I cannot wait'. You use it with the ending of the verb **čakati** in the person to whom you are referring, for example

Komaj čakamo.	We can't wait.
Komaj čaka.	(He or she) can't wait.

One's own

Possessive pronouns have a reflexive form **svoj**, **svoja**, **svoje**, which is used when the idea of possession is directed back to the subject, for example:

On se ne vozi s svojim avtom.	He doesn't drive his own car.
Ali imaš svojo sobo?	Do you have your own room?
Vsak mora imeti svoj potni list.	Everybody must have their own passport.

When you want to give your regards to someone

Pozdrav means 'greeting' and **pozdraviti** means 'to greet'. When you want to give someone your regards you use **pozdraviti** and the personal pronoun in the accusative form. Note how Barbara says to Ann: **Lepo te pozdravlja**. The person who will tell you this will say: (someone) **te/vas pozdravlja**. In the dialogue Barbara says **Tatjana te pozdravlja**.

It is a convention to say **Hvala enako** meaning 'Thank you, give her my regards too'.

In Slovene you are always talking 'with' somebody as opposed to 'to' somebody, as in English. When you say that you are talking to somebody you need to use the endings of the locative case; you can see more about this in lesson 11.

Exercise 11

Re-arrange these lines so that they will make up a conversation:

Dobro, hvala, in ti?
Pojdi k zdravniku!
Ne počutim se dobro.
Dober dan, kako si?
Mimogrede, Alenka te lepo pozdravlja.
Ja, nameravam iti jutri popoldne.
Hvala enako.

Exercise 12

(a) Križanka

1 to play
2 must
3 to recommend
4 to help
5 to come
6 to think
7 to stand
8 to have
9 to speak

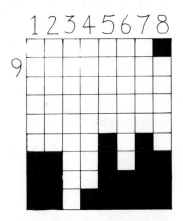

(b) Can you remember the Slovene for the words in italics? Test yourself!

1 You go for a drink with a friend where a sign in the bar says *No smoking*.
2 You are just about to park your car when you notice the sign *No parking*.

3 You are in a theatre and the performance is about to begin but your friend is still telling you something. Say to him *Stop talking*.
4 You think you are going to the lavatory in a restaurant when someone calls after you *Excuse me, no entry here*.
5 You are going away for some time and people say to you *Have a good trip and a pleasant holiday*.

Exercise 13

How could you say that the following people are in a hurry, using the personal pronouns?

1 we
2 you (familiar form)
3 he
4 she
5 you (polite form)

Exercise 14

Which in each line of words is the odd one out, and why?

1 kopalnica, kuhinja, dežnik, dnevna soba
2 mleko, radio, voda, kruh
3 dežuje, sneži, sporočilo, mrzlo je
4 povedati, pokazati, sosed, svetovati
5 šestič, četrtič, osmi, petič

Exercise 15

Pronunciation exercise. In this lesson you have learned that the letters **k** and **h** are prepositions both meaning 'to', as in 'I am going to my friend's place'. The preposition **h** is used before nouns starting with **k** or **g**; **k** is used before all other nouns. Let's practise reading out the sentences below, where these prepositions are used.

Ali greš k zdravniku?
Ne, k prijatelju grem.
Pridite h kosilu.
H gulažu jem zmeraj polento.
Po kosilu grem k Tatjani.
Jaz moram pa h gospodu Dolencu.

Dialogue for comprehension 🔲

It has been arranged during the day that Ann and Barbara will go to the opera on their own that evening. Ann organizes the evening. How are they going to go to town and why?

nesreča	accident

BARBARA: Prvič grem v opero v Londonu.
ANN: Ali greš v Ljubljani pogosto?
BARBARA: Ne, Tomažu opera ni všeč. Ampak velikokrat greva v kino. Ali greva sedaj z avtobusom?
ANN: Ne, z vlakom. Jaz imam avto, ampak promet tukaj je obupen. Moj avto je skoraj vedno v garaži. Raje se vozim z vlakom.
BARBARA: Ja, promet je res zelo gost. In vsi ti avtomobili na levi strani ceste. Vedno se mi zdi, da bo vsak trenutek nesreča.
ANN: Nisi navajena. Ali ti veliko voziš?
BARBARA: Ne, skoraj nikoli. Tomaž ima zmeraj avto. Vozi se v službo. In kadar greva kam skupaj, vozi on. Ali se nama mudi?
ANN: Ne, predstava se začne ob osmih, sedaj je ura šele šest.
BARBARA: Ali imava čas še za eno kavo?
ANN: Ja, če želiš, lahko greva v mestu na kavo.

7 Kako je bilo?

How was it?

In this lesson you will learn about:

- Ways of talking about past events
- More adjectives
- More time expressions
- How Slovene adverbs are formed
- Some members of a family
- How to say that something hurts you
- Some parts of the body

Dialogue 1 ▣

Ne vprašaj, kaj se je zgodilo

Don't ask what's happened

Tomaž and Barbara have returned from England. Eva, a friend of Barbara telephones her and asks about it

EVA: Kako je bilo?

BARBARA: Vse je bilo odlično, ampak imela sva slabo vreme. Tomaž je sedaj malo prehlajen in glava ga boli. Jutri dopoldne gre k zdravniku. Ali se je tvoja hčerka že vrnila iz študentskega izleta?

EVA: Ja, tudi ona se je imela lepo. Veliko je slikala. Moram ti pokazati fotografije.

BARBARA: Joj, jaz se jezim, zato ker sva midva pozabila fotoaparat.

EVA: Ne vprašaj, kaj se je zgodilo moji hčerki Sandri. Zadnji dan so ji ukradli fotoaparat. Šla je na stranišče in za trenutek ga je pustila na mizi v kavarni. In ko je prišla nazaj, ga ni več bilo.

BARBARA: Obupno! Ne moreš biti dovolj previden! Ali sta se vidva že odločila, kam gresta septembra?

EVA: Ne še točno, ampak verjetno greva nekam na jug.

EVA: *How was it?*

BARBARA: *Everything was wonderful but the weather was bad. Tomaž has flu now and a headache. He is going to the doctor's tomorrow morning. Has your daughter got back from her student trip yet?*

EVA: *Yes, she also had a good time. She took lots of photographs. I must show them to you.*

BARBARA: *Oh, I am annoyed because we forgot our camera.*

EVA: *Don't ask what happened to my daughter Sandra. On her last day she had her camera stolen. She went to the lavatory and left it on the table in the café for a moment. And when she came back it wasn't there any more.*

BARBARA: *Terrible! You can't be careful enough! Have you two decided yet where you're going in September?*

EVA: *Not exactly, but we're probably going somewhere south.*

Vocabulary

odlično	very well	**pozabiti**	to forget
prehlajen-a	to have flu	**fotoaparat**	camera
glava	head	**zgoditi se**	to happen
boli	hurts	**ukrasti**	to steal
vrniti se	to get back	**stranišče**	lavatory
slikati	to take photographs	**dovolj**	enough
pokazati	to show	**previden**	careful

Note: The Slovene word for lavatory is **stranišče**. However, on most public lavatories you will see the sign **WC** (pronounced 'vey tsay').

Language points

Past tense

To form the past tense in Slovene you use the present tense of the verb 'to be' plus the participle ending in **l**, which you form by dropping the **ti** ending of the infinitive and adding:

l to the macsuline form
la to the feminine form
lo to the neuter form
li to the plural form

For example:

delal/-a sem	I worked	**pisal/-a sem**	I wrote
delala je	she worked	**pisal je**	he wrote
delal je	he worked	**pisala je**	she wrote
delali smo	we worked	**pisali smo**	we wrote

There are a few exceptions to the rule for how the participle ending in **l** is formed. It will be helpful to you if you memorize them; you will need them for the formation of the future tense and the conditional.

	Masculine	Feminine	Neuter	Plural
iti	šel	šla	šlo	šli
priti	prišel	prišla	prišlo	prišli
reči	rekel	rekla	reklo	rekli
moči	mogel	mogla	moglo	mogli

Note how Barbara asks Eva in the dialogue **Ali se je tvoja hčerka že vrnila?**

Vrniti se is a reflexive verb meaning 'to return', 'to get back'. In the past tense, reflexive verbs are conjugated as follows:

1	jaz sem se vrnil/-a	vrnil/-a sem se
2	ti si se vrnil/-a	vrnil/-a si se
3	on se je vrnil	vrnil se je
	ona se je vrnila	vrnila se je
	ono se je vrnilo	vrnilo se je

1	midva sva se vrnila	vrnila sva se
2	vidva sta se vrnila	vrnila sta se
3	onadva sta se vrnila	vrnila sta se

1	mi smo se vrnili	vrnili smo se
2	vi ste se vrnili	vrnili ste se
3	oni so se vrnili	vrnili so se

Notice that the word order is different when you use the personal pronouns from when you don't, apart from the third person singular where **se** is placed in between the verb and the participle ending in **l**. In the negative form **se** is placed in front of the auxiliary and the verb when using the personal pronoun or between the negative auxiliary (**nisem, nisi**) and the verb when you aren't using the personal pronoun.

You put **ali** in front of the sentence to form a question in the past tense. To make a sentence negative you replace the positive form of the verb 'to be' by its negative equivalent. Here are a few examples:

Ali si bil-a v Angliji?	Have you been to England?
Ja, bil-a sem v Angliji.	Yes, I've been to England.
Ne, nisem bil-a v Angliji.	No, I haven't been to England.
Ali ste imeli lepo vreme?	Did you have good weather?
Ja, imeli smo lepo vreme.	Yes, we had good weather.
Ne, nismo imeli lepega vremena.	No, we didn't have good weather.
Ali se je tvoja hčerka že vrnila?	Has your daughter got back yet?
Ja, vrnila se je že.	Yes, she's already got back.
Ne, ni se še vrnila.	No, she hasn't got back yet.

Whilst there are several past tenses in English there is only one past tense in Slovene. Do not translate English auxiliary words like 'was, were, had'. The following sentences are all translated as **Delal je**:

He worked.
He was working.
He had been working.
He had worked.

You know the verbs **dežuje** (it rains) and **sneži** (it snows). They are irregular in the past tense and you say:

deževalo je	it rained
snežilo je	it snowed

Word order

Because every verb has its ending, which clearly indicates the person, and because all the nouns are declined, which indicates their function in a sentence, the word order in Slovene is less strict than the word order in English.

When personal pronouns in the accusative or dative case are used in the past tense the pronoun is usually placed between the auxiliary verb 'to be' and the participle, for example:

Včeraj sem jo videl.   I saw her yesterday.
Nisem mu pomagal.   I didn't help him.

How are you?

As in English, there are several ways of asking someone how they are. By now you have come across: **Kako si/ste?, Kako ti/vam gre?** In this lesson you will have noticed Eva saying **Tudi ona se je imela lepo**, meaning 'She also had a good time.' This is a more colloquial way of asking someone how they are, by using the verb **imeti** in reflexive form, for example:

Kako se imaš?   How are you?
Slabo, slabo se počutim.   Not well, I'm not feeling well. I
  Glava me boli.   have a headache.
Kako ste se imeli na dopustu?   How was your holiday?
  Na dopustu smo se imeli   We had a very good time on our
  zelo lepo.   holiday.

What is hurting you?

When you want to say that something hurts, you use the word **boli** and a personal pronoun in the accusative case depending on whom you are referring to. Notice how Barbara says **Glava ga boli**, meaning 'His head hurts.' You use this expression for other parts of the body, for example:

grlo	throat	**noga**	leg
zob	tooth	**trebuh**	belly
roka	hand, arm	**želodec**	stomach

The question 'What is hurting you?' is **Kaj te/vas boli?**

Passive

A passive construction does exist in Slovene but it is used much less than in English. Whilst in English it is very natural to use the passive in a sentence like 'I had my camera stolen or I was told, that . . .', you cannot use the passive in Slovene. You must not try to look for words with which you could express this idea word for word in a passive construction because it will not work. In sentences like the ones above you would use the word **nekdo** (someone, somebody) and you would say:

Nekdo mi je ukradel fotoaparat. Someone stole my camera.
Nekdo mi je povedal, da ... Someone told me that ...

More expressions about time

letos	this year
prihodnje/drugo leto	next year
lani	last year
pojutrišnjem	the day after tomorrow
včeraj	yesterday
predvčerajšnjim	the day before yesterday

In English 'a.m.' and 'p.m.' are used to describe the part of the day. Here are some expressions for the parts of the day:

zgodaj zjutraj	early in the morning	(4–7 a.m.)
zjutraj	in the morning	(7–9 a.m.)
dopoldne	in the morning	(9–11 a.m.)
opoldne	at noon	(12–2 p.m.)
popoldne	in the afternoon	(2–5 p.m.)
zvečer	in the evening	(6–9 p.m.)
pozno zvečer	late in the evening	(9–11 p.m.)
ponoči	during the night	

Adjectives and adverbs

In lesson 2 you learnt some adjectives and their opposite meanings. Here are a few more examples:

topel	warm	**mrzel**	cold
poln	full	**prazen**	empty
dolg	long	**kratek**	short
širok	wide	**ozek**	narrow

Some Slovene adjectives form their opposite meanings by adding the prefix **ne**. This occurs when the meaning is negative as in:

zanimiv	interesting	**nezanimiv**	uninteresting
prijazen	friendly	**neprijazen**	unfriendly
srečen	happy	**nesrečen**	unhappy
udoben	comfortable	**neudoben**	uncomfortable

All these adjectives are in the masculine form but you know that Slovene adjectives have a masculine, feminine or neuter form depending on the gender of the noun they modify. For example:

Masculine	Feminine	Neuter	
težek	težka	težko	difficult
lahek	lahka	lahko	easy
odličen	odlična	odlično	superb
prijazen	prijazna	prijazno	friendly
udoben	udobna	udobno	comfortable
prijeten	prijetna	prijetno	pleasant

The neuter form of the adjective is also the adverb in Slovene, for example:

tiho	quietly	glasno	loudly
hitro	quickly	počasi	slowly
razločno	clearly	nerazločno	unclearly

Prosim, govorite razločno.	Please speak clearly.
On govori zelo tiho, hitro in nerazločno.	He speaks very quietly, quickly and unclearly.
Ali je tukaj prosto ali zasedeno?	Is this place free or engaged?

The question 'how?' is **kako?** To this question you will need an adverb as an answer. You may remember the question **Kako si?** which you answer with **Dobro**, regardless of whether you are a man or a woman. This is because **dobro** is an adverb and also the neuter form of the adjective.

Note how Eva asks in the dialogue **Kako je bilo?** and Barbara answers **Bilo je odlično**.

Compass points

kompas	compass

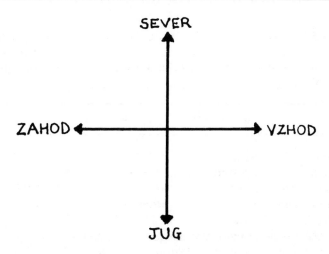

The adjectives of the points of the compass are:

severni	northern	**vzhodni**	eastern
južni	southern	**zahodni**	western

When you want to say that something is happening in one of these you use the preposition **na** and the nouns get the ending **u**:

na severu	in the north	**na vzhodu**	in the east
na jugu	in the south	**na zahodu**	in the west

When something is north of, south of, etc., you say:

severno od	north from/of	**vzhodno od**	east from/of
južno od	south from/of	**zahodno od**	west from/of

You can make compounds as follows:

severovzhod	north east
jugozahod	south west

You can also form adjectives which will, depending on the gender of the noun they modify, take appropriate endings:

severovzhoden/-dna/-o	northeastern *or* northeasterly
jugozahoden/-dna/-o	southwestern *or* southwesterly

You already know the names of some countries. Here is an additional list of some countries you may want to use; you will recognize their names, apart from, perhaps, **Madžarska** (Hungary): **Kanada, Finska, Švica, Irska, Nizozemska, Portugalska, Grčija, Švedska, Norveška, Škotska.**

Exercise 1

A family you know have just returned from their holiday. Talk to them about it!

kakorkoli	anyhow

ASK: 1 *How was it?*
Ne vprašaj! Imeli smo obupno vreme!
ASK: 2 *Did it rain?*
Ne, snežilo je!
ASK WITH AMAZEMENT: 3 *In June?*
Ja. Bilo je zelo mrzlo. Vse nas je ves čas zeblo.
SAY: 4 *But in the north it is usually like that.*
Ne sredi poletja! Kakorkoli, naslednjič gremo nekam na jug.
SAY: 5 *I'm also going to the south in October.*
O, kam pa?
SAY: 6 *To Greece.*

Exercise 2

You share a flat and your flatmate is always asking you questions about what you've done or what you will do. You answer them vaguely. Can you translate the sentences in italics, which are answers you could give her?

Kdaj si šel včeraj v službo?
1 *Early in the morning, at 6 o'clock.*
Ali si bil ves dan v službi?
2 *No, in the afternoon I was at my male friend's house.*
Kdaj si prišel domov?
3 *Late in the evening.*
Ali imaš danes popoldne čas?
4 *No, unfortunately not. I have a meeting this afternoon at 4 o'clock.*
Kaj pa jutri zvečer?
5 *No, I'm going to the cinema tomorrow evening.*

Exercise 3

You have just got back from your holiday and you meet a nosy neighbour who always asks you about what you are doing. You have to be polite and answer her questions:

1 Ali greste na sestanek?
   No, I had the meeting this morning.
2 Ali ste na dopustu?
   No, I was on holiday last week.
3 Kakšno vreme ste imeli?
   We had very nice weather.
4 Ali vam je bilo všeč v Španiji?
   Yes, we liked it very much.
5 Ali je vaša hčerka že doma?
   Yes, she came home early in the morning.

Exercise 4

Answer as suggested in full sentences:

vaja (f.) exercise

1 Kako bere Sonja? (*slowly and clearly*)
2 Kako poje Pavarotti? (*loudly*)
3 Kako je bilo v gledališču? (*interesting*)
4 Kako si se imela na dopustu? (*very well*)
5 Ali je bila ta vaja lahka ali težka? (*easy*)

Exercise 5

Which are the neighbouring countries of Slovenia? Fill them in!
(If you need help, see the map on p. 2).

1 Severno od Slovenije je ...
2 Južno od Slovenije je ...
3 Zahodno od Slovenije je ...
4 Vzhodno od Slovenije je ...

Dialogue 2 📼

Zaljubila se je

She fell in love

*On his way home from work, Tomaž met Sandra, Eva's daughter.
He asks about her holiday and she tells him how she has fallen in
love in Italy. As he gets home he tells Barbara about it*

Tomaž:	Na poti domov sem srečal Sandro, čisto po naključju. Zelo je rjava.
Barbara:	Ja, vem da je že doma. Eva mi je telefonirala. Ali ti je povedala, kaj se ji je zgodilo?
Tomaž:	Ja, zaljubila se je v enega Italijana.
Barbara:	A res? O tem nič ne vem. Eva ni ničesar omenila. Kaj ti je še povedala?
Tomaž:	Hoče se poročiti.
Barbara:	Ampak stra je komaj 18 let. Ali je povedala Evi?
Tomaž:	Dvomim.
Barbara:	Gotovo ne ve. Moram jo poklicati nazaj in ji povedati. Meni je samo povedala, kako so ji ukradli fotoaparat.

Tomaž:	*On the way home I met Sandra, quite by chance. She's very brown.*
Barbara:	*Yes, I know she's already at home. Eva telephoned me. Did she tell you what had happened to her?*
Tomaž:	*Yes, she's fallen in love with an Italian.*
Barbara:	*Oh really? I know nothing about this. Eva didn't mention anything. What else did she tell you?*
Tomaž:	*She wants to marry him.*
Barbara:	*But she's only nineteen. Did she tell Eva?*
Tomaž:	*I doubt it.*
Barbara:	*She certainly doesn't know. I must call her back and tell her. She only told me how they stole her camera.*

Vocabulary

srečati	to meet	**komaj**	only, hardly
čisto po naključju	quite by chance	**dvomiti**	to doubt
zaljubiti se	to fall in love	**nazaj**	back
poročiti se	to get married	**A res?**	Oh, really?

Language points

Call me!

As in English, there are two verbs to express 'to telephone someone':

telefonirati	to telephone
poklicati	to call

Notice how Barbara says to Tomaž **Moram jo (Evo) poklicati nazaj!** 'I must call her (Eva) back!'

Falling in love and getting married

The English prepositions in certain expressions do not correspond to the Slovene ones. In English you say 'to fall in love with' but in Slovene you say **zaljubiti se v**, in other words, in Slovene you fall in love *in* someone.

You know the words **mož** (husband) and **žena** (wife). When a woman gets married you use the verb **omožiti se**, and when a man gets married you use **oženiti se**. But for them both you use the verb **poročiti se**. **Poroka** means 'wedding'. **Ločiti se** means 'to get divorced'.

Note that these are all reflexive verbs. Look at the examples:

Marija se je lani omožila.	Maria got married last year.
Tim se hoče oženiti.	Tim wants to get married.
Darko in Simona sta se poročila.	Darko and Simona got married.
Tanja se je ločila.	Tanja got divorced.

When you are married or divorced you use:

biti poročen/-a	to be married
biti ločen/-a	to be divorced

By chance

The words for 'chance' are **naključje** or **slučaj**. When you want to say that something has happened by chance you say **po naklučju** or **slučajno**. Notice how Tomaž tells Barbara **Sandro sem srečal, čisto po naključju**, meaning 'I met Sandra by chance'. The word **čisto** in this context is an adverb, meaning 'quite', 'entirely', 'purely'. You can use it as in the following examples:

Čisto prav imaš!	You're quite right!
Čisto vse sem ti povedal.	I told you everything.

Clean/dirty

plaža	beach

The word **čisto** is also an adjective and it means 'clean' as opposed to **umazan** 'dirty'. For example:

Plaža je bila zelo umazana.   The beach was very dirty.
Njeno stanovanje je zmeraj čisto.   Her flat is always clean.

Members of a family

družina	family
starši	parents
oče ali ata in mama	father and mother
stari starši	grandparents
stari ata, oče (dedek)	grandfather
stara mama (babica)	grandmother
otroci	children
sin	son
hčerka	daughter
vnuki	grandchildren
vnuk	grandson
vnukinja	granddaughter
brat	brother
sestra	sister
teta	aunt
stric	uncle
sestrična	female cousin
bratranec	male cousin

You can find a few more family relations in the glossary at the back of the book.

The use of personal pronouns in the dative and in the accusative case

Look at the following examples:

(1) **Glava *ga* boli.**   He has a headache. (literally 'His head hurts *him*')

     Srečal sem *jo*.   I met *her*.
     Nisem *vas* videl.   I didn't see *you*.

(2) **Kaj se *mu* je zgodilo?**   What's happened *to him*?
     Povedal sem *ji*.   I told *her*.
     To sem *vam* dal že včeraj.   I gave this *to you* yesterday.

In the first list you see how the personal pronouns in the accusative case are used and in the second you see the use of personal pronouns in the dative case. You can construct more complex sentences using them both. In the dialogue, Eva could have said **Ukradli so ji ga**. **Ji** would refer to Sandra (from the context we know that she is talking about Sandra), **ga** refers to the camera (again, from the context we know she is referring to the camera). This is something Slovenes use all the time, in spoken and in written language. You may find it difficult at the beginning because of all the 'little words'. Let's have a look at another example: We can ask:

Kaj *se ji je* **zgodilo?** or **Kaj** *se mu je* **zgodilo?**

se in both sentences indicates a reflexive verb.
je indicates the past tense.
ji in the first sentence tells us we are asking about a woman, i.e. what has happened to her.
mu in the second sentence tells us we are asking about a man, i.e. what has happened to him.

All these words are called enclitics and you will see more about them in the lessons to come.

Exercise 6

Match the questions below with appropriate responses:

1 Kaj te boli?   (a) Ne, imeli smo slabo vreme.
2 Ali si dobre volje?   (b) Ne, neprijazen je bil.
3 Ali je bil natakar prijazen? (c) Včeraj, pozno zvečer.
4 Ali ste imeli lepo vreme?   (d) Glava me boli.
5 Kdaj je prišla Eva domov?   (e) Ne, slabe volje sem.

Exercise 7

Put the adjectives in brackets into the correct form in Slovene:

1 Že ves teden je (*bad*) vreme.
2 Ta cesta je zelo (*narrow*).
3 Tisti film je bil zelo (*uninteresting*).
4 Bila sem (*sure*), da je danes sreda.
5 Martin, ali si (*hungry*) ali (*thirsty*)?

Exercise 8

You have been invited to a wedding with a friend of yours where you hardly know anyone. A woman you meet is quite happy to tell your friend who is who and you have to listen to the conversation. Can you do it in Slovene?

1 THE WOMAN: Is Gregor your brother?
2 YOUR FRIEND: No, he is my cousin. But I haven't seen him for a very long time.
3 THE WOMAN: I know him. He was at school with my son. Do you know Irena?
4 YOUR FRIEND: Yes, she went to England for a year.
5 THE WOMAN: She has already come back.
6 YOUR FRIEND: Why didn't she stay there for a year?
7 THE WOMAN: Oh, I know but I can't tell you.

Exercise 9

You know the Slovene word for 'but'. Write down the following sentences connecting them with 'but', as in the example given below:

It was raining yesterday. It was warm.
Včeraj je deževalo, ampak bilo je toplo.

1 The weather was terrible. We had a good time.
2 It was very cold. In the north it is always like that.
3 My friend is already home. I haven't seen him yet.
4 I am going on holiday in August. I haven't decided yet where.
5 I worked all day. I'm not tired.

Exercise 10

An old friend wrote to you telling you about what has been going on in his life recently. Fill in the missing words given in brackets.

noseča	pregnant

1 Lani, septembra (*I got married*).
2 Prodal sem (*my old flat*) in kupil (*a small house*).
3 (*My parents*) so nama pomagali.
4 Kupila sva tudi avto ampak prejšnji mesec (*we had it stolen*).
5 (*This year*) nisva šla na dopust, zato ker je moja žena (*pregnant*).

Dialogue 3 📼

Kako mu je ime?

What is his name?

Sandra has arranged to meet her friend Sabina to tell her about her new love and after Sandra has been going on about him for hours Sabina manages to ask a few questions

SABINA: Kako mu je ime?
SANDRA: Emilio. Poglej! Tukaj sva na plaži!
SABINA: Ali je Italijan?
SANDRA: Ja. Iz Rima je.
SABINA: Koliko je star?
SANDRA: Dvaindvajset. Ali ti je všeč?
SABINA: Kje si ga spoznala? Ali je bil tudi on na izletu?
SANDRA: Ja, tudi on je študent. Študira arhitekturo. V Milanu. Zelo dobro igra kitaro in lepo poje.
SABINA: Ali je tudi on zaljubljen v tebe?
SANDRA: Prepričana sem. Zadnji dan sem mu podarila moj fotoaparat. Za spomin!

SABINA: *What's his name?*
SANDRA: *Emilio. Look! Here we're on the beach!*
SABINA: *Is he Italian?*
SANDRA: *Yes. He's from Rome.*
SABINA: *How old is he?*
SANDRA: *Twenty-two. Do you like him?*
SABINA: *Yes. Where did you meet him? Was he also on a trip?*
SANDRA: *Yes, he is also a student. He studies architecture. In Milan. And he plays the guitar very well and sings beautifully.*
SABINA: *Is he also in love with you?*
SANDRA: *I'm sure. The last day I gave him my camera. As a memento!*

Vocabulary

spoznati	to meet	**podariti**	to give as a present
kitara	guitar	**spomin**	memory, memento, souvenir

Language points

Negative questions

As in English, you can ask negative questions which usually suggest surprise. In Slovene you simply start the question with **ali** and put the verb into its negative form, for example:

Ali še nisi končal?	Haven't you finished yet?
Ali nisi bila v službi?	Haven't you been to work?
Ali ti ni pisal?	Didn't he write to you?

Where are they from?

The question 'Where are you from?' is **Iz kod si, ste, je . . . ?** The town or the country you will be given as an answer will be in the genitive case, about which you will see more later on. Most of the countries you have learned so far have ended in **a** and they will take an **e** ending in the genitive, if someone is from these countries, for example:

Ali si iz Italije?	Are you from Italy?
Ne, iz Španije sem. In ti?	No, I'm from Spain. And you?
Jaz sem iz Anglije, moja punca pa iz Francije.	I'm from England, and my girl-friend is from France.

Note how Sandra told Sabina that Emilio is from Rome (**iz Rima**). Masculine nouns take an **a** ending when you use them after the preposition **iz**, for example: **iz Rima**, **iz Londona**, **iz Pariza**, **iz Berlina**, **iz Madrida**, and so on. When the name of a town ends in **a** as, for example, in **Moskva**, the **a** ending will change to **e**: **iz Moskve**, **iz Lizbone**, **iz Ženeve**.

Describing people

The most common means of describing a person are by describing their hair, height, eyes, build, weight, and so on. Here are a few examples of how you can describe someone in Slovene:

On/ona ima dolge lase.	He/she has long hair.
kratke lase.	short hair.
Ima lepe/zelene/sive/modre oči.	He/she has beautiful/green/grey/blue eyes.

Zelo visok/-a je.	He/she is very tall.
Zelo majhen/-hna je.	He/she is very short.
Debel/-a je.	He/she is fat.
Vitek/-tka je.	
Suh/- a je. (*more colloquial*)	He/she is slim.

There is an expression **sem čisto suh/-a** meaning 'I'm broke, without any money'.

Do you play an instrument?

When you want to say that you play an instrument you use the verb **igrati** and the instrument will be in the accusative case, for example:

kitara	guitar
klavir	piano
harmonika	accordion
vijolina	violin

Emilio igra kitaro.	Emilio plays a guitar.
Ali igraš klavir?	Do you play the piano?
Moj stric igra harmoniko.	My uncle plays the accordion.

Exercise 11

1 Ask a friend who doesn't seem to you to be well *What is hurting you?*
2 Say to someone with whom you have to make an arrangement *Call me tomorrow!*
3 You have heard that something has happened to a female acquaintance of yours. Ask *What has happened to her?*
4 A male friend of yours has a new girlfriend. Ask him *Where did you meet her?*
5 Ask him also *Where is she from?*

Exercise 12

On your way home you overhear this conversation between two women on the train. Could you tell it to a Slovene friend of yours in Slovene?
A: Have you seen this film yet?
B: Yes, didn't I tell you?

A: Maybe, but I don't remember. I forget. Did you like it?
B: No, I didn't like it.
A: Why not?
B: It seemed to me to be boring.

Exercise 13

Križanka

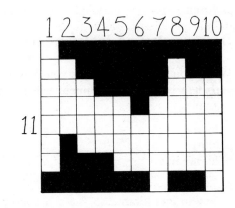

Down
1 traffic light
2 throat
3 aunt
4 tooth
5 exercise
6 dog
7 west
8 daughter
9 beach
10 guitar

What word do you get at 11 across?

Exercise 14

(a) Complete the sentences below with the following words: **visok,
težka, slabo, ozka, malo, suh**.

1 Eno . . . pivo, prosim.
2 Njen fant je zelo . . . in . . .
3 Imeli smo . . . vreme.
4 Ta ulica je zelo . . .
5 Ta vaja ni bila . . .

(b) Rewrite the sentences above and change the meaning by
replacing the words you filled in with their opposite meaning.

Exercise 15

Pronunciation exercise. The letter **l** has two sounds in Slovene.
When it is placed before a vowel or before the letter **j** it is
pronounced **l** as in **letalo, letališče, lani, glava, grlo, ljudje**. When
l is placed at the end of the word or before any other consonant
but **j** it is pronounced as **w** as in:

cel	all, whole

dopoldan	morning
popoldan	afternoon
cel dan	all day

In the past tense the participles ending in **l** denote masculine gender and are pronounced as **w** as in:

Tomaž mi je *povedal.*
Ali si *videl* Sandro?
Kupil sem si slovenski slovar.
Bil sem v službi.
Srečal sem Mateja.

Dialogue for comprehension 🔳

Barbara does not want to call Eva, Sandra's mother, because she does not want to interfere with Sandra's affairs but she feels she must talk to someone about this. She calls Sabina's mother in the hope that she will have learned something from her daughter. Find out what Sandra wants to do next and what has happened to the camera

pravzaprav	actually

BARBARA: Anita, živio. Nekaj ti moram povedati, pravzaprav, vprašati te moram.
ANITA: Ja, kaj?
BARBARA: Tomaž je včeraj na poti domov čisto slučajno srečal Sandro. Ali je Sandra kaj povedala Sabini o izletu?
ANITA: Ali misliš Emilio?
BARBARA: O, ali mu je ime Emilio?
ANITA: Ja, Sandra pravi, da ima dolge lase. Videla je slike. Baje piše pesmi in igra kitaro.
BARBARA: Ali Eva ve kaj o tem?
ANITA: Dvomim. Ampak Sandra hoče iti nazaj v Italijo.
BARBARA: Uboga Eva. Sigurna sem, da nič ne ve. Meni je samo povedala, kako so ji ukradli fotoaparat.
ANITA: Saj ji ga niso ukradli. Sandra mu ga je zadnji dan podarila, za spomin.

8 Moram se preseliti!

I must move!

Dialogue 1

Ta soba je premajhna!

This room is too small!

Robert, after five months in Slovenia, is still living in a hotel. He is desperate to find a flat but so far hasn't been successful. Matej goes to see him one afternoon with a piece of good news

MATEJ: Kako ti gre?

ROBERT: Poleti je tukaj zame prevroče. In ta soba postaja zares premajhna. Najbolj pogrešam pisalno mizo. Vse knjige in papirje imam na tleh.

MATEJ: Kot sem omenil po telefonu, včeraj zvečer sem srečal Sabino. Njena teta oddaja stanovanja in baje ima trenutno na razpolago eno garsonjero. Naslednji teden pa se nekdo izseli iz enega trosobnega stanovanja.

ROBERT: Kot veš, videl sem že sto stanovanj, ampak z vsakim je nekaj narobe. Ali je premajhno, ali predrago, ali pa predaleč iz mesta. Ali veš, kje je tisto trosobno stanovanje in koliko stane najemnina?

MATEJ:	Praktično v centru je. Nad eno pekarno. Ali imaš plan mesta?
ROBERT:	Ja, imam dva, ampak trenutno ne najdem nobenega.
MATEJ:	Ali si zainteresiran? Ali naj pokličem Sabino?
ROBERT:	Ja, prosim.

MATEJ:	*How is it going?*
ROBERT:	*In the summer it is too hot here for me. And this room is getting really too small. I miss the desk most. I have all my books and papers on the floor.*
MATEJ:	*As I mentioned on the telephone, I met Sabina last night. Her aunt lets flats and apparently she has a studio flat on offer at the moment and next week someone moves out of a three-room flat.*
ROBERT:	*As you know, I've seen a hundred flats already but there is something wrong with every one. It is either too small, too expensive, or too far out of town. Do you know where that three-room flat is and how much it costs?*
MATEJ:	*It is practically in the centre. Above a bakery. Do you have a plan of the town?*
ROBERT:	*Yes, I have two but at the moment I can't find either.*
MATEJ:	*Are you interested? Shall I call Sabina?*
ROBERT:	*Yes, please.*

Vocabulary

postajati	to become	**imeti na razpolago**	to have available
pogrešati	to miss	**garsonjera**	studio flat
pisalna miza	desk	**izseliti se**	to move out
papir	paper	**najemnina**	rent
oddajati stanovanja	to let flats	**pekarna**	bakery

Language points

To live somewhere

You have come across the verbs **živeti** and **stanovati**, both meaning 'to live'. They are marginally different in meaning. Compare these sentences:

Živim v Sloveniji.   I live in Slovenia.

Tim že dolgo živi v Šivici.	Tim has been living in Switzerland for a long time.
Stanujem v centru.	I live in the centre.
Moj stric sedaj stanuje v novi hiši.	My uncle lives in a new house now.

Živeti gives a wider implication; the noun **življenje** (life) comes from it. **Stanovati** tells you where someone lives; the noun **stanovanje** (flat) comes from it.

It is too . . .

When you want to say that something is 'too . . .' (as, for example 'too expensive') you put the prefix **pre-** in front of the adjective, for example:

To stanovanje je *predrago.*	This flat is too expensive.
Ta soba je *premajhna.*	This room is too small.
To je *predaleč* **iz mesta.**	This is too far out of town.

Houses and flats

You live either in a house (**hiša**), or in a flat (**stanovanje**). A block of flats is called **stanovanjski blok**, and you may be told **Stanujem v bloku** (I live in a block of flats). You can have a studio flat (**garsonjera**), a one-bedroom flat (**enosobno stanovanje**), a two-bedroom flat (**dvosobno stanovanje**), etc. When you have, say, a two-bedroom flat you don't count your kitchen and bathroom as a room but you do count the living-room. In other words a two-bedroom flat consists of a kitchen, bathroom and two rooms. You can have your own house or flat (**svojo hišo ali svoje stanovanje**) or rent one, which you express with **imeti v najemu**, in which case you pay rent (**najemnina**). For example:

> **V najemu imamo trosobno stanovanje v centru. Plačujemo visoko najemnino.**
> We are renting a three-bedroom flat in the centre. We pay a high rent.

When buying houses or flats people usually take on a mortgage (**kredit**).

Vrt means 'garden'. Almost all private houses have one and it usually has an area where there is lawn with trees, plants and flowers and an area where some basic vegetables are grown.

You may move into a furnished flat (**opremljeno stanovanje**), or into an unfurnished flat (**neopremljeno stanovanje**), in which case you will have to buy your own furniture (**pohištvo**). The names of the usual rooms in a flat or in a house are:

kuhinja	kitchen	**dnevna soba**	living room
kopalnica	bathroom	**otroška soba**	child's room
spalnica	bedroom	**stranišče**	lavatory

The words for basic furniture items are:

pohištvo	furniture	**postelja**	bed
miza	table	**kavč**	couch
stol	chair	**police**	shelves
omara	wardrobe	**kuhinjski elementi**	kitchen units

Other equipment and appliances you need in a house are:

štedilnik	cooker, stove	**pralni stroj**	washing machine
hladilnik	fridge	**sesalec**	vacuum cleaner
zmrzovalnik	freezer	**likalnik**	iron

Plural nouns

As in English, there are plural nouns in Slovene. This means that when a plural noun is the subject of the verb it is used with a plural verb e.g. 'police are . . .'. Plural nouns like this may not have a plural equivalent in Slovene. In Slovene, for example, **policija** is a singular noun and you say **policija je** (is) . . .

The words **vrata** (door) and **tla** (floor) are always plural in Slovene. When you use these nouns, the verb must also be in the plural, for example:

Vrata so odprta.	The door is open.
Tla so umazana.	The floor is dirty.

Let me tell you something

When you want to express a mild obligation, command or a wish you use the word **naj**, which you simply place in front of the verb in the present tense. In English you do this with words like 'may, let, should'. Here are a few examples using the word **naj**:

Kaj naj ti povem?	What shall I tell you?
Ali ga naj pokličem?	Shall I call him?

| **Ne, naj te on pokliče.** | No, let him call you. |
| **Naj se smeji!** | Let him smile! |

This is called optative. When it expresses an obligation it is translated with 'should', or 'shall'. Note how Matej asks Robert in the dialogue **Ali naj pokličem Sabino?** (Shall I call Sabina?)

Exercise 1

Here are a few comments on the dialogue **Ta soba je premajhna** (They are wrong). Can you correct and rewrite them?

1 Soba v hotelu je za Roberta prevelika.
2 Matej je včeraj popoldne srečal Sabino.
3 V Sloveniji je poleti za Roberta premrzlo.
4 Sabinina sestrična oddaja sobe.
5 Robert je takoj našel plan mesta.

Exercise 2

Tell your friend that:
1 your car is too old for the road;
2 your flat is too cold in the winter;
3 espresso coffee is too strong for you;
4 you never drive too fast;
5 that restaurant was too expensive.

Exercise 3

A colleague of yours has mentioned to you how he is about to move. Ask him few questions about it:

zavidati	to envy

1 YOU: *Did you buy a house or a flat?*
  HE: Kupil sem dvosobno stanovanje.
2 YOU: *Was it expensive?*
  HE: Ja. Vzel sem kredit.
3 YOU: *I'm sure you have a lot of work to do now.*
  HE: Ne vprašaj! Delam noč in dan.
4 YOU: *When are you moving?*
  HE: O, ne vem še. Sedaj moram kupiti pohištvo in še sto drugih stvari.

5 YOU: *Hm. . . . I don't envy you.*

Exercise 4

Choose the correct word in brackets in the summary of Robert's getting a flat:

1 Robert je končno dobil (*sobo, stanovanje, hišo*).
2 Zelo pogreša (*omaro, pisalno mizo, sesalec*).
3 Sabinina (*sestrična, sestra, teta*) oddaja stanovanja.
4 Trenutno ima na (*razpolago, ogledu, izbiro*) eno garsonjero in eno trosobno stanovanje.
5 Stanovanje je nad eno (*trgovino, pekarno, gostilno*).

Exercise 5

Križanka

1 kitchen
2 shelves
3 vacuum cleaner
4 cooker
5 table
6 chair
7 bedroom
8 furniture
9 couch
10 fridge

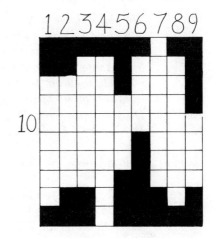

Dialogue 2

Stanovanje je kar lepo opremljeno

The flat is quite nicely furnished

Matej has arranged to meet Sabina that same evening and she took him round to see the flat. He thinks it might suit Robert very well and he telephones him back the following day to tell him what he thinks of it

MATEJ: Stanovanje je veliko, in kar lepo opremljeno. Najbolje je, če ga prideš sam pogledat.

ROBERT: Ali bo jutri zvečer kdo tam?

MATEJ: Sabina je rekla, da bo jutri ves dan tukaj. Pomagala bo čistiti. Zvečer imam tudi jaz čas. Če hočeš, lahko greva skupaj pogledat to stanovanje.

ROBERT: Ali veš, kakšna je cena?

MATEJ: Nič ne skrbi. Jaz sem jim povedal, da si moj dober prijatelj.

ROBERT: Ali bo jutri tudi lastnica tam? Moral jo bom spoznati.

MATEJ: Mislim, da. Ali boš okoli šestih v hotelu? Jaz lahko pridem po tebe.

ROBERT: Ja, če to ni pretežko. Če je bolje zate, se lahko dobiva kje v centru?

MATEJ: Ne, ne, jaz bom prišel v hotel. Ob šestih?

ROBERT: Odlično!

MATEJ: *The flat is large and quite nicely furnished. It is best if you come to have a look at it yourself.*

ROBERT: *Will anyone be there tomorrow evening?*

MATEJ: *Sabina said that she would be here all day tomorrow. She will help to clean. In the evening I have time too. If you want we can go there together to have a look at this flat.*

ROBERT: *Do you know what the price is?*

MATEJ: *Don't worry. I told them that you are a good friend of mine.*

ROBERT: *Will the owner be there tomorrow too? I'll have to meet her.*

MATEJ: *I think so. Will you be in the hotel around six o'clock? I can come and get you.*

ROBERT: *Yes, if that isn't too difficult. If it is better for you we can meet somewhere in the centre?*

MATEJ: *No, no, I'll come to the hotel. At six o'clock?*

ROBERT: *Excellent!*

Vocabulary

kar	quite	**lastnica**	owner
najbolje	best	**spoznati**	to meet
sam	alone, yourself	**bolje**	better
reči	to say	**zate**	for you
cena	price	**dobiti se**	to meet

Language points

Future tense

The future tense in Slovene is formed with the future tense of the verb 'to be' and the participle ending in **l**; that is the same participle that is used to form the past tense. The verb 'to be' in the future tense is conjugated as follows:

Singular	Dual	Plural
bom	bova	bomo
boš	bosta	boste
bo	bosta	bodo

As to how to form the participle ending in **l**, refer back to lesson 7, where you also learned a few irregular ones. Here is an additional list of the verbs which form their participle in a slightly irregular way:

Infinitive	1st person singular	Participle	
najti	*najdem*	**sem našel/-šla**	to find
odpreti	*odprem*	**sem odprl/-a**	to open
zapreti	*zaprem*	**sem zaprl/-a**	to close
nesti	*nesem*	**sem nesel/-sla**	to carry
prevesti	*prevedem*	**sem prevedel/-dla**	to translate

When you want to use 'to be' in the future tense you don't say **bom bil** but only **bom** which means 'I will be'. Note how Robert asks in the dialogue **Ali bo jutri zvečer kdo tam?** Matej asks him **Ali boš okoli šestih v hotelu?** But Matej says **Jaz bom prišel v hotel**. Apart from 'to be', verbs in the future tense are conjugated as stated above. Let's conjugate the verb **priti** (to come) in the future tense:

Singular		Dual		Plural	
(jaz)	bom prišel	(midva)	bova prišla	(mi)	bomo prišli
(ti)	boš prišel	(vidva)	bosta prišla	(vi)	boste prišli
(on)	bo prišel	(onadva)	bosta prišla	(oni)	bodo prišli

Word order

When you use the personal pronouns the word order in the future tense is usually as follows: personal pronoun, future tense of 'to be', participle, as in:

Jaz bom delal.   I will work.

When you don't use the personal pronouns the reverse of the above occurs as in:

Delal bom.   I will work.

Are you going to keep this in mind?

There is only one future tense in Slovene, always formed in the same way. In English you can express a future action with the verb 'to go' as in 'She is going to work tomorrow'. This construction *does not* exist in Slovene.

There is no future perfect tense in Slovene. A sentence like 'I will have learned this by tomorrow' is expressed with the only future tense which exists in Slovene: **To se bom naučil do jutri**. You may find this odd because by tomorrow this action will have been in the past, but that's the way it is!

On one's own or together

The word **sam/-a** means 'alone', 'by oneself', for example:

Danes sem sama doma.   I'm at home on my own today.
Po navadi grem sam v kino. I usually go to the cinema on my own.

The word **skupaj** means 'together', for example:

Skupaj sva šla v kino.   We (two) went to the cinema together.

Notice how Matej suggests to Robert **Če hočeš, lahko greva skupaj pogledat to stanovanje**.

Yes, quite

The word **kar** means 'quite', 'just', for example:

Kar povej ji!   Just tell her!

Kako si? Kar dobro.   How are you? Quite well.

Kar is also a conjunction word which you will meet later on.

Supine

The supine, like the infinitive, is a verbal form which does not indicate a person. The supine differs from the infinitive in that it doesn't have the final **i**, for example **gledat, govorit, pisat**.

The supine is used after verbs of motion, such as 'to go', 'to come', 'to drive', etc., for example:

Grem kupit par stvari.   I'm going to buy a few things.
Pridi me obiskat.   Come to visit me.

Note how Matej suggests to Robert:

Najbolje je, če ga *prideš* sam *pogledat*.
Če hočeš, *se* lahko *peljeva* skupaj *pogledat* to stanovanje.

(The verb and the supine are in italics in the sentences above.)

Exercise 6

Suppose you did the things below yesterday. How would you say them if you were going to do them tomorrow?

1 Kupil sem si tri knjige.
2 Ob desetih dopoldne sem šel v kavarno.
3 Ves popoldan sem se učil slovenščino.
4 V mesto sem se peljal z avtobusom.
5 Od sedmih do osmih zjutraj sem igral tenis.

Exercise 7

Davor is a student and is looking for a room. A friend of his tells him that there will soon be a room available in a flat where he lives. Can you put into Slovene the conversation they have had?

DAVOR: Where is the flat?
SERGEJ: Near the centre. Do you want to come to have a look at it?
DAVOR: Are you free this evening? Can I come to see you?
SERGEJ: Yes, if you want we can meet in the centre.
DAVOR: Yes, where?

SERGEJ: In the cafe 'Marija'.
DAVOR: How much does the rent cost?
SERGEJ: I'll tell you everything this evening.

Exercise 8

Are these statements about you true or false?

1	Stanujem v bloku.	T	F
2	Imam dvosobno stanovanje.	T	F
3	Moje stanovanje je v centru mesta.	T	F
4	Živim sam.	T	F
5	Nimam kuhinje.	T	F

Rewrite the ones which are false.

Exercise 9

Suppose this is a weather forecast for tomorrow. Can you fill in the missing words in Slovene, given in the box below, as indicated in brackets in English? Use each word once only.

Vremenska napoved za jutri

> V četrtek, sonce, okoli, bo, deževalo, popoldne, Temperature, dopoldne, od, do.

Jutri (1 *will*) po vsej Sloveniji (2 *rain*).
Temperature bodo (3 *from*) 18 (4 *to*) 21 stopinj celzija.
(5 *On Thursday*) bo delno jasno, (6 *in the afternoon*) bodo ponekod še manjše padavine.
(7 *The temperature*) bodo (8 *about*) 22 stopinj celzija.
(9 *In the morning*) bo pihal še veter ampak popoldne se bo pokazalo (10 *the sun*).

Exercise 10

Find out if the people below will go to the places indicated at the time given. The first sentence has been done for you.

1 Robert / to see the flat / tomorrow
   Ali bo Robert jutri šel pogledat stanovanje?
2 Davor / on holiday / next year

3 Sabina / to the theatre / tomorrow night
4 Sergej / to the cinema / tonight
5 Davor / to the doctor's / tomorrow morning
6 Barbara and Tomaž / to Spain / in September

Dialogue 3 🔲

Končno se selim!

I'm finally moving!

Robert and Matej have gone to the flat and had a look at it. Apart from a few things which will have to be arranged, Robert is quite pleased about it. He takes Matej, who has a few suggestions, for a drink

ROBERT: Na zdravje!
MATEJ: Na zdravje! Na tvoje novo stanovanje!
ROBERT: Hvala ti, Matej! To stanovanje ni samo lepo, ampak tudi poceni! In lepo diši, po kruhu.
MATEJ: Ja, povedal sem ti, spodaj je pekarna. Vsako jutro boš lahko imel sveži zajtrk.
ROBERT: Ja, ne bo mi treba skrbeti, da se bom zredil! Vsak dan bom hodil gor in dol po teh stopnicah. Škoda, da ni dvigala. In nekaj stvari bom moral kupiti.
MATEJ: Najbolje je, če se najprej vseliš in o vsem malo premisliš. Moji starši imajo mojo staro pisalno mizo na podstrešju. Lahko si jo izposodiš. In prepričan sem, da ti bo tudi Sabinina teta kaj posodila, če boš želel.
ROBERT: Ravno razmišljam, če se mi izplača kupiti vse, kar potrebujem. Ali je pohištvo drago ali poceni?
MATEJ: Odvisno, kaj kupiš.

ROBERT: *Cheers!*
MATEJ: *Cheers! To your new flat!*
ROBERT: *Thank you, Matej. This flat isn't only nice but is also cheap. And it smells nicely, of bread.*
MATEJ: *Yes, I told you, there is a bakery below. You'll be able to have a fresh breakfast every morning.*
ROBERT: *Yes, I won't need to worry that I am putting on weight. I'll be walking up and down these stairs every day. It's a*

> *pity there isn't an escalator there. And I'll have to buy a few things.*

MATEJ: *It is best if you move in first and think about everything a little. My parents have my old desk in the attic. You can borrow it. And I'm sure that Sabina's aunt will lend you something if you want.*

ROBERT: *I'm just wondering whether it's worth buying everything I need. Is furniture expensive or cheap?*

MATEJ: *It depends what you buy.*

Vocabulary

na zdravje	cheers	**premisliti**	to think over
svež	fresh	**podstrešje**	attic
zajtrk	breakfast	**izposoditi si**	to borrow
zrediti se	to put on weight	**posoditi**	to lend
stopnice	stairs	**razmišljati**	to think about
dvigalo	lift	**izplačati se**	to be worth while
nekaj stvari	a few things	**odvisno**	depends
vseliti se	to move in		

Language points

Up and down

You have learned that Slovene has two words for 'here' and 'there' depending whether the verb implies movement or not. The same applies to a few other words, like 'up' and 'down'. Notice how Robert says in the dialogue: **Vsak dan bom hodil *gor* in *dol* po stopnicah**. He will go **gor** but he will be **gori**. He will go **dol** but he will be **doli**. Look at some more examples:

Pridi sem!	Come here!
Tukaj sem!	I am here!
Ali greš danes ven?	Are you going out today?
Ne, včeraj sem bil ves večer zunaj.	No, I was out all evening yesterday.
Pridi dol!	Come down!
Vsi smo doli.	We're all down here.

Here are the words which are expressed with the same word in English but require different words in Slovene, depending on whether you go somewhere or whether you are somewhere.

You go	*You are*	
sem	**tukaj**	here
tja	**tam**	there
domov	**doma**	home
gor	**gori**	up (upstairs)
dol	**doli**	down (downstairs)
ven	**zunaj**	out

How much does it cost?

When asking this question you must put the verb into the third person singular when referring to one thing, as in:

Koliko stane ta knjiga?   How much does this book cost?

or into the third person plural when referring to more than two things, for example:

Koliko stanejo jabolka?   How much do apples cost?

You can also ask for the price (**cena**) as Robert did in the dialogue:

Kakšna je cena?   What's the price?

You may see notices in the shops:

posebna ponudba	special offer
ugodno	bargain
znižano	reduced
razprodaja	sale

Good/better/the best

You will learn how to form comparisons in lesson 13. As in English, the comparison for 'good' is irregular. It is as follows:

dober	boljši	najboljši
dobra	boljša	najboljša
dobro	boljše (bolje)	najboljše (najbolje)

Notice how Matej says to Robert:

Najbolje je, če ga (stanovanje) prideš sam pogledat.
It's *best* if you come to have a look at it yourself.

Robert asks Matej:

Če je *bolje* zate, se lahko dobiva kje v centru?
If it's *better* for you we can meet somewhere in the centre?

Not only . . . but also. . .

When you want to say that something is 'not only . . . but also . . .'
you use the words **ne samo . . . ampak tudi . . .** Notice how Robert
said in the dialogue:

Stanovanje *ni samo* lepo, *ampak tudi* poceni!

It smells nice/bad

There are two distinct verbs in Slovene describing a nice and a bad
smell:

dišati	smells nice
smrdeti	smells bad

Here are a few examples of how they are used:

smeti	rubbish

Tukaj nekaj smrdi.	Something smells here.
Smeti smrdijo.	The rubbish smells.
Kaj kuhaš? Lepo diši.	What are you cooking? It smells nice.

To lend/borrow

The verbs 'to lend' (**posoditi**) and 'to borrow' (**izposoditi si**) are
used in Slovene as in the following examples:

Ali mi lahko posodiš to knjigo?	Can you lend me this book?
Ne, ni moja. Marko mi jo je posodil.	No, it isn't mine. Marko lent it to me.
Ampak lahko si jo izposodiš v knjižnici.	But you can borrow it from the library.

One has to know these things

As in English, you can express an action which can be done by anyone. In English you use the impersonal 'one', or 'you' to express this. In Slovene you use the second person singular, for example:

Vsepovsod moraš biti previden. You must be careful every-where.

Nikoli ne veš. You never know!

You can also express things like this with the third person singular but you have to insert the word **človek** (men), for example:

Človek mora biti vsepovsod previden. One (lit. 'man') must be careful everywhere.

Človek nikoli ne ve. One (lit. 'man') never knows.

Slovene verbs

In this lesson you have come across **seliti se** (to move). By adding prefixes this verb has different meanings, for example:

seliti se	to move
preseliti se	to move *somewhere else*
odseliti se	to move *away*

The noun **odseljenci** (emigrants) comes from this.

priseliti se	to move *somewhere*

The noun **priseljenci** (immigrants) comes from this.

vseliti se	to move *in*
izseliti se	to move *out*

This happens with almost all Slovene verbs. Since in English only one verb exists for them all it is difficult to translate them. Let us take another example: **pisati** (to write).

vpisati se	to enrol
Ali si se *že* vpisal?	Have you *enrolled* yet?
podpisati	to sign
Podpišite tukaj, prosim!	*Sign* here, please!
prepisati	to copy
Prepiši mojo domačo nalogo!	*Copy* my homework!

*pri*pisati	to add
Nekaj moram še *pripisati*.	I must *add* something.

*od*pisati	to write back

Nisem imel časa, zato ti tako dolgo nisem *odpisal*.
I didn't have the time, that is why I didn't *write back* for such a long time.

*na*pisati

Danes sem *napisal* 200 strani.	Today I *wrote* 200 pages.
Pisal sem ves dan.	I've been writing all day.

By adding prefixes to **pisati** it will change the meaning, sometimes considerably and sometimes marginally. You must not think that you don't know the word when you come across it with its different prefixes. For the time being it is best if you look at the root of the verb, which you will recognize and which should give you an idea of what the verb could mean. As you have seen in the examples above, the verb has something to do with writing.

Is there such a construction in Slovene? No, there isn't

If you are thinking in English you must not try to translate literally sentences like:

Is there a shop close by here?	**Ali je tukaj blizu kakšna trgovina?**
There has been an accident.	**Zgodila se je nesreča.**
There is no one here today.	**Danes ni nikogar tukaj.**

Such a construction does not exist in Slovene, and when you want to express something like this you must not translate the word 'there' to do so but say it in another way. 'There' is understood in Slovene. Look at the examples on the right and see how this construction can be expressed in Slovene.

Exercise 11

Connect the following sentences with the conjunction given in brackets:
1 We can meet in a café. Is this better for you? (*if*)
2 The flat was big. It wasn't furnished. (*but*)
3 Robert has all his books and papers on the floor. The room in the hotel is too small for him. (*because*)

4 I told her. I didn't have the time. (*that*)
5 Come with us to the cinema. Do you have the time? (*if*)

Exercise 12

What answers on the right would be possible for the questions on the left?

1 Srečno pot!	(a) Ne, zelo nezanimiv je bil.
2 Kaj te boli?	(b) Dežuje, in mrzlo je.
3 Ali igraš klavir?	(c) Ne, to je moj bratranec.
4 Kam greš?	(d) Glava in grlo.
5 Ali je bil film zanimiv?	(e) Hvala.
6 Ali si prvič tukaj?	(f) Ne, kitaro.
7 Kakšno je danes vreme?	(g) V mesto.
8 Ali je to tvoj brat?	(h) Ne, drugič.

Exercise 13

Can you remember the Slovene for the words in italics? Test yourself!

1 You go for a drink with a friend where a sign in the bar says *No smoking*.
2 You are just about to park your car when you notice the sign *No parking*.
3 You are in a theatre and the performance is about to begin but your friend is still telling you something. Say to him *Stop talking*.
4 You think you are going to the lavatory in a restaurant when you see a sign *No entry*.
5 You are going away for some time and people say to you *Have a good trip and a pleasant holiday*.

Exercise 14

Complete these sentences with the following words: **predraga, predaleč, premrzlo, prevroče, prehitro.**

1 Njegov stric zmeraj vozi ...
2 Ne moreš it peš, ... je.
3 Stanovanje mi je všeč ampak najemnina je ...
4 Danes ne grem ven ... je.
5 Raje imam zimo, poleti je zame ...

Exercise 15 ▮▮

Pronunciation exercise. The letter **v** has different sounds in Slovene. When **v** is placed before a vowel or before the consonants **l** and **r** it is pronounced **v** as in 'villa'. Let's pronounce the following words:

veliko stanovanje
veter
človek nikoli ne ve
slabo vreme
ne vem
videl sem vas

When **v** is at the end of a word, when it stands after a vowel and when it stands before consonants (apart from **l** and **r**) **v** is pronounced like the English 'w' as in 'how':

Ali je bilo to vprašanje težko?
Rjav avto
To vsak ve!
Na zdravje!

Dialogue for comprehension ▮▮

Robert is very excited about having found a flat and he telephones a Slovenian friend, Špela, living in England to tell her about it. What does she say he will have to do when she next comes to visit?

ŠPELA: Prosim?
ROBERT: Špela, jaz sem.
ŠPELA: O, kako si?
ROBERT: Dobre volje sem. Končno se selim!
ŠPELA: Kam? Kdaj?
ROBERT: Mislim, da bom naslednji teden že tam. Matej mi je pomagal. Njegova prijateljica, pravzaprav njena teta oddaja stanovanja. Prejšnji teden se je nekdo izselil in trenutno ima na razpolago eno trosobno stanovanje.
ŠPELA: Ali ti je všeč? Ali je v centru?
ROBERT: Ja, kar veliko je in opremljeno je. Imel bom kuhinjo, zelo majhno kopalnico in tri sobe. Najbolj potrebujem pisalno mizo.
ŠPELA: O, vesela sem.

ROBERT: Mimogrede, baje vedno lepo diši, po kruhu. Spodaj je
pekarna.

ŠPELA: Torej ko pridem naslednjič, mi boš pripravil sveži zajterk.

ROBERT: Seveda!

9 Treba je napolniti hladilnik!

The fridge needs filling!

In this lesson you will learn about:

- How to use the genitive case
- Where and how to buy some food
- The way the Slovene words for 'to know' are used
- How to fill in a form
- More ways of expressing an obligation in a positive or in a negative way

Dialogue 1 🔲

Na tej glavni cesti je kar precej majhnih trgovin

There are quite a few small shops on this main road

Robert has moved into his flat and has met his neighbours Boštjan, Sergej and Davor, who are medical students sharing a flat next door to him. He meets Sergej just outside the block of flats one morning, who tells him where things in the area are

SERGEJ: Dobro jutro, zgodnji si. Ali si se že vživel?

ROBERT: Ja, kar. Končno imam več prostora. Ravnokar prihajam iz pekarne. Dopoldne nameravam iti nakupovat. Moram naponiti hladilnik.

SERGEJ: Ja, na tej glavni cesti je kar precej majhnih trgovin in velika samopostrežna je približno 200 metrov na ravnost in prva ulica na levo. Tam imajo dobro izbiro. Ni ti treba iti peš. Avtobusna postaja je pred trgovino.

ROBERT: Raje grem peš.
SERGEJ: In mesnica je tukaj za vogalom.
ROBERT: O, ne, ne bom je potreboval. Vegetarjanec sem.
SERGEJ: Moral boš iti na tržnico.
ROBERT: Ali je kje blizu?
SERGEJ: Ja, ... o, moj avtobus prihaja. Ali se hočeš oglasiti zvečer? Mislim, da bomo danes vsi doma.
ROBERT: Ja, kdaj?
SERGEJ: Vseeno je, kar pozvoni. Adijo!

SERGEJ: *Good morning, you're early. Have you got used to it yet?*
ROBERT: *Yes, quite. At last I have more space. I've just come from the bakery. In the morning I intend to go shopping. I must fill up the fridge.*
SERGEJ: *Yes, there are quite a few small shops on this main road and a big supermarket is approximately 200 metres straight down the road in the first street on the left. They have a good choice there. You don't need to walk. The bus stop is in front of the shop.*
ROBERT: *I prefer to walk.*
SERGEJ: *The butcher is here around the corner.*
ROBERT: *Oh no, I won't need it. I'm a vegetarian.*
SERGEJ: *You'll have to go to the fruit market.*
ROBERT: *Is it somewhere near?*
SERGEJ: *Yes, ... oh, my bus is coming. Do you want to come round in the evening? I think we'll all be at home.*
ROBERT: *Yes, when?*
SERGEJ: *It doesn't matter, just ring the bell. Bye!*

Vocabulary

biti zgodenj	to be early	**sampostrežna**	supermarket
vživeti se v	to get used to	**izbira**	choice
prostor	space	**ni treba**	there is no need to
ravnokar	just	**mesnica**	butcher's shop
napolniti	to fill up	**vseeno je**	it doesn't matter
glavna cesta	main road	**tržnica**	market

Language points

It is necessary to . . .

In lesson 4 you learnt that **morati** (must) is followed by the infinitive. Notice how Robert says **Moram napolniti hladilnik**.

An obligation is usually expressed with the verb **morati** in Slovene. In English you can express an obligation with other verbs like 'to have to, ought to, to be obliged to', which means that the same idea can be translated into English in different ways.

You have also learned that **morati** has no negative form and that you use **moči** (e.g. **nisem mogel**) to express an obligation in the negative sense.

You can express an obligation in a positive or in a negative sense with **treba je** or **ni treba**. This is an impersonal expression and it is used with the dative case and the infinitive, for example:

Ali ti je treba . . .?	Do you have to . . . ?
Ni mi treba . . .	I don't have to . . .
Ni ti treba . . .	You don't have to . . .

Notice how Sergej says to Robert in the dialogue **Ni ti treba iti peš** (You don't have to walk).

More uses of the infinitive

In lesson 4 you learnt that the verbs **morati**, **znati**, **smeti**, **moči**, **hoteti**, **želeti** are followed by an infinitive. Verbs which indicate a beginning (**začeti**), or an end (**končati**, **nehati**) are also followed by an infinitive, for example:

Začnimo jesti!	Let's start eating.
Nehal sem kaditi.	I stopped smoking.

There are phrases after which the infinitive is used. Here are a few:

biti primoran	to be obliged/forced to
biti sposoben	to be capable
imeti navado	to have the habit

You can use the infinitive where you would use a gerund in English as in:

sedeti	to sit

Kaditi (**je**) **prepovedano.**   *Smoking* prohibited.

Poleti je prijetno *sedeti* **zunaj.** In the summer *sitting* outside
                                            is pleasant.

Whilst you can use an infinitive in certain expressions in English
you cannot in Slovene. Instead you have to use a relative clause.
Look at the following examples:

Obljubil sem, da vas bom peljal na večerjo.
I promised to take you to have supper.

I don't mind

When you want to say that something doesn't matter, or that you
don't mind, you use the expression **biti vseeno** with the personal
pronoun in the dative case, for example:

Meni je vseeno.   I don't mind.

Njemu ni vseeno.   He does mind.

Notice how Sergej says to Robert **Vseeno je**, meaning 'It doesn't
matter'.

Ring the bell or knock on the door

Zvoniti means 'to ring' and **trkati** means 'to knock'. However, when
you tell someone to ring the bell or to knock on the door you use
these verbs with the prefix **po**, i.e. **pozvoniti** and **potrkati**. Notice
how Sergej says to Robert:

Kar pozvoni!   Just ring the bell!

He could have said:

Potrkaj na vrata!   Knock on the door!

Shopping for food

The word for 'a shop' is **trgovina**. You may want to go to a butcher
(**mesnica**), bakery (**pekarna**), delicatessen (**delikatesa**), fruit and
vegetable market (**tržnica**).

Plural of nouns

You know that Slovene nouns are masculine, feminine or neuter in gender and that they can appear in singular, dual or plural form. Let us take a look at how the plural of nouns is formed.

Feminine nouns ending in **a** change their ending to **e** in the plural form, for example:

hiš*a*	hiš*e*
prijateljic*a*	prijateljic*e*
nedelj*a*	nedelj*e*

Masculine nouns ending in a consonant usually take an **i** ending but there are exceptions, for example:

otrok	otro*ci*
prijatelj	prijatelj*i*

Neuter nouns ending in **o** or **e** take an **a** ending, for example:

mest*o*	mest*a*
dekl*e*	deklet*a*

To listen to/to hear

In English you use the verb 'to listen' with the preposition 'to' as in 'I'm listening to the radio'. In Slovene there is no preposition after **poslušati** (to listen), and you say **Poslušam radio**.

Here are a few more examples:

poročila	news

Kaj poslušaš?	What are you listening to?
Poslušam poročila.	I'm listening to the news.
Poslušaj me!	Listen to me!
Jaz nikoli ne poslušam radio.	I never listen to the radio.

When you want to say that you have heard something you use **slišati**.

Ali si slišal, kaj je rekla Eva?	Did you hear what Eva said?
Ne, nisem slišal. Nisem poslušal.	No, I didn't hear. I didn't listen.

Exercise 1

You are sharing a flat with a few people and things are never where they should be. Ask your flatmate if he has put the things below in the places indicated, using the verb provided. The first example has been done for you:

1 odnesti / knjige / dnevna soba
   Ali si odnesel knjige v dnevno sobo?

2 zapeljati / avto / garaža
3 dati / mleko / hladilnik
4 odnesti / dežnik / kopalnica
5 dati / časopis / miza
6 postaviti / rože / vaza

Exercise 2

Your flatmate told you that all the things you asked in exercise 1 have been done. What did he say to you? The first example has been done for you:

1 Knjige so v dnevni sobi.

Exercise 3

Davor and Sergej are planning to take a trip to Morocco (**Maroko**) during their summer holiday and are arranging things. As Davor gets home one afternoon he tells Sergej what he has found out. Can you put into Slovene what they were saying?

SERGEJ: Have you been to the travel agency?
DAVOR: Yes, I have. I asked how much the plane ticket costs.
SERGEJ: Is it cheap or expensive?
DAVOR: Very expensive. I think it is too expensive.
SERGEJ: Don't they have any charter flights?
DAVOR: Not in the summer.

Exercise 4

Ask your friend whether he has to do the following things. Use the expression **treba je**. The first example has been done for you:

v naprej	in advance
glasba	music

1 buy all these books
   Ali ti je treba kupiti vse te knjige?
2 smoke
3 reserve the ticket a month in advance
4 go to the cinema twice a week
5 work every evening
6 listen to the music all day

Exercise 5

Your friend answers that he doesn't need to do the things you were asking him about but he likes to do them. What did he say? The first example has been done for you
1 Ne, ni mi treba kupiti vse te knjige, ampak jaz rad kupujem knjige.

Dialogue 2 🔲

Ali znaš voziti po desni strani ceste?

Can you drive on the right side of the road?

Robert has decided to hire a car to help him move and do the shopping. As he gets to the Rent-a-Car office he sees Davor, one of his neighbours. Neither of them knows what the other is doing there but they tell each other

DAVOR: Robert, živio, ali me ne poznaš?
ROBERT: O, živio Davor, nisem te videl.
DAVOR: Ali si izposojaš avto?
ROBERT: Ja, izposodil si bom enega za en mesec. Ali ti delaš tukaj?
DAVOR: Ja, dvakrat na teden, zraven študija. Tako si zaslužim nekaj denarja. Najraje delam ob večerih, ko ni gneče. Včasih tudi študiram tukaj.
ROBERT: Lepo in pametno. Tudi jaz sem delal, ko sem bil študent.
DAVOR: Kaj si delal?

ROBERT: Prodajal sem kolesa, in tudi popravljal sem jih.
DAVOR: In sedaj hočeš avto. Ali znaš voziti po desni strani ceste?
ROBERT: Ja, seveda.

DAVOR: *Robert, hello, don't you know me?*
ROBERT: *Oh, hello Davor, I didn't see you.*
DAVOR: *Are you hiring a car?*
ROBERT: *Yes, I'll hire one for a month. Do you work here?*
DAVOR: *Yes, twice a week, alongside my studies. So I earn some money. I most like to work in the evening when it isn't busy. I study here sometimes as well.*
ROBERT: *Nice and clever. I also worked when I was a student.*
DAVOR: *What did you do?*
ROBERT: *I was selling bicycles, and also repairing them.*
DAVOR: *And now you want a car. Can you drive on the right side of the road?*
ROBERT: *Yes, of course.*

Vocabulary

izposoditi si	to borrow	**gneča**	a crowd of people
zraven	on the side, alongside	**pametno**	clever
zaslužiti	to earn	**popraviti**	to repair
nekaj	some		

Language points

Davor at the counter in the Rent-a-Car office gives Robert the following form to fill in:

Priimek	Surname
Ime	Name
Spol (moški, ženski)	Sex (m., f.)
Državljanstvo	Nationality
Rojstni datum	Date of birth
Rojstni kraj	Place of birth
Stalno prebivališče	Permanent address
Podpis	Signature
Datum	Date

Should you do anything official in Slovenia you will probably be asked to fill in such a form or one very similar. It is called **formular**, **obrazec**, **prijavnica**.

Vedeti/znati/poznati

You have come across these verbs: **vedeti**, **znati** and **poznati**. They are all translated as 'to know' in English, yet in Slovene they all have a different meaning. Look at the following examples.

Poznati means 'to know something or somebody':

Ali poznaš Ljubljano?	Do you know Ljubljana?
Robert ne pozna Sabine.	Robert doesn't know Sabine.

Vedeti means that you know something:

Ali veš, koliko je ura?	Do you know what time it is?
Ne, ne vem.	No, I don't know.

Znati means 'to know how to do something', as in:

Ali znaš voziti po desni strani ceste?	Can you drive on the right side of the road?
Ne, ne znam.	No, I can't.
Ali znaš igrati tenis?	Can you play tennis?

More about the Slovene verbs

Most Slovene verbs appear in two forms. One expresses an action which is limited, for example **prodati** (to sell). These are perfective verbs. Others express an action which is or was in progress, for example, **prodajati**. These are imperfective. Both **prodati** and **prodajati** are translated into English as 'to sell'. There is, however, a difference in meaning in Slovene. Notice how Robert tells Davor in the dialogue **prodajal sem kolesa**. This gives a sense of a continuing process, which is expressed with an imperfective verb. Robert could have said **Vsak dan sem prodal eno kolo** (Every day I sold one bicycle). This would give a sense of an action which was finished, and such an action is expressed with a perfective verb in Slovene. Here are a few examples of how perfective and imperfective verbs are used:

kupovati, kupiti
Kaj *kupuješ*?   What *are you buying?*
Kupil sem **avto.**   *I bought* a car.

pošiljati, poslati
Jane mi *pošilja* **novice iz**   Jane *is sending* me the news from
    Anglije.   England.
Jane mi je *poslala* **paket.**   Jane *sent* me a packet.

In the dialogue you came across the verbs **izposoditi si** and **popraviti** in their imperfective form. Here are some more examples of verbs which exist in two forms:

Perfective verbs (expressing an action which has been completed)	Imperfective verbs (expressing an action in progress)
prodati	prodajati
kupiti	kupovati
poslati	pošiljati
posoditi	posojati
izposoditi si	izposojati si
ostati	ostajati
plačati	plačevati
dobiti	dobivati
urediti	urejati

Which do you prefer or like most?

In lesson 5 you learnt how to express what you like (**imeti** *plus* **rad/-a**) and what you like doing (**rad/-a** *plus the verb in the form of the person you are referring to*). If you want to say that you like something or like doing something very much you put the adverb **zelo** (very) in front of **rad**, for example:

On se zelo rad vozi s kolesom.   He likes riding his bicycle very
    much.
Jaz imam zelo rad redeče vino.   I like red wine very much.

When you want to say that you prefer something you say **imeti raje** or **rajši**, as in:

Kaj imaš raje, kavo ali čaj?	Which do you prefer, coffee or tea?

To say that you like something most you put **naj** in front of **raje** or **rajši**, as in:

Najraje imam čaj z limono.	I like tea with lemon most.
Najraje igram kitaro.	I like playing the guitar most.

Raje, **rajši**, **najraje** and **najrajši** are adverbs and never change.

You have learned that to say that you like something you can use the expression **všeč mi je**, which takes a personal pronoun in the dative case. Another expression for liking something is **ugaja mi**, **ti**, which, again, you use with the personal pronoun in the dative case. Here are a few examples:

glasba	music
klasična glasba	classical music

Ali ti ugaja ta glasba?	Do you like this music?
Ne, žal mi je, ne ugaja mi.	No, I'm sorry, I don't like it.
Meni ugaja klasična glasba.	I like classical music.

The Slovene school system

Slovenes go to primary school (**osnovna šola**) at the age of six or seven, which is compulsory and lasts eight years. This primary school is sometimes called **osemletka** (the eight-years school). If you have completed primary school with good results you are able to go to the secondary school (**srednja šola**), usually for four years. These vary: some are orientated towards particular professions (like nursing, technology) and others are in the main preparation for universities. If you weren't quite as successful in your primary school you can go to a school which will train you for a particular job, like motor mechanics or hairdressing. The training normally lasts three years and the colleges are called **poklicna šola** (technical college).

Public education is free; in secondary schools and at universities you can get a grant (**štipendija**).

When you are in primary school you are in a **razred** (form). You will hear people say:

Metka je v petem/šestem razredu.
Metka is in the fifth/sixth form.

Above primary school you are in a **letnik** (year), for example:

V katerem letniku je Davor? Ne vem, mislim, da je v drugem.
In which year is Davor? I don't know. I think in the second.

What do you study?

You can ask somebody **Kaj študiraš/študirate?** and they will tell you the subject they study, which will be in the accusative case because it answers the question 'what?'. Here are a few subjects you can study:

zgodovina	history
pravo	law

You will recognize the names of the others major subjects. Note, however, how they are spelt in Slovene: **geografija**, **medicina**, **slovenščina**, **angleščina**, **ekonomija**, **matematika**, **fizika**, **biologija**, **kemija**.
   Diploma means 'degree' in Slovene. You may hear students say:

Kdaj si/boš diplomiral?   When did you/will you take your degree?

Diplomirati means 'to take one's degree'.

Exercise 6

Fill in the Slovene verbs for 'to know' in the correct person and tense in the sentences below

1 Ali ..., koliko je ura?
2 Ali ... Simono? Ne, ne ... je.
3 Ali ... igrati vijolino? Ne, ampak ... igrati klavir.
4 Nisem ..., da je Slovenija tako majhna.
5 (Jaz) ..., da nič ne ... (Sokrat).

Exercise 7

Choose the correct alternative from the words in italics:

1 Ne morem se *odločiti/odločati*.
2 Ali si že *prodal/prodajal* hišo?
3 Moj prijatelj me je povabil na večerjo. On je *plačal/plačeval*.
4 Žal mi je, ne morem ti *posoditi/posojati* te knjige. Jutri jo potrebujem.

5 Oprostite, kje lahko *kupim/kupujem* razglednice in znamke?

Exercise 8

What do the people below study? Make up similar sentences to the example which has been done for you:

Sergej/medicine
Sergej študira medicino.

1 Sabina/economy
2 Tanja/law
3 Milena/history
4 Ana/mathematics
5 Janez/biology

Exercise 9

You check into a hotel in Slovenia and you are given this form to fill in:

```
1 Priimek: ....................................
2 Ime: .......................................
3 Spol (moški, ženski): .........................
4 Državljanstvo: ..............................
5 Rojstni datum: ..............................
6 Rojstni kraj: ...............................
7 Stalno prebivališče: .........................
8 Podpis: .....................................
9 Datum: ......................................
```

Exercise 10

Choose the correct answer referring to the dialogues in this lesson:

1 Robert je zjutraj šel v
   (a) mesnico
   (b) pekarno
   (c) trgovino

2 Robert mora
   (a) kupiti radio
   (b) iti v mesnico

   (c) napolniti hladilnik

3 Kdo dela v Rent-a-Car pisarni?
   (a) Davor
   (b) Boštjan
   (c) Sergej

4 Kaj je delal Robert, ko je bil študent?
   (a) prodajal je avtomobile
   (b) prodajal je kolesa
   (c) popravljal je avtomobile

5 Za kako dolgo si bo Robert izposodil avto?
   (a) Za en mesec.
   (b) Za dva meseca.
   (c) Za tri mesece.

Dialogue 3

Ali sem jaz na vrsti?

Is it my turn?

Now that he has a car, Robert stops at his local fruit and vegetable market and buys a few things

BRANJEVKA:	Ali vam lahko postrežem, gospod? Sveže sadje imam, in zelenjavo. Poglejte!
ROBERT:	Ja, prosim. 2kg krompirja, 1kg paradižnika, 1kg jabolk in ½kg gob.
BRANJEVKA:	Gob pa danes na žalost nimam. Ali želite še kaj drugega? Lepe hruške imam.
ROBERT:	Ne, to je vse za enkrat, hvala.

(Robert then goes to the delicatessen counter of a shop.)

PRODAJALKA:	Želite, prosim?
ROBERT:	O, ali sem že jaz na vrsti? 20 dkg sira, 2l mleka in 2 jogurta prosim.
PRODAJALKA:	Izvolite! Želite še kaj drugega?
ROBERT:	Ne, hvala. Kje plačam?
PRODAJALKA:	Pri blagajni.

GREENGROCER:	*Can I get you anything, sir? I have fresh fruit and vegetables. Look!*
ROBERT:	*Yes, please. 2 kg of potatoes, 1 kg of tomatoes, 1 kg of apples and ½kg of mushrooms.*
GREENGROCER:	*Unfortunately I haven't got mushrooms today. Would you like anything else? I have nice pears.*
ROBERT:	*No, that's all for now, thank you.*

(Robert then goes to the delicatessen counter of a shop.)

ASSISTANT:	*Can I help you?*
ROBERT:	*Oh, is it my turn? 20 dkg of cheese, 2 litres of milk and 2 yoghurts, please.*
ASSISTANT:	*Here you are! Would you like anything else?*
ROBERT:	*No, thank you. Where do I pay?*
ASSISTANT:	*At the till.*

Vocabulary

branjevka	greengrocer	**hruška**	pear
postrči	to serve	**za enkrat**	for now
sveže sadje	fresh fruit	**biti na vrsti**	one's turn
zelenjava	vegetables	**sir**	cheese
krompir	potatoes	**jogurt**	yoghurt
paradižnik	tomato	**blagajna**	till
jabolko	apple	**dkg**	decagramme

Language points

Buying things

Bread, meat, fruit and vegetables are sold by the kilo in Slovenia. Liquid items such as milk or drinks are sold by the litre. At delicatessen counters sausages, cheese and salami are sold by grams or dekagrams.

Robert had a list of basic items he had to get at the shop:

Seznam	*Shopping list*
kruh	bread
mleko	milk
čaj	tea
kava	coffee
sir	cheese
jajca	eggs
salama	salami

Whose turn is it?

The word **vrsta** means 'line', 'queue'. You ask **Kdo je na vrsti?** meaning 'Whose turn is it?' You may get the answers:

Oprostite, sedaj niste vi na vrsti. Excuse me, it isn't your turn.
Ona je na vrsti. It is her turn.

Notice how Robert asks at the counter **Ali sem jaz na vrsti?**

The genitive case

You have come across expressions in which the genitive case was used. In Slovene the genitive case is used for the direct object of all negative verbs (e.g. **nimam časa**). It is used when in English you'd use the preposition 'of' (e.g. **v centru mesta**), which goes for all expressions of quantity. It is also used as the object of certain prepositions. This means that in all the above cases the nouns and the adjectives will take the following endings.

First declension
Feminine nouns ending in **a** will change their ending to **e**, for example:

Že dolgo nisem videl moje prijateljice Sabine.
I haven't seen my friend Sabine for a long time.

Second declension
Feminine nouns ending in a consonant will take an **i** ending, for example:

Veselim se pomladi.   I'm looking forward to spring.

Third declension
Masculine nouns will usually take an **a** ending, for example:

2 kg krompirja   2 kilos of potatoes

Fourth declension
Neuter nouns ending in **o** or **e** will take an **a** ending, for example:

Nismo imeli lepega vremena. We didn't have nice weather.
2 litra mleka.   2 litres of milk.

Personal pronouns in the genitive case are as follows:

Singular	Dual	Plural
mene (me)	naju	nas
tebe (te)	vaju	vas
njega (ga)	nju	njih
nje (je)		
njega (ga)		

With the exception of 'her', personal pronouns in the genitive case
are the same as personal pronouns in the accusative case.

Ali si jo videl?   Have you seen her?
Ne, nisem je videl.   No, I haven't seen her.

The prepositions used with the genitive case are:

od	from, of, since
do	to, until, up to, as far as
brez	without
iz	from, out of

Some prepositions are compounds:

izza	from behind
iznad	from above
izmed	among, out of
izpred	from before
izpod	from below

At what time?

In lesson 3 you learnt the cardinal and the ordinal numbers and a few basic expressions for how to tell the time. Look at the following times:

pol	half	**četrt**	quarter
tri četrt	three quarters		

Ura je štiri.
It is four o'clock.

Ura je pol dveh.
It is half past one.
(notice that you say 'half two'
meaning 'half to two')

Ura je četrt na eno.
It is quarter past twelve.
(notice that you say it is 'quarter onto
one' meaning 'quarter past twelve')

Ura je tri četrt na tri
It is quarter to three.
(notice that you say "it is three
quarters onto three' meaning
'quarter to three')

With **od** (from), **do** (until), **ob** (at), **po** (after), **pol** (half) the genitive or the locative endings of the numbers are used. The endings for the numbers from 1 to 12 are the same in the genitive and in the locative case: **enih, dveh, treh, štirih, petih, šestih, sedmih, osmih, devetih, desetih, enajstih, dvanajstih.**

When you use **na** (onto), as in **četrt na eno** (quarter past twelve) the only number which has a different ending is 'one', and you say:

Ura je četrt/tri četrt na eno, dve, tri ...

The prepositions **med** (between) and **pred** (before) take the accusative case, and you say:

Pridi med *eno* in *drugo.*	Come between *one* and *two.*
	tretjo in *četrto.*	*three* and *four.*
	peto in *šesto.*	*five* and *six.*
	sedmo in *osmo.*	*seven* and *eight.*

Ne pridi pred *deveto.*	Don't come before *nine.*
	deseto.	*ten*
	enajsto.	*eleven.*
	dvanajsto.	*twelve.*

Note that with prepositions **med** and **pred** you use ordinal numbers.

Exercise 11

Koliko je ura?

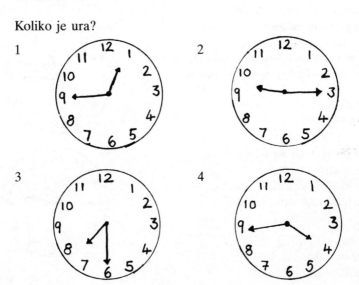

5 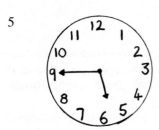   6

Exercise 12

Imagine you are in Slovenia for a week living in a self-catering apartment where you have to do your own shopping. Can you match the Slovene and the English words for the food items below which may be on your shopping list?

kava	milk
kruh	cheese
čaj	potatoes
mleko	eggs
jajca	tea
krompir	coffee
sir	bread

Exercise 13

You are doing some shopping in a big supermarket where you can get everything. How would you ask for the following items?

1 1 kg bread
2 2 litres of milk
3 1 yoghurt
4 10 dkg cheese
5 ½kg apples

Exercise 14

Here are a few adjectives. What words could they describe?

1 težek/-žka/-o
2 lep/-a/-o
3 dober/-bra/-o
4 nezanimiv/-a/-o
5 majhen/-hna/-o

Exercise 15 ▢▢

Pronunciation exercise. The Slovene **h** is always pronounced, as in English 'hello'. Here are a few more words where the letter **h** is present: **hvala, hčerka, zahvali se, hladilnik, hlače, hrana, hoteti, kuhati, kuhinja, kruh.**

Dialogue for comprehension ▢▢

That morning Robert promised Sergej that he would call by in the evening but Matej telephoned him in the afternoon and asked him if he would like to have supper with him and the Korens, who own the flat he is staying in. He still rings the students' door bell and tells the boys about it. Sergej, who answers the door, suggests that they could all go out to where they usually go on Friday evenings. What do they arrange to do on Friday?

SERGEJ: Dober večer, naprej!

ROBERT: Ne, na žalost ne morem. Prišel sem vam samo povedat, da danes nimam časa. Grem na večerjo. Ali poznate Sabino in njeno teto?

SERGEJ: Ne, jaz ne. Jaz sem se šele prejšnji mesec vselil. Ampak Boštjan in Davor jih poznata. Sabina študira pravo.

ROBERT: Ja, Matej je omenil, da je študentka. Baje je že tri leta v prvem letniku. Ampak to je vseeno! Hotel sem vas vprašati, če želite iti v petek zvečer ven jest. Jaz vas povabim!

SERGEJ: Ja, ampak ob petkih gremo mi po navadi v eno kavarno, kjer igrajo jazz. Če želiš, lahko prideš tudi ti.

ROBERT: Ja, najprej lahko gremo nekaj pojest.

SERGEJ: Vztopi za 5 minut! Vprašajva Boštjana in Davorja.

ROBERT: Res ne morem. Pozen sem že!

10 Obljubil sem, da vas bom povabil na večerjo

I promised to take you out for supper

In this lesson you will learn about:

- Words for food and drinks
- How to order a meal
- How to use the conditional
- Some adjectives describing food
- How to complain if something is not to your taste

Dialogue 1

Ali si že jedel?

Have you eaten yet?

As Robert promised, he is taking his three neighbours out for a meal. He rings their bell to arrange when and where they will go

BOŠTJAN: Robert, ravno se pogovarjamo o tebi. Vstopi!

ROBERT: Ali bomo šli ven jutri zvečer? Obljubil sem, da vas bom povabil na večerjo!

SERGEJ: Ja, in kam bomo šli?

ROBERT: Vi veste bolje kot jaz. Vi izberite restavracijo. Meni je vseeno. Lahko gremo tudi ven iz mesta, sedaj imam avto.

BOŠTJAN: Ali si že jedel? Pojej kaj z nami. Jaz sem ravnokar napravil narezek.

ROBERT: Ali si sami kuhate?
BOŠTJAN: Ja, jaz kuham, kot vidiš.
SERGEJ: Kadar kuha Boštjan, imamo vedno narezek.
BOŠTJAN: Po navadi jemo v študentski menzi. Ko jemo doma, jemo
               preproste stvari, jajca, testenine ...
ROBERT: In kdo pravi, da preproste stvari niso dobre?

BOŠTJAN: *Robert, we are just talking about you. Come in!*
ROBERT: *Are we going to go out tomorrow evening? I promised
               to take you to have supper.*
SERGEJ: *Yes, and where will we go?*
ROBERT: *You know better than I do. You choose a restaurant. I
               don't mind. We can also go out of town, I have a car now.*
BOŠTJAN: *Have you eaten yet? Have something with us. I've just
               done some sliced cold meat and cheese.*
ROBERT: *Are you cooking for yourself?*
BOŠTJAN: *I cook, as you see.*
SERGEJ: *When Boštjan cooks we always have 'narezek'.*
BOŠTJAN: *We usually eat in the student canteen. When we eat at
               home we eat simple things, eggs, pasta ...*
ROBERT: *And who says that simple things aren't good?*

Vocabulary

ravno	just	**študentska menza**	student canteen
obljubiti	to promise	**preproste stvari**	simple things
povabiti	to invite	**jajca**	eggs
izbrati	to choose	**testenine**	pasta
narezek	(see language points)	**solata**	salad

Language points

Meals

The words for meals are:

jed	meal	**kosilo**	lunch
obrok	course	**večerja**	supper
zajtrk	breakfast	**malica**	snack

There are some commonly used words in Slovene which don't have equivalents in English. One of them is **malica**. At every workplace and in schools there is time for **malica** at around 10 or 11 o'clock. It is a break when you have something to eat.

Narezek is something that Slovenes usually eat in the evenings. It is a plateful of sliced cold sausages, salami, meat, cheese, and so on.

Eating habits

In Slovenia the working day starts earlier than in England, at 7, 8, sometimes even 6 o'clock. Even people who have an optional one-hour flexitime usually prefer to start earlier so that they can make use of the afternoon that's left.

In general people don't have a big breakfast, they normally have a coffee and bread with butter (**maslo**) or margarine (**margarina**) and jam. **Marmelada** means 'jam' in Slovene. Naturally, there is a variety of jams. Here are some names for fruit and the adjectives which describe the type of jam:

marelica	apricot	**marelična marmelada**
sliva	plum	**slivova marmelada**
jagoda	strawberry	**jagodna marmelada**
malina	raspberry	**malinova marmelada**
borovnica	bilberry	**borovničeva marmelada**

Another common dish is **kompot** (stewed fruit), which is made of a variety of fruits. Below are the names for some more fruits and the adjectives which describe the salad. Note that the adjectives for jams are in the feminine form because **marmelada** is a feminine noun; the adjectives for fruit salads will be in the masculine form because **kompot** is a masculine noun.

sadje	fruit	**sadni kompot**
jabolko	apple	**jabolčni kompot**
breskev	peach	**breskov kompot**
hruška	pear	**hruškov kompot**
ananas	pineapple	**ananasov kompot**

The main meal of the day is usually **kosilo** (lunch), which people have as they get back from work. **Večerja** (supper) is a cold meal, often sliced salami, sausages and cheese, which is called **narezek**. However, when people work until later, or when the evening meal is a special occasion, they do have a bigger supper.

The verbs you will most often come across to do with meals are

jesti (to eat) and **piti** (to drink). They are both slightly irregular and are conjugated here for you:

Jesti

Present tense	Past/future tense
Singular	
jem	sem/bom jedel
ješ	si/boš jedel
je	je/bo jedel
Dual	
jeva	sva/bova jedla
jesta	sta/bosta jedla
jesta	sta/bosta jedla
Plural	
jemo	smo/bomo jedli
jeste	ste/boste jedli
jejo	so/bodo jedli

Note: **Je** can mean both 'he, she it *is*' and 'he, she, it *eats*'. The meaning of **je** depends on the context and on the pronunciation of the final **e**.

Piti

Present tense	Past/future tense
Singular	
pijem	sem/bom pil
piješ	si/boš pil
pije	je/bo pil
Dual	
pijeva	sva/bova pila
pijeta	sta/bosta pila
pijeta	sta/bosta pila
Plural	
pijemo	smo/bomo pili
pijete	ste/boste pili
pijejo	so/bodo pili

Useful expressions to do with eating are:

biti lačen/-čna	to be hungry
biti žejen/-jna	to be thirsty
biti sit/-a	to be full
zrediti se	to put on weight
shujšati	to lose weight

Slovenes eat a great variety of food; all kinds of meat dishes, fish, salads, potatoes prepared in a variety of ways. You can eat in all sorts of places.

If a waiter comes to you when you are at the door of a restaurant you say:

Mizo za dva/tri/štiri ...   A table for two/three/four ...

You can ask:

Ali je tista miza pri oknu rezervirana?
Is that table by the window reserved?

You may see a note on the table saying **Rezervirano**, meaning 'reserved'.

Whenever you ask if you can have something you can say:

Ali lahko dobim ...?   Can I have ...?

You may want to ask a waiter if he can recommend something:

Ali mi lahko kaj   Can you recommend something to
priporočate?   me?

You may want something small (a snack): **Nekaj malega**.

Tipping

Service is usually not included in the bill. You can give the waiter a tip (**napitnina**).

To do

There are a few verbs in Slovene which mean 'to do'. They are: **narediti, napraviti, storiti, delati**. The verbs **narediti, napraviti** and **storiti** are usually followed by an object; they imply that someone is getting something done. For example:

Ali si naredil vse, kar si mislil?	Did you do everything you meant to?
Ja, napravil sem vse.	Yes, I did everything.

As you know, **delati** also means 'to work'. When it means 'to do' it is translated into English in the progressive form, as in:

Kaj delaš danes?	What are you doing today?

Exercise 1

Match the names of the fruits below with their English equivalents. All the fruits are in the plural form:

jabolka	bilberries
hruške	plums
marelice	strawberries
slive	apricots
borovnice	apples
jagode	pears

Exercise 2

Boštjan surprised his fellow students and Robert one evening and made a large fruit salad. He had been to the fruit market in the morning, where he bought a variety of fruits. Put his request into English. Greet the greengrocer at the stall and ask if you can get:

1 1 kg apples
2 ½kg apricots
3 4 pears
4 2 peaches
5 1 pineapple

Exercise 3 ▮▮

You take a friend to a restaurant. As you enter, a waiter standing by the door greets you.

1 *Greet him back and ask for a table for two.*
  The waiter takes you to a table but you don't particularly want to sit there.

2 *Ask if that table by the window is free.*
Ne, na žalost je rezervirana. Ali želite sedeti tam (he points to another table).
3 *Say 'yes' and ask for the menu.*
Na mizi je.
4 *Ask him if he could recommend you something.*
Trenutno je čas kosila in imamo odlično izbiro. Vsa kosila so s tremi obroki.
5 *Say that you'd like something small. Tell him that you will look at the menu. Ask if you can order the drinks.*

Exercise 4

Can you make up questions to which you could get the following responses?

testenine	pasta

1 Kozarec vina, prosim.
2 Ja, rad imam testenine.
3 Jedilni list je na mizi.
4 Ne, nisem lačen. Pozno sem imel kosilo.
5 Ne, hvala. Ne pijem kave.

Exercise 5

Can you fill in a conjunction word in each of the sentences below as suggested by the English word in brackets?

1 Iskal sem te, (*but*) nisem te našel.
2 Bil sem v trgovini, ampak nesem kupil (*neither*) kruha (*nor*) mleka.
3 Poklical sem te, (*because*) ti moram nekaj povedati.
4 Kako si vedel, (*that*) sem doma?
5 Nisem se dobro počutil, (*that is why*) sem ostal doma.
6 Ostani še malo, (*if*) imaš čas.

Dialogue 2 📼

Ali imaš rad ribe?

Do you like fish?

Robert has left it to the boys to choose the place where they will go and, knowing that he doesn't eat red meat, they take him to a restaurant noted for fish

DAVOR: Ali bomo sedeli zunaj, ali bi šli raje noter?
ROBERT: Ostanimo zunaj, prijetno in toplo je.
DAVOR: Ja, in ni prepovedano kaditi!
ROBERT: Naročimo steklenico dobrega slovenskega vina. Ali bi vi raje pivo?
DAVOR: Ne, Boštjan in jaz bi vino, ampak Sergej danes ne bo pil ne vina ne piva.
ROBERT: Zakaj ne?
DAVOR: Ni mu dobro, že nekaj dni se ne počuti dobro.
ROBERT: Kaj bo pil?
DAVOR: Vprašali ga bomo, ko pride nazaj. Na stranišče je šel. O, natakar, ali lahko dobimo jedilni list, prosim?
NATAKAR: Ja, izvolite. Ali lahko prinesem pijačo?
ROBERT: Počakajmo Sergeja.
NATAKAR: Prišel bom nazaj.
ROBERT: Kaj je to 'prikuhe'?
DAVOR: To so jedi, ki jih dobiš zraven h glavni jedi. Robert, ta restavracija je znana po ribah. Ali imaš rad ribe?
ROBERT: Ja, zelo. O, tukaj vidim, 'ribe na žaru'.
DAVOR: Ja. Ali hočeš solato?
BOŠTJAN: Davor, pusti ga, naj se sam odloči! Ali ti že veš, kaj boš?

DAVOR: *Are we going to sit out or shall we go inside?*
ROBERT: *Let's stay outside, it's pleasant and warm.*
DAVOR: *Yes, and smoking isn't prohibited here.*
ROBERT: *Let's order a bottle of good Slovene wine. Or would you prefer to drink beer?*
DAVOR: *No, Boštjan and I would like wine but Sergej won't drink either wine or beer today.*
ROBERT: *Why not?*
DAVOR: *He isn't well. He hasn't been well for the past few days.*

ROBERT: *What will he drink?*
DAVOR: *We'll ask him when he gets back. He went to the lavatory. Oh, waiter, can we have the menu, please?*
WAITER: *Yes, here you are. Can I get you anything to drink?*
ROBERT: *Let's wait for Sergej.*
WAITER: *I'll come back.*
ROBERT: *What is this 'priduhe'?*
DAVOR: *These are the dishes you get with your main meal. Robert, this restaurant is noted for fish. Do you like fish?*
ROBERT: *Yes, very much. Oh, I see it here, 'grilled fish'.*
DAVOR: *Yes. Do you want a salad?*
BOŠTJAN: *Davor, leave him to decide. Do you know what you'll have?*

Vocabulary

sedeti	to sit	**prikuhe**	side orders
ostati	to stay	**jedi**	dishes
naročiti	to order	**glavna jed**	main meal
steklenica	bottle	**biti znan/-a**	to be famous/noted for
nekaj dni	few days	**ribe**	fish
jedilni list	menu	**na žaru**	grilled
prinesti	to bring	**pustiti**	to leave
pijača	drink		

Language points

Food and drink

A standard menu in Slovenia looks like this:

Jedilni list	Menu
Predjedi	*Starters*
Juhe	Soups
goveja juha z rezanci	beef soup with noodles
zelenjavna juha	vegetable soup
gobova juha	mushroom soup

Gotove jedi	*Prepared dishes*
kurja rižota	chicken risotto
dunajski zrezek	veal escalope
Jedi po naročilu	*Dishes to order*
goveji zrezki v omaki	beef in gravy
nadevan pečen piščanec	stuffed chicken
Prikuhe	*Side dishes*
riž	rice
krompir	potatoes
cmoki	dumplings
Solate	*Salads*
zelena solata	green salad
mešana solata	mixed salad
sezonska solata	seasonal salad
Zelenjava	*Vegetables*
špinača	spinach
fižol	beans
zelje	cabbage
Sladice	*Deserts*
torta	cake
sladoled	ice-cream
sadna kupa	fruit salad
jabolčni zavitek	apple strudel

A Slovene menu usually has a selection of **gotove jedi** and **jedi po naročilu**. The difference between the two is that the first are prepared, ready to be served, whilst the latter are usually more elaborate dishes for which you might have to wait a little longer.

You may need the following words to do with eating:

vilica	fork
nož	knife
žlica	spoon
žlička	teaspoon
krožnik	plate
kozarec	glass
servijeta	napkin, serviette

Talking about food

Whenever you ask for 'a glass of', 'a piece of', 'a plate of', the noun of whatever you are talking about will be in the genitive case in Slovene, for example:

kozarec vina, piva, vode ... a glass of wine, beer, water ...
kos kruha, peciva ... a piece of bread, cake ...

If a waiter should tell you that something is not on the menu, or if you want to say that you don't like something, the item will be in the genitive case because all the nouns followed by a negative verb are in the genitive case in Slovene.

Neither ... nor

You know that to express 'either ... or' you simply use **ali ... ali**. To express 'neither ... nor' you just use the words **ne ... ne** or **niti ... niti**. Here are some examples:

ne ti ne jaz neither you nor I
Nisem ne lačen, ne žejen. I'm neither thirsty nor hungry.

Niti gotovine, niti kreditne kartice nimam pri sebi.
I have neither cash nor my credit card on me.

Note how Davor says in the dialogue **Sergej ne bo pil ne vina ne piva**.

The conditional

The conditional in Slovene is formed with the word **bi**, which remains the same for all persons and numbers, and the participle ending in **l**, which you also use to form the past and the future tense. The word **bi** can be translated by 'would', 'should', 'if ... were'. Let's take the verb **pisati** in its conditional form:

Singular	Dual	Plural
jaz bi pisal/-a	midva bi pisala	mi bi pisali
ti bi pisal/-a	vidva bi pisala	vi bi pisali
on bi pisal	onadva bi pisala	oni bi pisali
ona bi pisala		
ono bi pisalo		

The uses of the conditional

The conditional is most often used in 'if' clauses. You know the word **če** (if), which usually introduces the 'if' clause. Whilst in English the past tense is used in the 'if' clause, in Slovene, the conditional of the verb is used in both the 'if' clause and the main clause, for example:

Če bi imel čas, bi šel na kavo.	If I had the time I'd go for a coffee.
Če bi vedela, bi ti povedala.	If I knew I'd tell you.

The personal pronouns are usually omitted and it depends on the context of the conversation in Slovene how they are translated into English. For example:

Če ne bi vedel ..., ne bi predlagal ...
If I didn't know ... I wouldn't have suggested ...

This sentence, out of context, could be translated in three ways:

If I didn't know ...
If you didn't know ....
If he didn't know ...

When you want to express a hypothesis in the future tense, you use the conditional in the 'if' clause, unlike in English, where you use the present tense. For example:

Če bo prišel, ga bom vprašal.	If he comes I'll ask him.
Če bo deževalo, bomo ostali doma.	If it rains we'll stay at home.

Regardless of which clause comes first, they are always separated by a comma.

You also use the conditional when you want to translate the following phrases: 'would like, could, ought' or 'should'. Here are a few examples:

Rad bi vedel ...	I would like to know ...
Rada bi ti pomagala ...	I would like to help you ...
Lahko bi mi povedal ...	You could have told me ...
Danes bi lahko šli ...	Today we could go ...
Morala bi teleforirati ...	I ought to telephone ...
Moral bi ti pokazati ...	I should have shown you ...

The pluperfect conditional does exist in Slovene but it is hardly used. Instead you use the present conditional, as discussed above.

Notice also how you can tell in Slovene whether a male or a female is speaking.

If I were you ...

To express this in Slovene you say **Če bi bil-a jaz na tvojem mestu ...** meaning literally 'If I were in your place ...' Here are some examples:

pozanimati se	to find out

Če bi bila jaz na tvojem mestu, bi se prej pozanimala.
If I were you I'd find out myself first.
Če bi bil jaz na tvojem mestu, bi šel sam.
If I were you, I'd go on my own.

Leave me to do this

When you want to tell someone to allow you or someone else to do something you use the verb **pustiti** (to let, to permit, to allow) in the imperative form and the personal pronoun in the accusative case, for example:

Pusti jo, naj posluša radio!   Let her listen to the radio!
Pusti jih, naj se igrajo!   Leave them to play!

Notice how Boštjan says to Davor in the dialogue **Pusti ga (Roberta), naj se sam odloči!**

If you want to tell someone to leave you alone you use the expression:

Pusti me pri miru!   Leave me alone!

Exercise 6

You are in a restaurant on your own. Look at the menu following dialogue 1 again and order yourself a three-course meal and something to drink.

Exercise 7 ▣▣

The waiter has brought the food but things are missing. Ask him for:

1 salt and pepper
2 some bread
3 another green salad
4 a knife and fork
5 a napkin

Exercise 8

Complete the second half of the sentence as suggested:

1 Če bi imel čas, *I'd look at the television.*
2 Če bi vedela, *she'd tell you.*
3 Če bi bil ta film dober, *I'd suggest you go to the cinema.*
4 Če bi imel njegovo telefonsko številko, *I'd call him.*
5 Če boš prišel jutri zvečer, *you could bring me that book.*

Exercise 9

You are talking to a colleague at work who says the things listed on the left to you. Which comments on the right could you use to answer him?

1 Danes je zelo mrzlo.
2 Danes nisem imel ne zajtrka ne kosila.
3 Kdaj igraš tenis?

4 Ne jem mesa.
5 Že ves teden delam od osmih do šestih.
6 Kakšne barve je tvoj novi avto?

(a) Ali si vegetarjanec?
(b) Moraš biti zelo utrujen.
(c) Ja, temperatura je minus pet stopinj celzija.
(d) Rdeč je.
(e) Ali si lačen?
(f) Spor~ladi in v jeseni.

Exercise 10

Križanka

1 menu
2 cabbage
3 steak
4 ice-cream
5 spoon
6 fork
7 knife
8 cheese
9 milk
10 rice
11 salad
12 cake

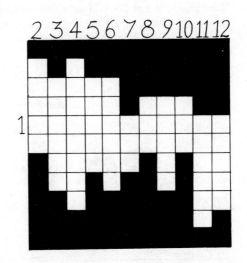

Dialogue 3

Dober tek!

Enjoy your meal!

The waiter has brought the food they ordered to the table and is asking them whether there is anything else they would like with it

NATAKAR: Ali bi še kaj drugega?
BOŠTJAN: Jaz čakam še na solato.
ROBERT: Sol in poper, prosim.
NATAKAR: Tukaj sta, na mizi. Solato bom takoj prinesel. Ali bi še kaj za piti?
ROBERT: Ja, še eno steklenico vina, prosim.
DAVOR: Ali lahko prinesete še nekaj kosov kruha?
NATAKAR: Črnega ali belega?
DAVOR: Vsakega malo. O, skoraj bi pozabil, ali lahko dobimo eno steklenico mineralne vode?
NATAKAR: Ja, prinesel jo bom. Dober tek!

WAITER: *Would you like anything else?*
BOŠTJAN: *I'm still waiting for my salad.*
ROBERT: *Salt and pepper, please.*
WAITER: *They are here, on the table. I'll bring the salad straight*

> *away. Would you like anything else to drink?*
> ROBERT: *Another bottle of wine, please.*
> DAVOR: *Can you bring a few more slices of bread?*
> WAITER: *Brown or white?*
> DAVOR: *Some of each. Oh, I almost forgot, can we have a bottle of mineral water?*
> WAITER: *Yes, I'll bring it. Enjoy your meal!*

Vocabulary

sol	salt	**mineralna voda**	mineral water
poper	pepper	**dober tek**	enjoy your meal
kos kruha	a slice of bread		

Language points

Dober tek!

This is a phrase said at the table almost without exception. Whether you are in a restaurant or at home or even if someone you know sees you eating, they will say **Dober tek!**, meaning 'Enjoy your meal!'.

Excuse me, waiter, this is no good!

If something is not as it should be or if you'd like to complain about a particular dish, you will have to call the waiter and tell him what is the matter with it. You address him with **Oprostite, ...** and tell him what there is wrong.

The following adjectives usually describe food:

kuhan/-a/-o	cooked
pečen/-a/-o	fried, baked
slan/-a/-o	salted
neslan/-a/-o	unsalted
kisel/-sla/-slo	sour
sladek/-dka/-dko	sweet
okusen/-sna/-sno	tasty

You know that to say that something is 'too . . .' you put the prefix **pre-** onto the adjective, as for example **preslan** (too salty), **presladek** (too sweet). To say that something is 'not . . . enough' you say **ni dovolj . . .**, for example:

Krompir ni dovolj kuhan.   The potatoes aren't cooked enough.

More about the conditional

In conversation you can omit the verb and only say **bi** when you know what you are referring to. This is particularly common in restaurants or in other places where you are served.

When you are offering something to somebody or asking them whether they would like something you also use **bi** without the verb. A waiter might ask you:

Ali bi še kaj drugega?   Would you like anything else?
Ali bi čaj ali kavo?   Would you like tea or coffee?

I almost forgot!

Very often the conditional is used with the word **skoraj** (almost, nearly). Here are some common expressions:

Skoraj bi zgrešil!   I almost missed it!

Notice how Davor says to the waiter:

Skoraj bi pozabil ...   I almost forgot ...

Exercise 11

Put the sentences below into the conditional, as in the example:

Nisem bil lačen, zato nisem jedel kosila.
Če bi bil lačen, bi jedel kosilo.

1 Nisi poslušala, zato nisi slišala.
2 Nisem vedel, zato ti nisem povedal.
3 Nisem je videl, zato je nisem pozdravil.
4 Okno je odprto, zato je tako mrzlo.
5 Nisem imel tvoje telefonske številke, zato te nisem poklical.

Exercise 12

Answer the questions below from the following dialogue in a restaurant between Oto and a waiter

OTO:	Kaj mi priporočate?
NATAKAR:	Naše ribe so zmeraj sveže.
OTO:	Ta teden sem imel za kosilo vsak dan ribe. Danes sem mislil naročiti nekaj drugega.
NATAKAR:	Ali želite kakšno solato?
OTO:	Ja, solato bom. In malo kruha.
NATAKAR:	In kaj bi pili?
OTO:	Sadni sok, prosim.

1 What does the waiter recommend Oto, and why?
2 How does Oto respond to the waiter's recommendation?
3 What does he eventually order to eat and to drink?

Exercise 13

A waiter brought you what you had ordered but things are not quite to your taste. Call him and tell him what the matter is with your dishes, following the example below:

potatoes   not cooked enough
Oprostite, natakar, ta krompir ni dovolj kuhan.

sploh ni	not at all

1 soup   unsalted
2 salad   too acid
3 steak   underdone
4 rice   too salty
5 vegetables   not cooked at all

Exercise 14

Which word in each line is the odd one out, and why?

1 kozarec, jabolko, krožnik, nož
2 omara, pisalna miza, stol, malica
3 zajtrk, večerja, večer, kosilo
4 predjed, prikuha, kosilo, sladica
5 slan, pečen, kruh, kisel

Exercise 15 ▣

Pronunciation exercise. The letter **e** is probably one of the most difficult to pronounce in Slovene. You must first remember that **e** is always pronounced as in 'Emma', and not as in 'Eve'. So, the differences with the letter **e** are really ones of stress and intonation.

You have seen that **je** can mean 'he, she, it is', or 'he, she, it eats', depending on how the final **e** is pronounced. When **je** means 'to be' the **e** is stressed but short:

Robert *je* v Sloveniji. Danes *je* bil v restavraciji. Tudi Davor *je* bil tam. Sergej se *je* slabo počutil.

When **je** means 'to eat' the **e** is stressed and long:

Robert ne *je* mesa ampak rad *je* ribe. Tudi Davor jih rad *je*. Vsak vegetarjanec ne *je* rib.

In some words, **e** is semi-pronounced, almost silent, as in: **pes**, **ves**, **zrezek**, **pesem**.

Let's pronounce a few more words and try to recognize the differences.

poglej!	velik	Eva	oče
žejen sem!	sestra	cena	vroče je
ne smej se!	učenec	lepa	hoče

Dialogue for comprehension ▣

They finished their meal and are now on their way to the place where jazz is played on Friday evening. They talk about the meal and Davor asks Robert when he will cook them a meal. See why he hasn't done it before, what he likes cooking best and what he will make

zdavnaj	long ago	**drobtine**	bread crumbs
pristna angleška/	a typical English/	**pommes frites**	chips
slovenska jed	Slovene dish	**mešati**	to mix

DAVOR: Robert, ali ti je bilo všeč?

ROBERT: Ribe so bile zelo dobre. Nisem navajen jesti ribe pripravljene na ta način. V Angliji dobiš ribe v drobtinah in pommes frites. Te so bile vsekakor boljše. Ampak mislil sem, da je bilo vino malo kislo.

DAVOR: Ja, mi po navadi pijemo to vino z malo mineralne vode.

ROBERT: Ali ga mešate?

DAVOR: Ja, temu se reče 'špricer'. Robert, kdaj nam boš ti skuhal kakšno pristno angleško jed?

ROBERT: Če bi imel več časa, bi to že zdavnaj napravil. Naslednji teden en večer!

DAVOR: Ali rad kuhaš?

ROBERT: Ja, kar. Najraje pripravljam sladice. Naredil bom kruhov narastek.

DAVOR: Kaj?

ROBERT: Boš videl!

11 Gripo imate!

You have flu!

In this lesson you will learn about:

- More parts of the body
- How to describe how you feel when you are ill
- The Slovene health resorts
- Words for some illnesses and adjectives describing what sort of illness someone has
- How verbal nouns are formed

Dialogue 1 ▣

Zelo slabo se počutim

I'm feeling terrible

Robert wakes up one morning feeling terrible and on his way to work he goes to the chemist to get some medicine

LEKARNAR: Dobro jutro.

ROBERT: Dobro jutro. Ali bi lahko dobil aspirin ali kakšne podobne tablete. Zelo slabo se počutim. Vso noč nisem spal. Bruhal sem in drisko imam.

LEKARNAR: Ali imate temperaturo?

ROBERT: Ne vem, nisem si je izmeril.

LEKARNAR: Kako dolgo se že počutite slabo?

ROBERT: Od včeraj. Želodec me boli in v glavi se mi vrti. Vse vidim megleno.

LEKARNAR: Mislim, da je najbolje, če greste k zdravniku, gospod. On vas bo pregledal in predpisal zdravila.

CHEMIST:	*Good morning.*
ROBERT:	*Good morning. Could I have some aspirin or some similar tablets. I'm feeling terrible. I couldn't sleep all night. I was vomiting and I have diarrhoea.*
CHEMIST:	*Do you have a temperature?*
ROBERT:	*I don't know, I didn't take it.*
CHEMIST:	*For how long have you been feeling ill?*
ROBERT:	*Since yesterday. I have a stomach ache and I feel dizzy.*
CHEMIST:	*I think it is best if you go to the doctor, sir. He'll check you and prescribe medicine.*

Vocabulary

podoben	similar, alike	**meglen**	foggy, hazy
izmeriti(si)	to take one's	**pregledati**	to examine
temperaturo	temperature	**predpisati**	to prescribe
vrteti (se)	to turn	**zdravila**	medicine
lekarna	chemist	**bruhati**	to vomit
gripa	flu	**driska**	diarrhoea

Language points

Parts of the body

Refer back to lesson 7, where you learnt some parts of the body. Here are a few more:

telo	body	**lice – lica**	cheek/-s
obraz	face	**uho – ušesa**	ear/-s
hrbet – križ (*coll.*)	back	**oko – oči**	eye/-s
nos	nose	**las – lasje**	hair
vrat	neck	**zob – zobje**	tooth/teeth
usta	mouth		

Note that even though there is a dual form in Slovene parts of the body of which there are two are most often referred to in the plural. You would, for example, say: **Ušesa/oči/lica me bolijo** (My ears/eyes/cheeks hurt).

Here are some parts of the body which are normally used in the plural. This means that they are followed by a verb in the plural, and you say:

Rebra me bolijo!		My ribs hurt!	
pljuča	lungs	**usta**	mouth
jetra	liver	**rebra**	ribs

At the chemist

Lekarna means 'dispensing chemist' (you may hear people calling it **farmacija** or **apoteka**). In Slovenia, **lekarna** is a place where you go primarily for **zdravila** (medicine). It is a great offence to a **lekarnar** or a **farmacevt** (a pharmacist) if you think of them as shop assistants. They are specially trained and can help you with minor illnesses. They know – or should know – what they are talking about. However, if you should need a **recept** (a prescription) for your medicine you will have to see a doctor. If you are in a really bad way you can **poklicati zdravnika na dom** (call a doctor to your home). Otherwise you go to see a doctor, in which case you will have to wait in a **čakalnica** (waiting room).

During non-working hours you will always find a **dežurni zdravnik** (duty doctor) and a **dežurna lekarna** (duty chemist) in town. You will be able to find out from the paper which doctor and chemist are on duty on particular weekends or holidays. If your illness is more serious you may need to go to the **bolnišnica** (hospital).

Komu sem podoben? (Who do I look like?)

The expression **biti podoben** means 'to resemble', 'to look like', and it is followed by a noun in the dative case. For example:

Komu je podobna Sabina?	Who does Sabina look like?
Sabina je podobna mami.	Sabina looks like her mother.
očetu	her father.
Sandri.	Sandra.
Robertu.	Robert.

More about personal names when used with case endings

You may find it odd how personal names and names of places change. They take the endings of the case they are in, which is determined by their function. Let's take the names **Sabina**, **Sandra** and **Robert**. Here are six sentences where these names have been used in all six Slovene cases

1 Sabina, Sandra in Robert so na Bledu.
2 Sabine, Sandre in Roberta nikoli ni dobiš po telefonu.
3 Zahvaliti se moram Sabini, Sandri in Robertu.
4 Ali si videl Sabino, Sandro in Roberta?
5 Na zabavi sem bil pri Sabini, Sandri in Robertu.
6 Zvečer grem v kino s Sabino, Sandro in Robertom.

Unstressed words (enclitics)

Some words, like **se**, **ji**, **ga**, **si**, etc., are never stressed. They include
the following.

The short form of the personal pronouns: these can only be used
when you know who you are talking about. They cannot stand at
the beginning of a sentence.

Ali ga vidiš?	Do you see him?
Ne vidim ga.	I don't see him.

Most prepositions: these precede the word they refer to:

V službi sem bil.	I was at work.
Ali si šel na banko?	Did you go to the bank?

The forms of the verb 'to be': these follow the subject or the predicate of its verb:

Kako si?	How are you?
Utrujen sem. In kako ste vi?	I'm tired. And how are you?

Conjunctions: these are most often placed before the word they
refer to. Some do occur at the beginning of the sentence.

Ali ti, ali on.	Either you or him.
Dobro veš, da oba ne moreta.	You know well that you both can't.

Relative pronouns

Relative pronouns are words which connect the ~~bordinate with
the main clause. Relative pronouns usually qualify nouns and in
Slovene they are declined. The relative pronouns used most often,
'who' and 'which', are translated by **ki** and **kateri** in Slovene. Look
at these examples:

To je knjiga, *ki jo že dolgo* **iščem.**	This is the book I've been looking for for a long time.

To so knjige, *ki jih že* dolgo iščem.   These are the books I've been looking for for a long time.

Ki is declined by adding the forms of the personal pronoun in the correct case to it.

To je lekarna, *v kateri* sem kupil zdravila.   This is the chemist where (literally 'in which') I bought some medicine.

To je študent, *s katerim* živim.   This is the student with whom I live.

Kateri is declined like all adjectives; its ending depends on what it refers to in the first part of the sentence.

When you want to say, for example:

He who is rich has power.   **Kdor je bogat, ima moč.**

What you said is not true.   **Kar si rekel, ni res.**

you use the relative pronoun **kdor** for people and **kar** for things.

In questions **kateri?** means 'which?' or 'what?' and it is also declined. For example:

Kateri dan je danes?   What day is it today?

Katera hiša ti je bila najbolj všeč?   Which house did you like best?

Exercise 1

(a) How would you ask your friend:

1   Who do you look like?
2   Who does he/she look like?
3   Who does Anna look like?

(b) How would you tell him/her that:

1   your brother looks like your mother.
2   your cousin (female) looks like your aunt.

Exercise 2

Fill in the missing words in this summary of dialogue 1:

Robert je zjutraj šel v (1 . . .), zato ker se je slabo (2 . . .) Kupiti (3 . . .) je hotel aspirin ali kakšne podobne (4 . . .) Bolel (5 . . .) je želodec in v glavi se (6 . . .) je vrtelo. Vse je (7 . . .) megleno.

Exercise 3

Fill in the correct forms of the suggested verbs in the correct form:

1 Ali lahko (mi) ... darila tukaj? (*to buy*)
2 Zakaj se ne moreš ... ? (*to decide*)
3 Ali lahko (jaz) ... angleško? (*to speak*)
4 Ali ... pride tudi moj prijatelj? (*can*)
5 Danes oni ... priti. (*cannot*)

Exercise 4

Match the Slovene words for the parts of the body with the English ones:

usta	face
zob	neck
lasje	eye
hrbet (križ)	body
obraz	mouth
vrat	tooth
oko	hair
telo	back

Exercise 5 ▄▄

How would you tell someone that the following parts of the body hurt?

1 your tooth
2 your stomach
3 your ears
4 your back
5 everything

Dialogue 2 🔲

Poklical bom zdravnika

I'll call the doctor

Robert goes straight home from the chemist and knocks on his neighbours' door. Boštjan comes out and knows there is something the matter with Robert

BOŠTJAN: Robert, kaj ti je?

ROBERT: Sam ne vem. Bil sem v lekarni, kjer so mi rekli, naj grem k zdravniku. Vedno slabše se počutim. Na poti domov sem se začel potiti.

BOŠTJAN: Uleži se. Bom jaz poklical zdravnika. Si si izmeril vročino? Ali imaš termometer?

ROBERT: Ja, ampak bog ve kje. Nujno moram poklicati Mateja. Ne bom mogel iti na sestanek, komaj stojim.

BOŠTJAN: Vstopi! Ti bom dal termometer.

ROBERT: Ne vem, če bom preživel.

BOŠTJAN: Ne bodi neumen. Gripo imaš! V kolikor jaz vem, jo ima pol mesta. Zaradi gripe ne boš umrl.

BOŠTJAN: *Robert, what's the matter with you?*

ROBERT: *I don't know myself. I've been to the chemist where they told me that I should go to the doctor. I am feeling worse all the time. I started to sweat on the way home.*

BOŠTJAN: *Lie down. I'll call the doctor. Did you take your temperature? Do you have a thermometer?*

ROBERT: *Yes, but God knows where. I must call Matej urgently. I won't be able to go to the meeting, I can hardly stand up.*

BOŠTJAN: *Come in, I've got a thermometer.*

ROBERT: *I don't know if I'll survive.*

BOŠTJAN: *Don't be stupid. You have flu. As far as I know half of the town has it. You won't die from flu.*

Vocabulary

potiti se	to sweat	**neumen**	stupid
uleči se	to lie down	**v kolikor**	as far as
vročina	temperature (more colloquial)	**zaradi**	because of
termometer	thermometer	**umreti**	to die
bog ve!	God knows!	**izmeriti si**	to take one's
preživeti	to survive	**vročino**	temperature

Language points

How do you feel?

If you are unwell it is important to be able to describe how you feel. Here are some expressions:

Ne počutim se dobro.	I'm not feeling well.
Bolan/lna sem.	I'm ill.
Prehlajen/-a sem.	I have a cold.
Glava/grlo/želodec/vse me boli.	My head/throat/stomach/everything hurts.

If you don't know the name of the part of the body which hurts you can always point to it and say:

Tukaj me boli.	It hurts here.

Here are some verbs which describe a physical state:

kašljati (kašljam)	to cough
kihati (kiham)	to sneeze
bruhati (bruham)	to vomit

The verb **zboleti** means 'to get ill'; **bolezen** means 'illness'. The verb **ozdraviti se** means 'to get well'; **zdravje** means 'health'.

If you know what your illness is, here are the names of some specialist doctors you might need:

zdravnik	a general term for a health doctor
otroški zdravnik	a paediatrician
kirurg	a surgeon
zobozdravnik	a dentist
ginekolog	a gynaecologist
psiholog	a psychologist
psihiater	a psychiatrist

More about adjectives and demonstrative pronouns

You know that in Slovene adjectives take endings depending on the gender of the noun they modify. Some adjectives are proper adjectives, like **lep**, **dober**, **majhen**, and so on; whereas words like **takšen** or **tak** (such), **neki** (some), and all adjectives which indicate possession like **moj**, **tvoj**, **naš**, are pronominal adjectives. They also have to agree with the noun they modify and they give you an answer to the questions **kakšen?** (what?, what kind of?), **kateri?** (which one?), **čigav** (whose?).

In lesson 2 you learnt that in Slovene there are three kinds of demonstrative pronoun which qualify nouns. Because they can qualify a noun in the singular, dual or plural, they have the following forms.

	Singular	*Dual*	*Plural*
m.	ta, tisti, oni	ta, tista, ona	ti, tisti, oni
f.	ta, tista, ona	ti, tisti, oni	te, tiste, one
n.	to, tisto, ono	ti, tisti, oni	ta, tista, ona

Tisti and **oni** are both translated by 'that' in English. In Slovene, **tisti** points to things which are a little further away; **oni** points to things which are very far away. For example:

Te tablete lahko kupiš, tiste pa ne.	You can buy these tablets, but not those.
One, ki sem jih jemal lani, so bile dobre.	Those I was taking last year were good.

Note: In Slovene the verb you use to say that you are taking some pills is **jemati** (**tablete**).

In some cases, however, you use **ta** in Slovene where you would use 'that' in English. For example:

Ali si mu povedal to?	Did you tell him that?
To ni bilo prav.	That wasn't right!

The pronoun **tak/-a/-o** (such) is a demonstrative pronoun and it points to quality. For example:

Taki avtomobili so dragi.	Such cars are expensive.
Take obleke so mi všeč.	I like such dresses.

The pronoun **tolik/-a/-o** (such) is also a demonstrative pronoun and it points to quantity. For example:

Že dolgo ni zapadlo toliko snega.	It's a long time since so much snow has fallen.
Toliko jih je bilo!	There were so many of them!

Here are the forms of the pronouns **tak** and **tolik**:

	Singular	*Dual*	*Plural*
m.	tak, tolik	taka, tolika	taki, toliki
f.	taka, tolika	taki, toliki	take, tolike
n.	tako, toliko	taki, toliki	taka, tolika

As far as I know

You will have noticed how Boštjan said in the dialogue: *V kolikor jaz vem*, jo (gripo) ima pol mesta. The expression 'as far as I know' is **v kolikor jaz vem**. Here are some examples:

V kolikor jaz vem, ima v jeseni veliko ljudi gripo.
As far as I know, a lot of people have flu in autumn.
V kolikor jaz vem, je to zaradi spremembe vremena.
As far as I know, this is because of the change in the weather.
V kolikor jaz vem, gripa ni huda bolezen.
As far as I know, flu isn't a dangerous illness.

Komaj

Komaj means 'hardly', 'scarcely', as in:

Komaj čakam! I can hardly wait!
Komaj vidim! I can hardly see!

Note how Robert says in the dialogue **Komaj še stojim!**
When you use **komaj** in Slovene you don't start the sentence with the personal pronoun as you do in English; the personal pronoun is indicated in the verb.

If you want to say that you can hardly wait for something to happen you have to use a relative clause, as in:

Komaj čakam, da bo zima. I can hardly wait for the winter.
Komaj čakam, da pridejo. I can hardly wait for them to come.

Zaradi

Zaradi means 'because of' and it is followed by a noun in the genitive case. Note how Boštjan tells Robert in the dialogue **Zaradi gripe ne boš umrl!**

Exercise 6

Sabina has applied for a temporary job during her summer holiday. She was asked what she does in her spare time and has made a list of things she could put down on her application form. Can you fill in the verbs (given below in their infinitive form) in the first person singular as she would use them?

poslušati, gledati, kuhati, brati, igrati, učiti se

1 ... knjige.
2 ... klavir.
3 ... glasbo.
4 ... televizijo.
5 ... tuje jezike.
6 Rada ...

Exercise 7

People in the office are curious as to why Robert is not at work. They know you spoke to him but you don't really know much. Answer their questions saying that 'As far as you know ...':

1 he is ill.
2 he has flu.
3 he will telephone again.
4 he is going to see the doctor.
5 he will be here tomorrow.

Exercise 8

(a) Say the words in italics in another way, following the example which has been done for you:

Zaradi slabega vremena smo ostali doma.
Zato ker je bilo slabo vreme, smo ostali doma.

1 *Zaradi bolezni* prejšnji teden nisem bil v službi.
2 *Zaradi visokih cen* si nisem nič kupil.

(b) Tell your friend that:

1 you can hardly wait for tomorrow.
2 you can hardly wait for spring.

Exercise 9

Match the questions you were asked (on the left) to the answers you could give (on the right):

1 Kako dolgo se že slabo počutiš?   (a) Zato ker nimam časa.
2 Ali imaš temperaturo?   (b) Vrat in hrbet.
3 Ali si bil v lekarni?   (c) Ja, kupil sem si tablete proti boličinam.
4 Kaj te boli?   (d) Od srede.
5 Zakaj ne greš k zdravniku?   (e) Ne vem. Nisem si je izmeril.

Exercise 10

Peter invited Helena out one day. She clearly didn't want to accept the invitation. Look at the way the conversation went:

PETER: Helena, ali hočeš iti danes zvečer v kino?
HELENA: Ne, žal mi je. Že ves teden se slabo počutim. Grlo me boli. In v kolikor vem, bo danes zvečer deževalo.

Suppose you were invited somewhere and you didn't want to accept the invitation. Can you think of some excuses you could give? Write them down.

Dialogue 3 ▣

Napisal vam bom recept

I'll write out a prescription for you

The doctor arrived quite quickly and he is speaking to Robert

ZDRAVNIK: Kaj vas boli?
ROBERT: Najbolj me boli želodec. Ves čas mi gre na bruhanje. In komaj se premikam.
ZDRAVNIK: Ali ste si izmerili vročino?
ROBERT: Ja, 39 je. Ampak mene zebe, kar trese me.
ZDRAVNIK: Odprite usta! Globoko dihajte! Hudo gripo imate. Teden dni ostanite doma, na toplem. Napisal vam bom recept. Trikrat na dan vzemite po eno tableto. Če boste začeli kašljati, vzemite tudi dve žlički sirupa, vsakih šest ur. Čez en teden pridite na pregled.

DOCTOR: *What is hurting?*
ROBERT: *The worst pain is in my stomach. I want to vomit the whole time. And I can hardly move.*
DOCTOR: *Have you taken your temperature?*
ROBERT: *Yes, it is 39.*
DOCTOR: *Open your mouth! Take a deep breath! You have bad flu. Stay at home for a week, and keep warm. I'll write you a prescription. Take one tablet three times a day. If you start coughing take two spoonfuls of the syrup, every six hours. Come for a check-up in a week.*

Vocabulary

premikati se	to move	**pregled**	check-up, medical examination
tresti (se)	to shake	**pregledati**	to examine
dihati	to breathe	**tablete**	tablets

Note: **recept** means both a prescription and a cooking recipe.

Language points

Every day, every six hours . . .

When you want to say that something takes place at a given interval you use the word **vsak** (every). Whilst the word *every* never changes in English, its Slovene counterpart **vsak** changes according to gender, case and number. Here are a few examples:

Vsako leto grem na dopust.	I go on holiday every year.
Vsakih šest mesecev grem k zobozdravniku na pregled.	I go to the dentist every six months for a check up.
Vsak dan se učim slovenščino.	I'm learning Slovene every day.

What sort of illness do you have?

Here are some adjectives which describe what sort of illness you may have:

ozdravljiv/-a/-o	curable	**nevaren/-rna/-o**	dangerous
neozdravljiv/-a/-o	terminal	**resen/-sna/-o**	serious
nalezljiv/-a/-o	contagious		

The verbs used when you are ill are:

zboleti	to become ill	**zdraviti se**	to be cured, to be treated
biti bolan/bolna	to be ill		
zdraviti	to cure, to treat	**ozdraviti**	to get well

Some nouns coming from these verbs are:

zdravnik	doctor (male)	**zdravilo**	medicine
zdravnica	doctor (female)	**zdravilišče**	spa, health resort
zdravje	health		

How words are formed

New words in Slovene are formed with suffixes. Let's look at some words you know:

učiti	pisati	pismo	delati
učitelj	pisarna	pismonoša	delo
učiteljica	pisatelj		delavec
učenec			delavka
			delodajalec

We will not go into the various rules for how these words are
formed. The important thing for you is that when you come across
a word which you think you don't know look at it and see if you
can recognize a part of it. In the words above, you may not know
the word **pismonoša**. You do, however, know the words **pismo** (a
letter) and the verb **nositi** (to carry). **Pismonoša** means 'postman'.
Delodajalec means 'employer'; it is formed from the words **delo**
(work) and **dajati** (to give). **Delojemalec** means 'employee'; it is
formed from the words **delo** and **jemati** (to take).

Verbal nouns

Verbal nouns (gerunds) are nouns which denote a verbal action
(e.g. English 'cooking, walking, singing'). In Slovene, most verbal
nouns are formed by replacing the **ti** ending of the infinitive with
a **nje** or **tje** ending. For example:

kuhati	*kuhanje*	cooking
peti	*petje*	singing
potovati	*potovanje*	travelling
parkirati	*parkiranje*	parking
nakupovati	*nakupovanje*	shopping

All of these verbal nouns are neuter in gender. Here are some
verbal nouns which are formed slightly irregularly:

živeti	*življenje*	living
kaditi	*kajenje*	smoking
čistiti	*čiščenje*	cleaning
trpeti	*trpljenje*	suffering

Verbal nouns can mean an action (i.e. shopping, cleaning) or something that is in some way connected with that action, for example:

meniti	*mnenje*	view, opinion
dovoliti	*dovoljenje*	permit, licence
presenetiti	*presenečenje*	surprise
prijaviti	*prijava*	declaration
delati	*delo*	work
prositi	*prošnja*	application, request
pogovarjati se	*pogovor*	conversation

Slovene health resorts

There is a number of thermal spas in Slovenia. One of the best known is Rogaška Slatina, which was developed as a fashionable spa in the nineteenth century and attracted such patients as the composer Franz Liszt and the Austro-Hungarian emperor.

There are other modernised spas. People still come to these spas to treat rheumatism and a variety of other ailments. The spas have increased their popularity by offering the same sort of facilities as you would find in an English health club, like slimming courses, massage, stress therapies and so on.

Positive and negative verbs

Used with a positive verb, the direct object is in the accusative case, for example:

Imam veliko *denarja*.	I have a lot of money.
Rada pijem *kavo in čaj*.	I like drinking coffee and tea.
Danes zvečer imam *čas*.	I have time this evening.

Used with a negative verb, the direct object is in the genitive case, for example:

Nimam *nič denarja*.	I have no money.
Nimam rada *ne kave ne čaja*.	I like neither coffee nor tea.
Ti *nikoli nimaš časa*.	You never have time.

Keep in mind that all negative words like **nič**, **nihče**, **nikoli**, always take a negative verb in Slovene.

Exercise 11

How many words for parts of the body can you spot in this word search? (Look only down and across.)

N	O	G	A	A	T	N	O	S	L
P	R	S	T	V	Č	O	V	Z	K
U	T	Š	R	Z	A	U	I	O	O
S	I	Ž	E	L	O	D	E	C	B
T	E	Z	B	L	K	B	R	M	R
A	P	O	U	H	O	D	D	M	A
N	T	B	H	K	R	I	Ž	A	Z

Exercise 12

Several people telephoned Robert at work during the week he was ill. Suppose you answered the telephone. Complete the following dialogue:

Dober dan, Zmago Kovač pri telefonu. Ali je Robert tam?
1 *Tell him that he isn't in the office today.*
Ali bo jutri tam?
2 *Say that it would be better if he tried next week. Tell him that he is ill.*
O, ali veste kaj mu je?
3 *Tell him that he has flu.*
Ali imate morda njegovo telefonsko številko od doma?
4 *Say that you're sorry but you don't have it. Tell him that he telephoned this morning and told you that he would be back on Monday.*
Če bo še poklical ga lepo pozdravite.
5 *Say that you will.* (But by then you have forgotten what his name was.) *Ask him politely if he could tell you again what his name is.*

Exercise 13

(a) Where would you go if you needed something listed in the left column? Pair off the sentences:

Če bi		*bi šel/šla*
1 potreboval – a zelenjavo	(i)	na trg
2 moral – a kupiti kruh in mleko	(ii)	v lekarno
3 potreboval – a znamke in pisma	(iii)	v trgovino
4 moral – a zamenjati denar	(iv)	na pošto
5 potreboval – a zdravila	(v)	na banko

(b) Now rewrite the sentences saying that you can do or get things on the left at places on the right.

Exercise 14

You know that the English preposition 'of' is not translated into Slovene; instead the noun in the genitive case indicates it. Can you put the nouns in brackets below into the genitive case. These are all very commonly used groups of words.

predsednik	president
član	member

konec	of the film	**člani**	of the family
konec	of the week	**center**	of the town
predsednik	of the country	**začetek**	of the performance

Exercise 15 🔘

Pronunciation exercise. Like **e**, the letter **o** has a few sounds in Slovene. Let's try to pronounce the words where **o** is used. It can be narrow and stressed, as in the words **nos, zob, morje, kos, mož, noč, osem, sto, goba, olje, opera**; or long, broad and stressed, as in the words **roka, noga, ona, otok, soba**.

There aren't many words with a double vowel or consonant in Slovene. Where they appear, they are pronounced as one long sound of that letter as in:

priimek	surname	**oddaja**	broadcasting
pooblastiti	to authorize	**oddati**	to give in, away
pooblastilo	authorization	**oddahniti se**	to take a rest, to
oddelek	department		recover breath

Dialogue for comprehension 🔘

*As Robert was told he did go to see the doctor in a week's time. In the waiting room (**v čakalnici**) he spoke to a woman who told him about someone she knows who has had the same terrible flu for a long time already. See why she thinks Robert recovered so quickly*

kosti	bones

ROBERT: Oprostite, ali me bodo poklicali?
GOSPA: Ja, ali še nikoli niste bili tukaj?
ROBERT: Ne, zdravnik je prejšnji teden prišel k meni na dom.
GOSPA: Ali se vam je kaj hudega zgodilo?
ROBERT: Ne, gripo sem imel. Ampak komaj sem se premikal. Vse me je bolelo in v glavi se mi je vrtelo. Moj sosed je poklical zdravnika.

GOSPA: Ja, ja, poznam to gripo. Moja sodelavka je že dva tedna doma. Kiha in kašlja, baje jo vse kosti bolijo. Ali se tudi vi tako počutite?

ROBERT: Ne, jaz sem že zdrav. Veliko bolje se počutim. Prišel sem samo na pregled.

GOSPA: Imeli ste srečo. Mladi ste še! To pomaga!

12 Nekaj imam v načrtu!

I have something planned!

In this lesson you will learn about:

- How to use the locative case
- The prepositions **v** and **na**
- How to book accommodation
- How to report what other people have said
- The reflexive verbs

Dialogue 1 📼

Lahko bi prenočili na Bledu!

We could stay the night by lake Bled!

During the summer holidays Sabina has a job as a receptionist in a hotel by lake Bled. Robert often goes there for the day, and one Saturday Sergej suggested how they could play a little trick on Sabina

SERGEJ: Robert, ali imaš kaj v planu za danes popoldne?

ROBERT: Ne, zakaj?

SERGEJ: Po kosilu bi lahko šli na Bled. Sabina začasno dela na Bledu, v enem hotelu ob jezeru v recepciji.

ROBERT: Ja, gospa Koren je zadnjič omenila, da tam dela.

SERGEJ: Jaz imam nekaj v načrtu! Danes bi lahko vsi štirje prenočili na Bledu.

ROBERT: Ne vem, če bomo dobili sobo. Sedaj je turistična sezona in gotovo je vse zasedeno.

SERGEJ: Privat se zmeraj kaj dobi. Ampak najprej bomo poizkusili v hotelu, kjer dela Sabina. Ti boš šel v recepcijo, tebe Sabina ne pozna. Po angleško jo vprašaj, če ima prosto sobo za štiri osebe za eno noč.

ROBERT: Ali zna angleško?

SERGEJ: Bomo videli!

SERGEJ: *Robert, do you have anything planned for this afternoon?*

ROBERT: *No, why?*

SERGEJ: *We could go to lake Bled after lunch. Sabina has a temporary job in reception at a hotel by the lake.*

ROBERT: *Yes, Mrs Koren mentioned last time that she is working there.*

SERGEJ: *I have something planned. All four of us could stay the night in Bled today.*

ROBERT: *I don't know if we'll get a room. It is now the tourist season and surely everything must be booked.*

SERGEJ: *You can always stay in a private home. But first we'll try in the hotel where Sabina works. You go to the reception, she doesn't know you. Ask her in English if she has a room for four for a night.*

ROBERT: *Can she speak English?*

SERGEJ: *We'll see!*

Vocabulary

imeti v planu *or*	to have planned	**prenočiti**	to stay overnight
imeti v načrtu		**poizkusiti**	to try
začasno	temporary	**oseba**	person
jezero	lake		

Language points

Do you have anything planned?

The words **plan** and **načrt** mean 'plan'. If you want to ask or tell someone about your or their plans you use the expressions **imeti v planu**, or **imeti v načrtu**. For example:

Ali imaš za danes kaj v planu?   Do you have anything planned for today?

Ne, ničesar nimam v planu, zakaj?   No, I have nothing planned. Why?

Jaz imam nekaj v načrtu.   I have something planned.

You can also use the verbs **planirati** or **načrtovati**, for example:

Kaj *planiraš/načrtuješ* **za jutri?**   What are you *planning* for
tomorrow?

What has been happening lately?

You know that if you put **č** on the cardinal numbers (as in **prvič**,
drugič, **tretjič**, etc.) this means 'for the first, the second, the third
time'. **Zadnjič** means 'for the last time'.
Zadnjič can also mean 'the other day', as in:

Zadnjič sem jo videl.   I saw her the other day.
Zadnjič sva šla na kavo.   We went for a coffee the other day.

Note how Robert says in the dialogue **Gospa Koren je zadnjič omenila...** You will be able to distinguish from the context of your conversation whether **zadnjič** means 'for the last time' or 'the other day'.
If you want to say that something has been happening recently,
you use the expression **zadnje čase**, as in:

Zadnje čase te nič ne vidim.   I haven't been seeing you recently.

If you want to say that something has happened just at the right
time you use the expression **ravno v pravem času**, as in:

Ravno v pravem času si prišel.   You came just at the right time.

To be doing something permanently or temporarily

The adjective **stalen/-lna/-o** means 'permanent' and the adjective
začasen/-sna/-o means 'temporary'. Here are a few examples of
how they are used:

Sabina ima začasno službo.   Sabina has a temporary job.
Ali je to tvoja stalna služba? Is this your permanent job?
Začasno stanujem tukaj.   I am living here temporarily.
To je moj stalni naslov.   This is my permanent address.

In which language did they tell you this?

When you want to say that something has been said in a particular language you use the preposition **po**, as in:

po angleško	in English
po slovensko	in Slovene
po nemško	in German

Notice how Sergej says to Robert!:

Po angleško jo vprašaj ...   Ask her in English ...

The locative case

The locative case is used only as the object of the following prepositions:

pri (by, with, at): **Bil sem pri zdravniku** (I've been at the doctors).

po (on, by, after): **Po kosilu gremo na Bled** (We're going to lake Bled after lunch).

ob (at, on, when expressing time): **Ob petkih delam do treh** (I work until three on Fridays); (by, when expressing location): **Ta hotel je ob jezeru** (This hotel is by the lake).

o (about, concerning): **Ali veš kaj o tej knjigi?** (Do you know anything about this book?).

If the prepositions **v** or **na** tell you where something is they take the locative case. If, however, they answer the question 'where to?', i.e. if they indicate direction, they take the accusative case (see lesson 6). Here are a few more examples:

Accusative	*Locative*
Lahko bi šli na Bled.	**Na Bledu je trenutno vse zasedeno.**
We could go to Bled.	Everything is booked in Bled at the moment.
Gremo v hotel!	**Prenočili bomo v hotelu.**
Let's go to the hotel.	We'll stay the night in a hotel.
Ti boš šel v recepcijo.	**Sabina dela v recepciji.**
You'll go to reception.	Sabina works in reception.

You may find it difficult to distinguish when to use **v** and when **na**. There isn't a rule you could follow to know when to use which preposition. Here are some examples of prepositions with places which are very commonly used:

Grem v Slovenijo	I'm going to Slovenia
v kino	to the cinema
v trgovino	to the shop
v kuhinjo	to the kitchen
v posteljo	to bed
v službo	to work

Grem na dopust	I'm going for a holiday
na koncert	to the concert
na vrt	to the garden
na nogometno tekmo	to the football match
na banko	to the bank
na pošto	to the post office

The nouns above are all in the accusative case because you are going to these places and the verb which is used implies movement. If you wanted to say that you are at these places, you would use the same prepositions, but the nouns would be in the locative case.

Keep in mind that **na** can also mean 'on', as in **na mizi** (on the table).

The endings in the locative case are as follows:

The first and the second declensions (feminine nouns)
Feminine nouns take an **i** ending in the singular and an **ah** ending in the dual and plural.

Singular		*Dual*	*Plural*	
hiša	*pri hiši*	hiši	hiše	*pri hišah*
miza	*pri mizi*	mizi	mize	*pri mizah*

The third declension (masculine nouns)
Masculine nouns take an **u** ending in the singular and an **ih** ending in the dual and in the plural.

Singular		*Dual*	*Plural*	
stric	*pri stricu*	strica	strici	*pri stricih*
kozarec	*pri kozarcu*	kozarca	kozarci	*pri kozarcih*

The fourth declension (neuter nouns)
Neuter nouns take an **u** ending in the singular and an **ih** ending in the dual and in the plural.

Singular		Dual	Plural	
mesto	*pri mestu*	mesti	mesta	*pri mestih*
drevo	*pri drevesu*	drevesi	drevesa	*pri drevesih*

The dual and plural endings of the locative case happen to be the same. This is not always the case. We will look into how the dual and the plural of other cases are formed later on.

Personal pronouns in the locative case

Singular	Dual	Plural
pri meni	pri nama	pri nas
pri tebi	pri vama	pri vas
pri njem	pri njima	pri njih
pri njej		
pri njem		

The preposition **pri** has been used in all the above examples. Depending on the context of your conversation, you can use any other preposition which takes the locative case and the ending will be the same.

Demonstrative pronouns are very often used as adjectives in the locative case and they have the following endings:

Masculine and neuter nouns in singular: **tem** (e.g. **pri tem hotelu**).
Feminine nouns in singular: **tej** (e.g. **pri tej hiši**).
Dual and plural nouns for all three genders: **teh** (e.g. **pri teh ljudeh**).

The interrogative pronouns in the locative case are **pri kom** (by whom) or **pri čem** (by what).

Exercise 1

Someone wants to meet you but you can't make it because of other engagements in your diary. Tell him what you are doing at the times given below

1	Wednesday afternoon	you are at a meeting
2	Friday	you have something planned
3	next week	you are not in town
4	Thursday evening	you are going to the cinema

5 on Mondays   you usually play basketball

Exercise 2

Anja, a friend of Sabina, does not know what Sabina is doing during the summer. She telephones Sabina's home and Sabina's mother tells her where Sabina is. Fill in Sabina's mother's lines:

ANJA: Dober večer, ali bi lahko govorila s Sabino?
MAMA: 1 *Sabina is not at home. Who is calling?*
ANJA: Jaz sem Anja, njena prijateljica iz univerze. Ali bo jutri doma?
MAMA: 2 *No, Sabina has a temporary job in Bled.*
ANJA: O, nisem vedela. Kaj pa dela?
MAMA: 3 *She is working in a hotel by the lake, at reception.*
ANJA: Zanimivo, kako dolgo bo tam delala?
MAMA: 4 *Two months, until October.*
ANJA: Ali ji je všeč?
MAMA: 5 *She says yes, but she has a lot of work. Now is the tourist season.*

Exercise 3

Choose the correct alternative, referring to the dialogue:

1 Sabina ima *stalno/začasno* službo na Bledu.
2 Dela *v enem hotelu/v eni trgovini*.
3 Dela *v pisarni/v recepciji*.
4 V turistični sezoni so sobe po navadi *zasedene/proste*.
5 *Robert/Sergej* ima nekaj v planu.

Exercise 4

You are enquiring about hotel accommodation over the telephone. Ask the person who answers the phone:

1 if you could ask her something in English.
2 if she could tell you when the tourist season there is.
3 if she thinks that they would have a room free in August.
4 if she could tell you what the prices are.
5 whether you could book the room now.

Exercise 5

(a) Tell your friend that you would like to have a house:

reka	river

1 by a lake.
2 on the main road.
3 by the river.

(b) Tell him also where you went yesterday:

1 to the doctor.
2 to the hairdresser.
3 to your mother's place.

Dialogue 2 🔘🔘

Ali imate rezervacijo?

Do you have a reservation?

Robert does go to the reception where Sabina works, and tries to book a room for the night. Sabina, whom he doesn't know, is trying to help him but there is no free room. She makes other suggestions

ROBERT: Dober dan.
SABINA: Dober dan, želite prosim?
ROBERT: Ali imate prosto sobo za štiri osebe za eno noč?
SABINA: Ali imate rezervacijo?
ROBERT: Ne, na žalost je nimam.
SABINA: Žal mi je, toda trenutno nimamo nobene proste sobe. Sredi turistične sezone smo in ob jezeru je vse zasedeno.
ROBERT: Ali mislite, da ne bo nihče v zadnjem trenutku odpovedal?
SABINA: To se redko zgodi. Ampak če želite, lahko izpolnite prijavnico. Kako dolgo bi radi ostali?
ROBERT: Samo eno noč. Samo prenočišče z zajtrkom bi radi.
SABINA: Jaz bom obdržala ta formular. Pokličite proti večeru! Ampak mislim, da je najbolje, če se med tem pozanimate, kje so privatne sobe. Vem, na primer, da imajo

tukaj še prostor. Lepa hiša je in ni daleč od jezera. Poizkusite!

ROBERT: *Good afternoon.*

SABINA: *Good afternoon, how can I help you?*

ROBERT: *Do you have a room for four for one night?*

SABINA: *Do you have a reservation?*

ROBERT: *No, unfortunately I don't.*

SABINA: *I'm sorry but we don't have any empty rooms at the moment. We are in the middle of the tourist season and all the hotels on the lake are fully booked.*

ROBERT: *Don't you think that someone might cancel at the last minute?*

SABINA: *That happens rarely. But if you like you could fill in this form. How long would you like to stay?*

ROBERT: *Only one night. We only want bed and breakfast.*

SABINA: *I'll keep this form. Call towards the evening. But I think that it is best if in the meantime you find out about private rooms. I know, for example, that they have vacancies here. It's a beautiful house and it isn't far from the lake. Try it!*

Vocabulary

rezervacija	reservation	**redko**	rarely
toda	but	**prenočišče z**	bed and breakfast
sredi	in the middle	**zajtrkom**	

nihče	no one, nobody	**obdržati**	to keep
v zadnjem	at the last	**proti večeru**	towards the evening
trenutku	minute	**pozanimati se**	to find out
odpovedati	to cancel	**na primer**	for example

Language points

Booking a room

In most major tourist centres you will find a **turistična agencija** (tourist agency) or some kind of tourist information office. There are different places of accommodation. In larger towns you will find hotels, and you may come across **motels**, which are the equivalent of the English bed and breakfast. Private houses let rooms and they will have a sign outside, usually in English and German. If you only want bed and breakfast you ask for **prenočišče z zajtrkom**, literally meaning 'accommodation for the night with breakfast'.

Some useful phrases when you check in are:

Ali imate prosto sobo za enega/dva/tri .. ?	Do you have a room for one/two/three ...?
Rad-a bi enoposteljno sobo.	I would like a single room.
dvoposteljno sobo.	double room.
sobo s kopalnico.	room with bathroom.
sobo z balkonom.	room with balcony.
Ali je v sobi radio/televizor?	Is there a radio/television in the room?
Ali lahko vidim sobo?	May I see the room?
Koliko časa boste ostali?	How long will you stay?
Kakšna je cena za eno noč	What is the price for one night?
en teden?	one week?
Moja prtljaga je ...	My luggage is ...
Če boste kaj potrebovali, pokličite recepcijo!	If you should need anything, call reception!

Breakfast

In most places you will be given a continental breakfast, i.e. bread, butter and jam, tea or coffee and some juice. You may be able to order a more substantial meal, which will be eggs, ham and a variety of salami, cheese and a variety of rolls.

How to complain

You may come across difficulties, in which case you will have to complain. If something doesn't work you say **... ne dela!**
Here are a few things which may not work:

luč	light
kurjava	heating
prha, tuš	shower

You may find that something is broken, in which case you say ...
je pokvarjen/-a/-o.
Other things which may go wrong are:

Okno/omara se ne odpre/zapre.   The window/wardrobe won't open/close.
Vrata se ne zaklenejo/odklenejo.   The door won't lock/unlock.

More about reflexive verbs

You know that when a verb is reflexive it is either preceded or followed by **si** or **se**. Some verbs only exist in reflexive form, for example:

prepirati se	to argue	**smejati se**	to laugh
bati se	to be afraid	**počutiti se**	to feel

You use the reflexive verb when there is no object in the sentence to describe what is happening, as in:

Trgovina se odpre ob osmih.   The shop opens at eight.
Banka se zapre ob šestih.   The bank closes at six.
Okno se ne odpre/zapre.   The window won't open/close.

When there is an object by which the action is carried out the verb is not reflexive, as in:

Trgovino odprejo ob osmih.   They open the shop at eight.
Vratar zapre banko ob šestih.   The doorman closes the bank at six.
Vsako jutro odprem/zaprem okno.   I open/close the window every morning.

In some cases **se** or **si** can be replaced with **sebe** or **sebi** and mean 'myself, yourself, himself', etc.

Sebe poglej!   Look at yourself!

Ona vidi samo sebe!	She only looks after herself!
Sam sebi (si) pomagaj!	Help yourself!

Note: The expression **Sam/-a si pomagaj** is an insulting expression. You must not use it when you want to express the English 'Help yourself' as in 'Here are some cakes and biscuits on the plate. Help yourself!' In such instances you can say **Postreži-te si!** The Slovene **Sam/-a si pomagaj** doesn't have this meaning!

But

In the dialogue you will have noticed Sabina say **Žal mi je, toda trenutno nimamo nobene proste sobe.** You know the word **ampak** meaning 'but'; **toda** is another word for 'but'. You may also see the word **a**, also meaning 'but'. You can use **ampak**, **toda** or **a** when you want to say 'but'. **Ampak** is the most common one in the spoken language.

Exercise 6

You want to stay the night:

RECEPTIONIST:	Dober večer. Želite, prosim?
YOU:	1 *Return his greeting and ask if there is a room free.*
RECEPTIONIST:	Ja, imamo. Sobo s kopalnico. Za kako dolgo bi jo želeli?
YOU:	2 *Say for one night. Ask what the price is. And ask if he would like your passport.*
RECEPTIONIST:	Ja, prosim. Jutri ga boste dobili nazaj. Ali bi izpolnili ta formular?
YOU:	3 *Say yes, of course. Ask what time breakfast is.*
RECEPTIONIST:	Od pol sedmih do devetih zjutraj.
YOU:	4 *Ask him if he knows where you could get something light to eat now.*
RECEPTIONIST:	Če želite večerjo, restavracija je v hotelu.
YOU:	5 *Thank him and on your way to your room just ask, by the way, if there is a telephone in your room.*

Exercise 7

You are staying in a hotel and late in the evening you realize that lots of things are not working. You telephone the reception and they tell you to make a list of the faults and someone will see to them in the morning. Of course, the list has to be in Slovene. How will you write down the following?

1 The light in the bathroom doesn't work.
2 The television is broken.
3 The window in the bedroom won't open.
4 The door in the bathroom won't lock.
5 There is no telephone in the room.

Exercise 8

How could you phrase questions in order to get the words in italic as an answer? One example has been done for you.

Sebastjan stanuje *pri stricu.*
Kje stanuje Sebastjan?

1 To je *gospod Kočevar.*
2 *Jutri zjutraj* grem k zdravniku.
3 Ime mi je *Danjela.*
4 Avtobusna postaja je *za tistim hotelom.*
5 Nadja je ostala doma, *zato ker se je slabo počutila.*

Exercise 9

Re-arrange these lines so that they will make a coherent telephone conversation:

Za koliko oseb?
Ja, je. Želite, prosim?
Ne, pokličite turistične informacije. Njihovo številko imam, če želite.
Prosim?
Za dve osebi.
Dobro jutro, ali je to hotel 'Lev'?
Trenutek, prosim. Žal mi je, ampak naslednji konec tedna je vse zasedeno. Poizkusite hotel 'Slon'!
Rad bi rezerviral sobo za naslednji konec tedna.
Tja sem že poklical in tudi oni imajo vse zasedeno. Ali imate morda informacije o privatnih sobah?
Tisto številko imam sam. Hvala, nasvidenje.

Exercise 10

Write a short dialogue for the scenes below:

1 A stranger stops you on the street and asks you where the 'Kaj' restaurant is but you don't know.
2 You are about to go out and your friend seems to be looking for something. Ask her what she is looking for and, as she tells you that she is looking for her umbrella, tell her that you have seen it in the bathroom.
3 You are in a hotel and you want to go out to eat. Ask the receptionist which restaurant she would recommend and when she tells you about a new one round the corner noted for fish ask her whether it is cheap or expensive.

Dialogue 3 ▣

Vprašal sem, če imajo sobo za štiri

I asked if they had a room for four

Sergej, Boštjan and Davor are anxiously waiting for Robert in front of the hotel. As he comes out they ask him lots of questions about his conversation with Sabina

SERGEJ: Kaj je rekla?
ROBERT: Vprašal sem jo, če imajo prosto sobo za štiri za eno noč.
SERGEJ: In?
ROBERT: Vprašala me je, če imam rezervacijo. Povedal sem ji, da je nimam in rekla je, da trenutno nimajo nobene proste sobe in da je ob jezeru vse zasedeno.
SERGEJ: Ali si jo vprašal, če morda ve, kje bi lahko prenočili?
ROBERT: Ja, predlagala je, naj poizkusimo to privatno hišo. Baje imajo še prostor. Vprašal sem jo tudi, če ne misli, da bo kdo odpovedal.
SERGEJ: In kaj pravi?
ROBERT: Pravi, da se to redko zgodi. Ampak kljub temu sem izpolnil prijavnico. Rekla je, naj proti večeru pokličem.
SERGEJ: Ja, poklicali bomo, verjetno zastonj, ampak kdo ve? Do večera se lahko marsikaj zgodi!

SERGEJ: *What did she say?*

ROBERT: *I asked her if they had a room free for four for a night.*
SERGEJ: *And?*
ROBERT: *She asked me if I had a reservation. I told her that I didn't and she said that they haven't got any empty rooms at the moment and that everything by the lake was booked.*
SERGEJ: *Did you ask her where we could stay the night?*
ROBERT: *Yes, she suggested that we should try a private house. They still have room here, apparently. I also asked her if she thought that someone would cancel at the last minute.*
SERGEJ: *And what did she say?*
ROBERT: *She said that that rarely happens. But in spite of this I have filled in a form. She said that we should call towards the evening.*
SERGEJ: *Yes, we will call. Most probably in vain but who knows? Lots of things can happen before the evening.*

Vocabulary

redko	rarely	**zastonj**	in vain
kljub temu	in spite of this	**marsikaj**	many things

Language points

Zastonj

The word **zastonj** has two meanings. It can mean 'in vain', as in:

Zastonj čakaš na ta avtobus. Ob nedeljah ne vozi!
You are waiting for the bus in vain. It doesn't run on Sundays!

Zastonj can also mean that something is free (of charge), as in:

'Koliko si plačal za to?' – 'Bilo je zastonj.'
'How much did you pay for this?' – 'It was free!'

This happens often, rarely, sometimes

The word **pogosto** means 'often' and **redko**, **redkokdaj** mean 'rarely', 'seldom'. If you want to say that something happens often or seldom you use the reflexive verb **zgoditi se** (to happen) in the third person singular and the above adverbs. For example:

To se redko zgodi.	This rarely happens.
To se pogosto zgodi.	This often happens.
To se ne zgodi pogosto.	This doesn't happen often.

Marsi/kaj/kje/kdaj/kdo

The prefix **marsi** in front of some pronouns tells you 'many a . . . ': for example, note how Sergej says in the dialogue **Do večera se lahko *marsikaj* zgodi!**

Direct and reported speech

In direct speech we repeat the words of the person who has said them, for example:

Sabina je rekla: 'Trenutno nimamo nobene proste sobe.'

In indirect (or reported) speech we only give the exact meaning of what they have said, without repeating it word by word.

We can report statements, questions and commands. In English the tense which you use when you report someone's words changes but in Slovene this is much simpler. You use the same tense as was used in the original statement. The only change is the person, which is replaced by the third person.

What someone originally said or asked is usually reported with **reči** (to say), **povedati** (to tell), **praviti** (to say), **vprašati** (to ask).

Statements

Direct speech
Sabina je rekla: 'Trenutno nimamo nobene proste sobe.'
Sabina said: 'We have no rooms available at the moment.'

Indirect speech
Sabina je rekla, *da* trenutno nimajo nobene proste sobe.
Sabina said *that* they had no rooms available.

Notice that in Slovene the only difference between the sentences above is the conjunction **da** and *the change of the personal pronoun*.

Questions

Direct speech
Sabina je vprašala: 'Ali imate rezervacijo?'
Sabina asked: 'Do you have a reservation?'

Indirect speech
Sabina je vprašala, *ali* (*če*) *ima* rezervacijo.
Sabina asked *whether he had* a reservation.

When you report a question, you only change the verb into the third person in Slovene. The correct word to use is **ali**, which indicates a question. However, colloquially **če** is used much more often.

Commands

Direct speech
Sabina je rekla: 'Pokličite proti večeru!'
Sabina said: 'Call (telephone) towards evening!'

Indirect speech
Sabina je rekla, (*da*) *naj pokličem* proti večeru.
Sabina said that I should call towards evening.

When you report advice or a command you were given by someone, the imperative form of the verb which the person used is replaced by the present tense and the word **naj** (see lesson 8) is put in front of it. Colloquially, you will hear people use the conjunction word **da**, which is optional. When you give a command in Slovene you cannot use the infinitive as you do in English. Instead, you put the verb into the form of the person to whom you are referring, for example:

Rekel mi je, naj grem v trgovino.   He told me to go to the shops.

Exercise 11

You are on holiday with your friend and you have gone to the reception desk of an hotel. Report back to him what has been said.

(a) You asked:

1 Do you have a double room free for a week?
2 What is the price?
3 At what time is breakfast served?

(b) The receptionist told you (use **reči**):

1 We have two single rooms.
2 The price is the same.
3 The rooms are large and nicely furnished.

Exercise 12

Whilst the students are waiting for Robert in front of the hotel where Sabina works they are gossiping about her.

Put their words into Slovene.

družiti se	to mix with

1 Sergej told her to study more.
2 Boštjan told her not to work this summer.
3 Davor told her not to mix with Sandra.

Sabina gave sharp answers to each of them. Put into reported speech what she said:

brigati se za sebe	to mind one's own business
poizkati si	to find (something for oneself)

4 to Sergej: to mind his own business.
5 To Boštjan: to find himself a girlfriend.

Exercise 13 🔲

A colleague of yours, Monika Černe, telephones one morning and you answer the telephone. She says:

Dobro jutro, ali lahko poveš direktorju, da danes ne bom prišla v službo. Bolna sem. Že od včeraj se zelo slabo počutim. Kašljam in kiham, glava me boli in ponoči sem bruhala. Dopoldne bom šla k zdravniku in popoldne bom še enkrat poklicala.

Can you go to the director and tell him in your own words what she told you?

Exercise 14

The words on the left are things and people. Match them with the places on the right where you could find them.

avto	restavracija
omara	gostilna
receptor	garaža

pivo	pošta
zrezek	knjigarna
znamka	hiša
knjiga	hotel

Exercise 15 ▐▌

Pronunciation exercise. The Slovene **j** is always pronounced as in the English words 'yes', and 'yellow' and *not* as the French *j*!

Let's pronounce the following words: **junij**, **julij**, **jug**, **dežuje**, **ključ**, **knjiga**.

J is also pronounced in country names, e.g. **Anglija**, **Slovenija**, **Španija**, **Italija**; and in people's names: **Marija**, **Katja**, **Manja**, **Tanja**, **Sonja**.

Dialogue for comprehension ▐▌

On the way to the house Sabina suggested that Robert should tell the boys about a hotel where he once stayed. Make a list of all the things that went wrong there.

kakor hitro	as soon as
tuširati se	to have a shower
teči	to run

ROBERT: Upam, da bo ta privatna hiša boljša od tiste, kjer sem lani enkrat prenočil.

SERGEJ: Kaj je bilo narobe?

ROBERT: Vse je bilo narobe. Bilo je pozimi, zelo mrzlo je bilo in kurjava ni delala. Okno v moji sobi se ni zaprlo. Luč v kopalnici je bila pokvarjena in v temi sem se tuširal. Tuš je delal, ampak kakor hitro se je kdo nad nami tuširal, voda ni več tekla. Nekaj je bilo narobe tudi s straniščem: kopalnica je smrdela. In za vogalom je bila ena gostilna, odprta vso noč. Glasba je bila zelo glasna. Nihče ni mogel spati.

SERGEJ: Zakaj niste šli tudi vi v tisto gostilno?

ROBERT: Jaz sem ves dan delal in zvečer sem bil utrujen. Hotel sem se odpočiti. In tudi moji prijatelji so bili utrujeni.

SERGEJ: Danes zvečer bom za glasbo poskrbel jaz. Ti nisi utrujen in vsi bomo imeli zabavo.

ROBERT: Ali ne gremo jutri zgodaj zjutraj na jezero?

SERGEJ: Ja, ali ne veš, da vsako jezero izgleda najbolje iz terase kakšne kavarne?

13 Vse najboljše za rojstni dan!

Happy birthday!

In this lesson you will learn about:

- How to use the instrumental case
- How to compare adjectives and adverbs
- Personal and national celebrations

Dialogue 1 🔊

Kje je darilo za Roberta?

Where is the present for Robert?

Robert did not realize that the reason they wanted to go to lake Bled was because they had discovered that Saturday was his birthday. Sabina knew that he would come to the hotel and it was she who was organizing the party at Sandra's parents' house at lake Bled, the house where she had suggested they should stay. She and Sandra are just getting the last things ready before the guests arrive

SABINA: Upam, da ne bodo prišli pred osmo. Kje je darilo za Roberta? Zaviti ga je treba!

SANDRA: Pod temi papirji je. Jaz ga bom zavila.

SABINA: Dobro, jaz pa bom med tem pripravila mizo.

SANDRA: Miza je že pripravljena, samo kozarci še manjkajo. Nisem jih našla.

SABINA: Morali bi biti v eni škatli v dnevni sobi.

SANDRA: Tja nisem pogledala.

SABINA: Jaz bom šla po njih.

SANDRA: Ali pridejo z avtom, ali s taksijem?

SABINA: Pojma nimam. Sergej je samo rekel, da naju bodo prej poklicali.
SANDRA: Če se bodo spomnili!

SABINA: *I hope they won't come before eight. Where is the present for Robert? We must wrap it.*
SANDRA: *It's under these papers. I'll wrap it.*
SABINA: *Alright. I'll prepare the table in the meantime.*
SANDRA: *The table is prepared, only the glasses are missing. I couldn't find them.*
SABINA: *They should be in a box in the living-room.*
SANDRA: *I didn't look there.*
SABINA: *I'll fetch them.*
SANDRA: *Are they coming by car or by taxi?*
SABINA: *I haven't a clue. Sergej only said that they will give us a ring before to warn us.*
SANDRA: *If they remember!*

Vocabulary

pred	before	**manjkati**	to be missing
darilo	present	**škatla**	box
zaviti	to wrap	**pojma nimam**	I haven't a clue
med tem	in the meantime		

Language points

I hope so, I think so

When you want to tell someone that you hope or think something, you must make a relative clause, for example:

Upam, da bo jutri lepo vreme! I hope the weather will be nice tomorrow.
Upam, da ne bo deževalo! I hope it won't rain.

Mislim, da pridejo vsi! I think they're all coming.
Mislim, da so bili včeraj v kinu. I think they were in the cinema yesterday.

If you want to say that you hope or think so, you say:

Upam, da.	I hope so.
Mislim, da.	I think so.

Something is missing!

The verb **manjkati** means 'to be missing'. When you want to say that something or someone is missing you use this verb in the third person singular. Keep in mind that the present continuous tense does not exist in Slovene and you must therefore not translate the English auxiliary 'is'. For example, you say:

Nekaj/nekdo manjka!	Something/someone is missing!
Kdo/kaj manjka!	Who/what is missing?
Manjka mi časa/denarja.	I'm short of time/money.

I haven't a clue!

As in English, there are several colloquial expressions for saying 'I don't know'. Notice how Sabina says in the dialogue **Nimam pojma!**, meaning 'I have no idea'.

Here are a few more expressions which you may hear people say:

Sanja se mi ne!	I don't even dream about it!
Nimam blage veze!	I have no idea!
Nimam ideje!	I have no idea!
Nimam pojma!	I haven't a clue!

Will you remember?

The words for 'to remind' and 'to remember' are another example of how in Slovene, when you change a prefix or when a verb is reflexive, it has a different meaning. Look at these examples:

Ali se spomniš?	Do you remember?
Ne, ne spomnim se.	No, I don't remember.
Spomni me!	Remind me!
Ne morem si zapomniti!	I can't remember.
Zapomni si!	Remember!

The verb **spomniti** when used with an object, as in 'Spomni me!' means 'to remind'. **Spomniti se**, as in **Ali se spomniš?** or **Ne spomnim se!**, means 'to remember'. **Zapomniti si** also means 'to remember', as in **Ne morem si zapomniti!**

The instrumental case

Like the locative case, the instrumental case is used as the object of certain prepositions. It is called instrumental case because it is used when you name an instrument by means of which a particular action is carried out. Look back at lesson 3, where you learnt how to use this case with the means of transport. The prepositions which are followed by the instrumental case are listed below:

s/z
Both of the above prepositions mean 'with', 'by means of'. The preposition **s** is used before all unvoiced consonants, which are: **c, č, s, š, f, h, k, p** and **t**.

The preposition **z** is used before all vowels (**a, e, i, o, u**) and all voiced consonants (**b, d, g, j, l, m, n, r, v, z, ž**). For example:

z roko	by hand
z avtobusom	by bus
z vlakom	by train
z mano	with me
s knjigo	with (a/the) book
s profesorjem	with (a/the) professor
s Sabino	with Sabina
s tabo	with you

nad (over, above): **Nad nami je še eno stanovanje** (There is another flat above us).

pod (under): **Nekaj je pod mizo** (Something is under the table).

med (during, between, among): **Med nami je zmeraj tako** (Among us it is always like that).

za (behind, beyond, after): **Nekdo je za vrati** (Someone is behind the door); **Za zimo pride pomlad** (After winter comes spring).

pred (in front of, before): **Čigav avto stoji pred hišo?** (Whose car is in front of the house?).

The endings in the instrumental case are as follows:

The first and the second declension (feminine nouns)
Feminine nouns take an **o** ending in the singular, an **ama** ending in the dual and an **ami** ending in the plural.

Singular		Dual		Plural	
mama	z *mamo*	mami	z *mamama*	mame	z *mamami*
teta	s *teto*	teti	s *tetama*	tete	s *tetami*

There are quite a few exceptions to this rule among the nouns of the second declension.

The third and the fourth declension (masculine and neuter nouns)
Masculine and neuter nouns take an **om** or **em** ending in the singular, an **oma** or **ema** ending in the dual and an **i** ending in the plural.

Singular		Dual		Plural	
nož	z *nožem*	noža	z *nožema*	noži	z *noži*
mesto	z *mestom*	mesti	z *mestoma*	mesta	z *mesti*

Personal pronouns in the instrumental case

Singular	Dual	Plural
z mano	z nama	z nami
s tabo	z vama	z vami
z njim	z njima	z njimi
z njo		
z njim		

The prepositions **s** and **z** are used above. They can be replaced by other prepositions used with the instrumental case.

The interrogative pronouns in the instrumental case are **S kom** (with whom) and **S čim** (with what).

Exercise 1

Answer these questions relating to dialogue 1. Some information you are asked is not given in the dialogue, in which case you answer that you don't know.

1 Kdo bo zavil darilo za Roberta?
2 Zakaj Sandra ni postavila kozarcev na mizo?
3 Kaj sta Sandra in Sabina kupili Robertu?
4 Kje so kozarci?
5 Ali bo Sergej telefoniral, preden pridejo?

Exercise 2

How would you tell someone the following?

1 that you can't remember how much you paid for that book.
2 that you can't remember what your secretary's surname is.
3 to remind you to telephone your mother.
4 to remind you to go to the bank.
5 that you can't remember how to say this in Slovene.

Exercise 3

How would you answer the questions below (use the clues in brackets)?

na sprehod	for a walk

1 Kje si parkiral avto?
   (*in front of the house*)
2 Kako si šel v službo?
   (*by train*)
3 Ali si zamenjal denar?
   (*Yes, I went to the bank during my break.*)
4 Kdaj prideš jutri domov?
   (*not before six*)
5 Psa moram peljati na sprehod.
   (*I'll come with you.*)

Exercise 4

From the conversation between Sandra and Sabina, say what they bought Robert and why.

SANDRA: Ali misliš, da mu bo ta knjiga všeč?
SABINA: Ne vem. Kupila sem jo zato, ker je enkrat omenil, da rad kuha.
SANDRA: Ampak v tej knjigi so same solate!
SABINA: Ali ne veš, Robert je vegetarjanec!

Exercise 5

Sabina and Sandra have found the glasses and they are now talking about the drinks. From the dialogue below make a note of where the different drinks are

klet	cellar

SABINA: Sok je v hladilniku. In pivo tudi.
SANDRA: Iščem mineralno vodo.
SABINA: Na mizo sem jo že postavila. In kje je vino?
SANDRA: Belo vino je v kleti, rdeče pa v eni škatli v kuhinji.

Dialogue 2

Kaj boš oblekla?

What will you wear?

Sabina and Sandra have prepared the table and the room; now it is time for them to get dressed. Of course, they have a few problems

SABINA: Sandra, jaz ne vem kaj naj oblečem.
SANDRA: Lahko si izposodiš mojo rdečo obleko. Meni je premajhna.
SABINA: Jaz sem večja od tebe, meni bo prekratka.
SANDRA: Poizkusi tisto črno krilo, ki je sicer eno izmed mojih najcenejših kril, ampak najdaljše.
SABINA: Zelo mi je všeč. Ali se ga kupila na razprodaji?
SANDRA: Ja.
SABINA: In kaj boš ti oblekla?
SANDRA: Te hlače in en velik pulover ali bluzo, zato ker sem se zredila.
SABINA: Obleči tega, ta je najlepši.
SANDRA: Tega sem veliko nosila, ko sem prišla nazaj iz Italije. Takrat sem bila bolj rjava in bolj suha.

SABINA: *Sandra, I don't know what to wear.*
SANDRA: *You can borrow my red dress. It is too small for me.*
SABINA: *I am taller than you, it will be too short for me.*
SANDRA: *Try that black skirt, which is one of my cheapest skirts but it is the longest I have.*

SABINA: *I think it's a very nice skirt. Did you buy it in a sale?*
SANDRA: *Yes.*
SABINA: *And what will you wear?*
SANDRA: *These trousers and a big jumper or a blouse because I've put on weight.*
SABINA: *Wear this one, it's the nicest.*
SANDRA: *I wore it a lot when I came back from Italy. But I was browner and slimmer then.*

Vocabulary

obleči	to wear	**bluzo**	blouse
obleka	dress, suit	**hlače**	trousers
poizkusiti	to try	**pulover**	pullover
krilo	skirt	**katerega?**	which one?
sicer	namely	**nositi**	to carry, to wear

Language points

Shopping for clothes

Browsing around clothes shops, you will be approached by a shop-assistant. You can tell them:

Samo gledam, hvala.	I'm just looking, thank you.
Iščem . . .	I'm looking for . . .
Ali lahko pomerim . . .?	May I try . . .?

A shop-assistant may ask you:

Katero številko želite?	What size would you like?
V kakšni barvi želito to . . .	In what colour would you like this . . .

If you are lucky, you can find things

na razprodaji	in a sale
po znižani ceni	reduced
po polovični ceni	half price

Obleka

You may find it confusing, but **obleka** means both a dress for a woman and a suit for a man. Here are some more words for items of clothing:

sandali	sandals	**majica**	T-shirt, vest
škornji	booth	**spodnje perilo**	underwear
šal	scarf	**nogavice**	socks
rokavice	gloves	**kravata**	tie

Nositi

The verb **nositi (nosim)** means 'to carry', as in:

Kaj nosiš v tej veliki torbi?   What are you carrying in this big bag?

Nositi can also mean 'to wear', as in:

Najraje nosim hlače.   I like wearing trousers best.
Poleti nosim krila.   I wear skirts in the summer.

You also use **nositi** to say that you wear spectacles, as in:

očala	spectacles

Ali nosiš očala?   Do you wear spectacles?
Ja, slabo vidim. Že dolgo jih nosim.   Yes, I see badly. I've been wearing them for a long time.

Comparison of adjectives and adverbs

The three degrees of comparison are:

1 the positive
2 the comparative
3 the superlative

When you want to compare adjectives or adverbs in English you either add '-er' and '-est' to the adjective (as in 'cheap, cheaper, the cheapest') or you add 'more' and 'most' in front of them (as in 'expensive, more expensive, the most expensive'). A similar, but not identical method, is used in Slovene.

To form the comparative in Slovene you add the following suffixes to the positive: **-ši, -ji, -jši.**

To form the superlative you simply put **naj** in front of the comparative. Look at the following examples:

lep	beautiful	**lepši**	**najlepši**
mlad	young	**mlajši**	**najmlajši**
kratek	short	**krajši**	**najkrajši**
slab	bad	**slabši**	**najslabši**
dolg	long	**daljši**	**najdaljši**

drag	expensive	**dražji**	**najdražji**
visok	high	**višji**	**najvišji**
velik	big	**večji**	**največji**
lahek	easy	**lažji**	**najlažji**

nov	new	**novejši**	**najnovejši**
star	old	**starejši**	**najstarejši**
bogat	rich	**bogatejši**	**najbogatejši**
reven	poor	**revnejši**	**najrevnejši**

Which suffix is added and how some adjectives alter or shorten when the suffix has been added must be memorized.

The comparative can also be formed with the word **bolj** (more) and the superlative with the word **najbolj** (the most), for example:

rjav	brown	**bolj rjav**	**najbolj rjav**
jezen	angry	**bolj jezen**	**najbolj jezen**
razočaran	disappointed	**bolj razočaran**	**najbolj razočaran**
zaskrbljen	worried	**bolj zaskrbljen**	**najbolj zaskrbljen**

The endings **-ši, -ji** and **-jši** are added only when an adjective denotes the quality of something. All other adjectives form their comparative and superlative with the helping word **bolj** and **najbolj**.

When you compare things you use the following conjunction words:

The positive

Anglija je tako velika *kot* Italija.   England is as big as Italy.

The comparative

Anglija je večja *kot* Slovenija.   England is bigger than
**   *od* Slovenije.**   Slovenia.

The superlative

Amerika je največja *izmed* teh držav.   America is the biggest
**   *od* teh držav.**   of all these countries.
**   *med* temi državami.**

Notice that the endings of nouns change depending on which preposition you use. The endings of adjectives in their comparative and superlative forms also change.

Comparison of adverbs

You know that the neuter form of an adjective is also an adverb. They usually end in **o** (**dobro, veliko, lepo**). Adverbs are words which you don't decline. They can tell us location (**kam, doma, domov**), manner (**hitro, počasi**), reason (**zato**). You have already learned how you compare the adverbs **dobro** and **rad**. Here are some more adverbs and their comparative and superlative forms.

veliko	a lot	**več**	**največ**
zelo	very	**bolj**	**najbolj**
malo	a little	**manj**	**najmanj**
daleč	far	**dlje**	**najdlje**
blizu	close by	**bliže**	**najbliže**

More about the conjunction words

In Slovene there are two types of conjunction words: coordinate and subordinate. Coordinate conjunctions can express:

Supplement: these tell us that there is something else, for example: **Davor *in* Sergej.** Other words which can express supplement are **pa**, meaning 'and'. **Pa** is used more colloquially. The word **ter** is used as the last conjunction when you are listing things, for example: **Kupil je kruh, krompir, sol, poper ter maslo.**

Choice: **ali ... ali** meaning 'either ... or' expresses a choice. **Ali** on its own, meaning 'or', also expresses a choice.

Opposition: we have very often used the word **ampak**; its synonyms are **toda**, **a**, **vendar**.

Degree: **ne ... ne**, or **niti ... niti** mean 'neither ... nor'. The words **ne samo ... ampak tudi ...** mean 'not only ... but also'.

Cause: there are a few words with which you can express cause. Among the common ones are **namreč** (namely), **sicer** (or else), **kajti** (for). Here is an example: **Pohiti, sicer boš zamudil avtobus!**

Subordinate conjunctions introduce a subordinate clause. The conjunction **da** (that) introduces almost all types of subordinate clauses. The words **ki**, **kateri**, **kdor**, **kar** are all translated by 'which' and introduce a subordinate clause. Other subordinate conjunctions express:

> *time:* **kadar**, **ko** (when)
> *condition:* **če** (if)
> *cause:* **ker**, **zato ker** (because)
> *comparison*, as you have seen above.

Exercise 6

Match the Slovene words with the English ones:

hlače	tie
bluza	skirt
kravata	scarf
krilo	shoes
čevlji	blouse
rokavice	trousers
šal	gloves

Exercise 7

Ask your friend which she prefers wearing:

kostim	suit (for a woman)
leče	contact lenses

1 shoes or sandals
2 blouses or pullovers
3 skirts or trousers
4 dresses or suits
5 glasses or contact lenses

Exercise 8 🔳

You are walking round town and you see some nice things in a window (**v izložbi**). You enter the shop and you are approached by a shop-assistant. Fill in your part of the conversation.

razprodano	sold out

PRODAJALKA: Želite, prosim?
YOU: 1 *Tell her that you are just looking.*
PRODAJALKA: Sedaj imamo razprodajo. Vse je po polovični ceni.
YOU: 2 *Tell her that you are looking for a jumper for your brother.*
PRODAJALKA: Katero številko želite?
YOU: 3 *Tell her that you don't know. Ask if you could see some men's jumpers.*
PRODAJALKA: Kakšne barve ga želite?
YOU: 4 *Say in blue or in brown.*
PRODAJALKA Na žalost imamo samo še male številke. Veliko je že razprodano.
YOU: 5 *Thank her and say that you will have a look somewhere else.*

Exercise 9

Fill in the comparative of the suggested adjectives and adverbs in the sentences below. The adjectives in brackets are all in the masculine form. Keep in mind that these will have different endings depending on the gender of the noun

1 Ali je tvoje novo stanovanje ... ali ... od prejšnjega?
  (*small*, *big*)
2 Ali je ta hotel ... ali ... od jezera?
  (*close*, *far*)
3 Ali je tvoja nova služba ... ali ... ?
  (*good*, *bad*)
4 Ali je v tej trgovini zelenjava ... ali ...?
  (*cheap*, *expensive*)
5 Ali si bil lani ... ali ... .?
  (*rich*, *poor*)

Exercise 10

Robert asks Davor a few questions about lake Bled. Fill in his part
of the conversation

globok	deep
svet	world

ROBERT: 1 *Is lake Bled the largest lake in Slovenia?*
DAVOR: Ne vem, mislim da.
ROBERT: 2 *Is it the most beautiful one?*
DAVOR: Veliko ljudi tako pravi. Meni je bolj všeč Bohinj. Ni daleč
od tod.
ROBERT: 3 *If it isn't far we could go there one day. I like lakes. I
always wanted to see lake Baikal. That is the deepest lake.
It is also the coldest.*
DAVOR: Jaz sem mislil, da je Loch Ness najglobje jezero?
ROBERT: 4 *No, Loch Ness is the deepest and the longest lake in
Scotland but not in the world.*

Dialogue 3 💿

Na zdravje!

Cheers!

*People have already begun to arrive at the party. As Robert and the
students enter the house they all sing happy birthday to him*

ROBERT: Ne vem, kaj naj rečem.
SERGEJ: Nič ne reci! Sedi in vzemi svoj kozarec! Danes je tvoj
rojstni dan!
SANDRA: Počakaj, počakaj, Sergej! Robert, ali nam boš povedal,
koliko si danes star?
ROBERT: Morala boš malo počakati, Sandra. Najprej bom nekaj
popil!
SERGEJ: Kje je vino?
SANDRA: Tukaj!
SERGEJ: Robert, to je najboljše slovensko vino. Ampak preden
je zares dobro, moraš popiti nekaj kozarcev!

ROBERT: Hvala. Hvala vsem! Na zdravje!

ROBERT: *I don't know what to say!*
SERGEJ: *Don't say anything! Sit down and take your glass! It's your birthday!*
SANDRA: *Hold on, Sergej! Robert, will you tell us how old you are today?*
ROBERT: *You'll have to wait a bit, Sandra. I'll have something to drink first!*
SERGEJ: *Where is the wine?*
SANDRA: *Here!*
SERGEJ: *Robert, this is the best Slovene wine! But you have to drink a few glasses before it becomes really good!*
ROBERT: *Thank you. Thank you all! Cheers!*

Language points

Birthday cards

Robert received quite a few cards for his birthday. Here are some examples showing you how to write a birthday card:

Vse najboljše za tvoj rojstni dan   All the best on your birthday.

Sabina in Sandra

Vse najboljše, Robert!   All the best, Robert!

Sergej, Davor, Boštjan

K tvojemu rojstnemu dnevu ti želimo vse najboljše
We wish you all the best on your birthday.

Družina Koren

Vse najboljše means 'All the best'.

Describing a person

You should by now be able to describe a person's physical appearance; here are some more words you can use, some of which are for when you want to describe someone's character:

značaj	character	**postava**	figure

vedenje	behaviour	**polt**	complexion
dobro srce	good heart		

In Slovene, you can describe someone by saying that they have some of the above characteristics, in which case the nouns will be in the accusative case; or that they are of the above characteristics, in which case the nouns will be in the genitive case, for example:

Davor ima lep značaj.	Davor has a nice character.
Davor je lepega značaja.	Davor is of a nice character.
Sandra ima temno polt.	Sandra has a dark complexion.
Sandra je temne polti.	Sandra is of a dark complexion.

Personal celebrations

Most people celebrate their birthday (**rojstni dan**). The fiftieth birthday is the biggest celebration; you are celebrating **abrahama** then. Other important celebrations are:

Matura: You have a 'matura dance' when you finish your secondary education, at the age of eighteen or nineteen.

Diploma: This is when you graduate.

Zaroka: 'engagement': most people give a party when they get engaged

Poroka 'wedding'.

Srebrna poroka (literally 'a silver wedding'): this is an occasion to celebrate – you've been married for twenty-five years

Zlata poroka (literally 'a golden wedding'): you've been married for fifty years.

Krst 'christening'.

Not a celebration but another event when a family gets together is **pogreb** (funeral).

What do Slovenes celebrate?

'A national holiday' is **državni praznik**. Together with those, there are a few other days in the year which Slovenes celebrate:

31. december	**silvestrovo**	New Year's Eve
1. januar	**novo leto**	New Year's Day
8. februar	**Prešernov dan**	Prešeren Day
		This is a Slovene day of culture, a day when the greatest Slovene poet, France Prešeren, was born.

april (varies from year to year)	**velika noč**	Easter
27. april		This commemorates the day of uprising against the occupying powers in the Second World War
1. maj	**praznik dela**	May Day
25. junij	**dan državnosti**	Slovenia day
1. november	**dan mrtvih**	Day of remembrance of the dead
24. december	**božični večer**	Christmas Eve
25. december	**božični dan**	Christmas Day
26. december	**dan samostojnosti**	Independence Day

Spelling in Slovene

You know that the days of the week and the months of the year are spelt with a small letter in Slovene. The national holidays, likewise, are spelt with a small letter, unless, of course, they appear at the beginning of a sentence. Inhabitants of countries are spelt with a capital letter (e.g. **Anglež**, **Slovenka**), but the languages are spelt with a small letter (e.g. **Govorim angleško/slovensko**).

More about dates

The question **Katerega smo danes?** (What date is it today?) can be answered in two ways: you know that you can say **Danes je ...**; however, it is much more common to say **Danes smo ...**, in which case the numbers will take the genitive ending. Look at the example:

25.4.
Danes je petindvajseti četrti
Danes smo petindvajsetega četrtega

Exercise 11

Katerega smo danes? (Use **smo**.)

1 16.5.
2 24.3.
3 9.7.
4 31.6.
5 4.1

Exercise 12

Which verb do you think would fit best in the sentences below?

1 Tone zelo rad ... zanimive knjige.
2 Njegova mama je učiteljica. ... matematiko in fiziko.
3 Letos si moram ... nov plašč.
4 Ali ... očala?
5 Naslednji teden ... na poroko. Ne vem, kaj naj ...

Exercise 13

Fill in the personal pronouns in the gaps in the sentences below:

1 Jaz ne poznam Sabine. Ali ... ti poznaš?
2 Telefonirati moram Matjažu. Nekaj ... moram vprašati.
3 Peter mi je že pred dvema mesecema posodil to knjigo, ampak nisem ... še prebral.
4 Grem k Borisu. Nekaj ... moram povedati.
5 Kje je darilo? Zaviti ... je treba.
6 Ali poznaš Simono?
   Ja, poznam ... , ampak že dolgo ... nisem videl.

Exercise 14

Change the meaning of the sentences below by replacing the word in italics with its opposite meaning:

1 Danes sem *dobre* volje.
2 *Prižgi* radio!
3 Ali je danes pošta *zaprta*?
4 Ta restavracija je zelo *daleč*, in *draga je*.
5 Zelo *slabo* govoriš slovensko.
6 Ta avtobus vozi *hitro* in *nikoli nima zamude*.

Exercise 15 ▄▄

Pronunciation exercise. You know that **s** and **z** are prepositions, both meaning 'with'. You use **s** before nouns which start with unvoiced consonants (these are **c, č, s, š, f, h, k, p, t**) and **z** before nouns which start with a vowel (**a, e, i, o, u**) or with a voiced consonant (these are **b, d, g, j, l, m, n, r, v, z, ž**).
   Here are some sentences using these prepositions. Read them out

svinčnik	pencil
led	ice

Ali prideš z mano, ali greš z njo?
S tabo pridem.
Ali bi čaj z limono?
Ne, čaj z mlekom bom.
Ali si zadovoljen z novo službo?
Rad jem solato s kisom in oljem.
Najraje pišem s svinčnikom.
Ali bi sok z ledom?

Dialogue for comprehension 🔘

Robert comes down to breakfast the next day at 10:30 and makes himself some black coffee. He has a headache. As he is recovering, Sergej and Davor come downstairs, looking even worse. Robert asks them a bit about Slovene celebrations. Why did they think Robert's birthday was special?

vzrok	reason

ROBERT: Ali vse rojstne dneve tako praznujete?
SERGEJ: Ne, tvoj rojstni dan je bil poseben.
ROBERT: Zakaj?
SERGEJ: Zato, ker boš kmalu šel nazaj v Anglijo. Ne moremo čakati na tvoj petdeseti rojstni dan, zaroko ali poroko.
ROBERT: Ali v Sloveniji praznujete državne praznike?
SERGEJ: Ja, ampak če ni nobenega... Tvoj rojstni dan je prišel zares v pravem času!
ROBERT: In kaj, če nima nihče rojstnega dneva?
SERGEJ: O, mi zmeraj najdemo kakšen vzrok za praznovanje.

Reference grammar

Adjectives

Since adjectives qualify nouns they also have three gender endings.
The same applies to possessive pronouns (e.g. his, her) – they must
agree with the noun in gender, case and number. For example:

m.	*dober* **dan**	good day
f.	*dobra* **večerja**	good supper
n.	*dobro* **jutro**	good morning

(see lessons 2, 7, 8)

Adverbs

In Slovene the neuter form of an adjective is also an adverb, for
example: *Dobro* **kuhaš!** (You cook well!).

(see lessons 7, 8)

There are adverbs which never change their form, for example
blizu (close by), **daleč**, (far away), **zelo** (very), **prvič** (for the first
time), and so on.

Article

Slovene has no article, neither indefinite (English 'a') nor definite
(English 'the').

Cases

Words in sentences or expressions stand in a relationship which is
determined by the meaning we want to put across. In English this

relationship is indicated by word order and prepositions whilst in Slovene it is indicated by case endings.

In the Slovene language there are six cases, each of them having a particular function. The nouns and other parts of the sentence which qualify them change with their function in a sentence.

The cases are:

1 nominative (**imenovalnik**) (see lesson 2);
2 genitive (**rodilnik**) (see lesson 9);
3 dative (**dajalnik**) (see lesson 6);
4 accusative (**tožilnik**) (see lesson 5);
5 locative (**mestnik**) (see lessons 6, 12);
6 instrumental (**orodnik**) (see lessons 3, 13).

Comparison

There are two ways of forming comparatives and superlatives of adjectives and adverbs:

1 The comparative is formed with suffixes **-ejši**, **-ši** and **-ji**, depending on the adjective. Superlatives in this case are formed by adding the prefix **naj** to the comparative.

hiter	hitrejši	najhitrejši
slab	slabši	najslabši

2 With **bolj** (more) and **najbolj** (the most) placed in front of the adjective or the adverb:

rjav	bolj rjav	najbolj rjav
razočaran	bolj razočaran	najbolj razočaran

(see lesson 13)

Conjunction words

There are two types of conjunction in Slovene: coordinate and subordinate. Among the most commonly used coordinate conjunctions are **in** (and), **ampak** (but), **ali ... ali** (either ... or), **ne samo ... ampak tudi** (not only ... but also).

Subordinate conjunctions always introduce a subordinate clause. The conjunction **da** (that) introduces almost all types of subordinate clause. Some others are **če** (if), **kadar**, **ko** (when).

(see lesson 13)

Declensions

All Slovene nouns are divided into four groups called declensions. They are:

First declension: into this group come nouns of feminine gender ending in **a**.
Second declension: into this group come nouns of feminine gender ending in a consonant.
Third declension: into this group come nouns of masculine gender.
Fourth declension: into this group come nouns of neuter gender.

All Slovene nouns can be declined in the singular, dual and plural.

Demonstrative pronouns

There are three types of demonstrative pronoun in Slovene:

1 **Ta**, **ta**, **to**
   tisti, **tista**, **tisto** (for things which are a little further away);
   oni, **ona**, **ono** (for things which are very far away).
2 **Tak/-a/-o** (indicates a quality).
3 **Tolik/-a/-o** (indicates quantity).

(see lesson 11)

Gender of nouns

Unlike English, the Slovene language distinguishes three genders: masculine, feminine and neuter. Masculine gender refers to male persons and most male animals; and female gender refers to female persons and most female animals. The gender of other inanimate objects and abstract nouns must be memorized. The endings in the nominative singular can be helpful in determining the gender:

1 nouns ending in **a** are usually feminine;
2 nouns ending in **e** or **o** are usually neuter;
3 nouns ending in a consonant are either masculine or neuter.

(see lesson 1)

Interrogative pronouns 'who' and 'what'

The interrogative pronouns **kdo?** (who?) and **kaj?** (what?) are declined in all six cases as follows:

1 **kdo** or **kaj**;
2 **koga** or **česa**;
3 **komu** or **čemu**;
4 **koga** or **kaj**;
5 **pri kom** or **pri čem**;
6 **s kom** or **s čim**.

Number

Nouns, adjectives and pronouns have different number forms. Unlike most languages, Slovene has, beside the singular and plural, dual forms.

Dual is an ancient Slavic form which has been lost in most languages but is still in use in Slovene. All Slovene nouns, verbs and pronouns have, in addition to the singular and the plural, the *dual form*, which is used when one talks about two things or two people. This increases the number of Slovene grammatical forms enormously.

Whilst in English you use the plural 'we', when you mean two people you need to use the *dual form* 'the two of us' in Slovene. In other words, Slovene has:

singular form (one person or one thing);
dual form (two people or two things) (see lesson 5);
plural form (more than two people or things).

Personal pronouns

When personal pronouns are the subject of a sentence they can be omitted because the ending of the verb indicates the person. In Slovene they are declined in the singular, dual and plural in six cases as follows:

Nom.	Gen.	Dat.	Acc.	Loc.	Instr.
Singular					
jaz	mene	meni	mene	pri meni	z mano
ti	tebe	tebi	tebe	pri tebi	s tabo
on	njega	njemu	njega	pri njemu	z njim
ona	nje	njej	njo	pri njej	z njo
ono	njega	njemu	njega	pri njemu	z njim
Dual					
midva	naju	nama	naju	pri nama	z nama
vidva	vaju	vama	vaju	pri vaju	z vama
onadva	njiju	njima	njiju	pri njiju	z njima
Plural					
mi	nas	nam	nas	pri nas	z nami
vi	vas	vam	vas	pri vas	z vami
oni	njih	njim	njih	pri njih	z njimi

Prepositions

Prepositions are words (such as 'to', 'from', 'without') which govern nouns or pronouns and adjectives modifying them. Particular prepositions are used in specific cases, with few exceptions, as follows:

Genitive: **brez** (without), **od** (of, since, from), **do** (to, until, as far as), **mimo** (past, by), **zaradi** (because of), **okoli** (about, around), **blizu** (close by), **sredi** (in the middle of), **iz** (from, of, out of), **izza** (from behind), **izpod** (from below), **iznad** (from above).

Dative: **k/h** (to), **kljub** (in spite of), **proti** (towards, to, against).

Accusative: **čez** (across, over), **med** (between, among), **skozi** (through). The prepositions **po** (for), **v** (in, to), **na** (on, upon, at, in), **ob** (at, on), **za** (for), **pred** (before, in front of), **pod** (under, below), **nad** (above, over) are used with the accusative case when they express an aim or a direction.

Locative: **pri** (at, by, near), **o** (about, at, on). The prepositions **na**, **ob**, **po** and **v** are used with the locative case unless they express an aim or a direction.

Instrumental: **z/s** (with, by means of). The prepositions **za**, **nad**, **pod**, **pred** and **med** are used with the instrumental case when they mean time.

Reporting speech

What someone originally said is usually reported with **reči**, **povedati**, **vprašati**. When reporting what other people have said you use the same tense as was used in the original statement. The only change is that of the personal pronoun.

(see lesson 12)

Sentence patterns

Forming questions

Questions in Slovene are formed:

1 With the question word **ali**, which is used in all tenses and for all persons:

Ali si danes doma? (present tense)
Ali je bil včeraj doma? (past tense)
Ali boste jutri doma? (future tense)

2 With interrogative pronouns. Some commonly used interrogative pronouns are

kdo	who	**kateri**	which, which one
kaj	what (see	**kako**	how
	interrogative	**koliko**	how much,
	pronouns		how many
	'who' and	**kakšen**	what kind of
	'what')	**čigav**	whose
kam	where to	**zakaj**	why
kje	where	**od kod, iz kod**	from where

3 By the intonation of your voice: e.g. **Danes si doma?**

Negative statements

Apart from the three verbs which form their negative in the present tense in one word (**nisem, nimam, nočem,**) you negate a present-tense statement by putting **ne** in front of the verb: **ne vem** (I don't know), **ne vidim** (I don't see).

In the past tense you negate a statement with the negative form of the auxiliary 'to be' and the participle in **l**: **nisem vedel** (I didn't know), **nisem videl** (I didn't see).

In the future tense you negate a statement by putting **ne** in front of the auxiliary 'to be' in the future tense and the participle in **l**: **ne bom vedel** (I won't know), **ne bom videl** (I won't see).

Double negative: the double negative is used in Slovene. This means that negative words such as 'never' and 'nothing' require a negative verb, for example:

Še nikoli nisem bil tukaj.	I've never been here before.
Nihče ga ni videl.	Nobody saw him.

Word order

By and large, word order is fairly flexible in Slovene. Because of the case and verb endings it means that you cannot get the meaning of the sentence wrong. There are, however, some rules.

Especially where unstressed words (enclitics) are used, the word order changes; enclitics can never stand at the beginning of a sentence.

The verb

The principal verbal forms in Slovene are the infinitive and the present tense of the first person singular ending in **m**. From them all other verbal forms are derived.

Biti *(to be)*

As in most languages the verb 'to be' is irregular. It is best to learn it by heart so that you can recognize and recall the form you need at all times.

Positive form		*Negative form*	
Singular			
1 **jaz sem**	I am	**jaz nisem**	I am not
2 **ti si**	you are	**ti nisi**	you are not
3 **on je**	he is	**on ni**	he is not

ona je	she is	**ona ni**	she is not
ono je	it is	**ono ni**	it is not

Dual

1	**midva sva**	we two are	**midva nisva**	we two are not
2	**vidva sta**	you two are	**vidva nista**	you two are not
3	**onadva sta**	they two are	**onadva nista**	they two are not

Plural

1	**mi smo**	we are	**mi nismo**	we are not
2	**vi ste**	you are	**vi niste**	you are not
3	**oni so**	they are	**oni niso**	they are not

The infinitive

Infinitives are those parts of a verb which do not indicate a person. In English they are preceded by 'to', as in 'to work'. Slovene infinitives end in **ti** or **či**, for example **delati**, **pisati**, **reči**. There are verbs such as 'must', 'to wish', 'to want' which are always followed by an infinitive.

(see lessons 4, 9)

When a verb is finite it must agree with the subject of the sentence in person and number (see tenses).

Participle in l

You form the participle in **l** by dropping the **ti** or **či** ending from the infinitive and adding:

- **-l** for masculine ending (e.g. **delal**);
- **-la** for feminine ending (e.g. **delala**);
- **-lo** for neuter ending (e.g. **delalo**);
- **-li** for plural ending (e.g. **delali**).

(see lessons 7, 8)

Supine

Like the infinitive, the supine is a verbal form which does not indicate a definite person. It differs from the infinitive only in that it does not have the final **i**. The supine is used after verbs of motion.

(see lesson 8)

Verbal noun

The Slovene verbal nouns correspond to English nouns ending in '-ing' ('writing, singing'). Most of the Slovene verbal nouns are formed by dropping the **ti** ending from the infinitive and adding **nje**. For example:

kaditi	*kajenje*
pisati	*pisanje*

(see lesson 11)

Verbal aspect: perfective and imperfective verbs

Perfective verbs usually mean a beginning or an end of an action, whilst imperfective verbs indicate a repeated or a continuous action. Perfective verbs are formed by changing the suffix of the imperfective verb (for example, **kupovati** – **kupiti**) or by dropping the prefix (for example, **odpotovati** – **potovati**). Some Slovene verbs have either only the perfective or only the imperfective form but most verbs appear in both forms.

(see lessons 8, 9)

Tenses

Slovene has four tenses:

1 present tense;
2 past tense;
3 future tense;
4 pluperfect tense.

Present tense: The present tense, together with the infinitive, is the main verbal form in Slovene. All other verbal forms are derived from these. The verb endings in the present tense are:

Singular	Dual	Plural
1 jaz dela*m*	midva dela*va*	mi dela*mo*
2 ti dela*š*	vidva dela*ta*	vi dela*te*
3 on dela (no ending, only stem)	onadva dela*ta*	oni dela*jo*

Past tense: The past tense is formed with the present tense of the verb 'to be' and the participle in **l**.

(see lesson 7)

Future tense: The future tense is formed with the future tense of the verb 'to be' and the past active participle. The forms of the verb 'to be' in the future are:

Singular	Dual	Plural
jaz *bom*	midva *bova*	mi *bomo*
ti *boš*	vidva *bosta*	vi *boste*
on *bo*	onadva *bosta*	oni *bodo*

(see lesson 8)

Pluperfect tense: the pluperfect tense exists in Slovene but it is not used in spoken Slovene. We have not looked into how it is formed in this book.

Mood

Mood is a term applied to verbs. Slovene has three moods:

1 *Indicative*, which expresses a fact in whichever tense.
2 *Imperative*, which expresses a command, advice, a wish. The imperative is formed from the present tense of the verb by dropping the **m** or **im** ending from the first person singular and adding different forms for different persons.

(see lesson 4)

3 *Conditional*, which expresses a hypothesis, e.g. something that might have happened. The conditional is formed with the word **bi**, which remains the same for all persons and numbers, and the participle in **l**.

(see lesson 10)

Voice

The term voice applies to verbs. Slovene has two voices: active and passive. The subject of an active verb is the noun which carries out the action, e.g. **Kuham kosilo** (I'm cooking a lunch), where the subject is shown in the verb ending. In the passive the subject receives the action, e.g. *Kosilo* **je kuhano** (*The lunch* is cooked). This is an example where you do use the passive in Slovene, but on the whole the passive is rarely used.

(see lesson 7)

Key to exercises

There is a variety of exercises in this book. Model answers are given below. In certain instances, such as when you are asked to construct an answer to a question, there is no single correct answer. It follows that in such cases an answer that differs from the model is not necessarily wrong.

Lesson 1

1

Živio, kako si? Zelo dobro, hvala, in ti? Zelo sem utrujen.

2

1 Dobro jutro. 2 Na svidenje. 3 Živio! 4 Lahko noč. 5 Dober dan. 6 Dober večer. 7 Lahko noč.

3

1 Živio, ali si v Italiji? Živio, ali si v Ljubljani? Živio, ali si na letališču? Živio, ali si v restavraciji? Živio, ali si v gostilni? 2 Ali je Milan v Nemčiji? Ali je Milan v Sloveniji? Ali je Milan v Angliji? Ali je Milan v Ameriki? Ali je Milan v Španiji? 3 Ali sem na letališču? Ali sem v Ljubljani? Ali sem v Sloveniji? Ali sem doma? Ali sem v gostilni?

4

1 Ja, on je utrujen. 2 Ja, ona je v Angliji. 3 Ja, ona je v Sloveniji. 4 Ja, mi smo danes doma.

5

si; dobro, ti; hvala, v; je; v.

6

1 je; 2 je; 3 smo; 4 sem; 5 je; 6 sem.

7

To je moja žena. To je Robert. To je moj prijatelj. To je gospod Koren. To je moj mož.

8 (translation of the statements)

1 I'm a bit tired today. 2 My wife is in Germany. 3 I am in England. 4 I'm not at work today. 5 I'm very busy today.

9

Ali je Bojan doma? Ali je gospa Kobal doma? Ali je Marija doma? Ali je gospod Koren doma? Ali je gospa Koren doma?

10

Gospod Dolenc ni v službi. Jana ni v službi. Samo ni v službi. Moja žena ni v službi. Gospa Koren ni v službi.

11

1 a; 2 a; 3 b; 4 a; 5 b.

12 (translation of the questions)

1 Are you in England? 2 Is your wife in Slovenia? 3 Are you tired today? 4 Are you at work? 5 Are you at home this evening?

13

1 d; 2 a; 3 b; 4 e; 5 c.

14

1 f; 2 n; 3 m; 4 f; 5 m; 6 m; 7 n.

Translation of the dialogue for comprehension

Mr Stopar:	Hello, Robert. How are you?
Robert:	I'm fine. And you?
Mr Stopar:	Oh, I'm not very well today. I'm very tired. Please come in.
Robert:	Thank you very much.
Mr Stopar:	Robert, this is my wife.
Robert:	Nice to meet you.
Mrs Stopar:	Nice to meet you Robert.
Mr Stopar:	And this is my friend, Tomaž Rataj.
Tomaž Rataj:	Hello, Robert. How are things going? Is your girlfriend here?
Robert:	No, she isn't here.
Tomaž Rataj:	Is she in Ljubljana?
Robert:	No she isn't in Slovenia. She is in England. Is your wife here?
Tomaž Rataj:	No, she is not. She is at work today.
Robert:	Is she in Ljubljana?
Tomaž Rataj:	Yes, she is at work at the Brnik airport. I also work at the Brnik airport but I am at home today. I am very tired.
Robert:	Oh, we're all very tired today.

Lesson 2

1

Tuesday – **torek**; on Saturday – **v soboto**; Wednesday – **sreda**; on Sundays – **ob nedeljah**; Friday – **petek**; Monday – **ponedeljek**.

2

Miran, ali imaš v torek čas? Miran, ali imaš v soboto čas? Miran, ali imaš ob nedeljah čas? Miran, ali imaš v petek čas? Miran, ali imaš ob ponedeljkih čas?

3

Žal mi je, ampak v torek nimam časa. Žal mi je, ampak ob petkih nimam časa. Žal mi je, ampak v nedeljo nimam časa. Žal mi je, ampak ob sobotah nimam časa. Žal mi je, ampak v ponedeljek nimam časa.

4

1 V ponedeljek sem v službi. V sredo sem v službi. V petek sem v službi.

2 Moja prijateljica je v torek doma. Moja prijateljica je v četrtek doma. Moja prijateljica je v soboto doma.

5

Sabina v torek nima časa. Denis nima sreče. Denis ob sredah nima časa. Sabina ima smolo. Sabina je v četrtek ves dan doma in tudi Denis ima v četrtek zvečer cas.

6

1 Patrice je Francoz, ampak njegova punca ni Francozinja. 2 Vittorio je Italijan, ampak njegova punca ni Italijanka. 3 Martin je Anglež, ampak njegova punca ni Angležinja. 4 Jaroslav je Rus, ampak njegova punca ni Rusinja. 5 Pedro je Španec, ampak njegova punca ni Španka.

7

1 To je Lynda. Ona je Angležinja. 2 To je Pamela. Ona je Američanka. 3 To je Gusti. Ona je Nemka. 4 To je Maria. Ona je Španka. 5 To je Laura. Ona je Italijanka.

8

Prosim!
Žal mi je, ampak jutri zvečer nimam časa.
Ja, prav. V četrtek sem ves dan doma.
Ali je Angležinja?

9

1 Darko, ali si v torek zvečer doma? 2 Lara, ali si v četrtek zvečer doma? 3 Peter, ali si v ponedeljek zvečer doma? 4 Darja, ali si v soboto zvečer doma? 5 Nataša, ali si v petek zvečer doma?

10

imaš; nimam; sem; imam; sem; je; je.

11

1 Ja, Tim ima prav. 2 Ne, ona nima sreče. 3 Ne, danes zvečer nimam časa. 4 Ja, to je res. 5 Ne, to ni prav. 6 Ja, to je važno.

12

1 To je nemogoče. 2 To ni res. 3 Ampak to je zelo pomembno. 4 To ni prav. 5 Imaš prav.

13

majhen avto; dobro jutro; lepa hiša; veliko mesto; težka lekcija; slabo vreme.

14

Španka	Slovenec	sreda	Anglija	policija
Francozinja	Anglež	ponedeljek	Francija	gasilci
Slovenka	Francoz	sobota	Nemčija	pomoč na cesti
Nemka	Američan	četrtek	Rusija	prva pomoč

Translation of the dialogue for comprehension

SECRETARY: Hello?

DENIS: Good day, Denis Golob speaking. Is Matej Novak there?

SECRETARY: Just a moment, please.

MATEJ: Hello?

DENIS: Hello Matej, Denis here.

MATEJ: Oh, you're back, how are you?

DENIS: Excellent. And how are you?

MATEJ:	I'm very busy. I have a lot to do at work and Robert is here in Slovenia.
DENIS:	Who is Robert?
MATEJ:	Robert is a friend of mine. He's from England. His mother is Slovene. And this weekend his girlfriend Jane is coming as well.
DENIS:	Oh, this Englishman is unlucky. The weather is very bad.
MATEJ:	You're right. It's been raining the whole week.
DENIS:	When is Jane coming?
MATEJ:	On Thursday afternoon.
DENIS:	Is she English?
MATEJ:	Yes, she's English.
DENIS:	Do you have anything planned for Friday evening?
MATEJ:	Not yet.
DENIS:	My friend Sabina is coming to see me. She speaks very good English. Come and have supper, all of you!
MATEJ:	Oh, thanks. Do you have time on Saturday? I have a new car and we are probably going for a trip somewhere.
DENIS:	But Matej, don't you have your football training on Saturdays?
MATEJ:	Yes, but that is not important!

Lesson 3

1

1 a, b; 2 b, c; 3 b, c; 4 a, b; 5 b, c.

2

1 Avtobus ima včasih zamudo. 2 Vlak ima včasih zamudo. 3 Letalo ima včasih zamudo.

3 (examples)

1 Oprostite, ali ima avtobus ob petkih vedno zamudo? 2 Ura je že deset. Zelo pozni smo! 3 Hvala. 4 Ne, Anglež sem.

4

The numbers are said as follows:

1 dvesto štiriinsedemdeset osemsto sedemintrideset; 2 dvesto triinpetdeset osemsto sedeminpetdeset; 3 dvesto sedeminštirideset dvesto štiriindevetdeset; 4 sto štiriinosemdeset devetsto šestindvajset; 5 dvesto štiriinšestdeset nič sedeminpetdeset.

You can also read out the numbers individually.

5

Danes je:

1 peti november, tisoč devetsto šestindevetdeset; 2 sedemindvajseti junij, tisoč devetsto štiriindevetdeset; 3 enaintrideseti december, tisoč devetsto triinsedemdeset; 4 dvanajsti maj, tisoč osemsto petinštirideset; 5 triindvajseti oktober, tisoč osemsto triinsedemdeset.

6

Ura je petnajst in petdeset minut. Ura je šestnajst in deset minut. Ura je dvaindvajset in trideset minut. Ura je dvanajst in petnajst minut. Ura je osemnajst in petinštirideset minut.

7

1 avtobus; 2 vlak; 3 avto; 4 letalo; 5 leto; 6 sobota; 7 ura; 8 mesec.

8

1 devetintrideset; 2 šestindvajset; 3 sedeminšestdeset; 4 dvainšestdeset; 5 dvaintrideset.

9 (examples)

1 Dober dan. 2 Ja, je. 3 Ne, Anglež sem. 4 Ja, malo razumem. Ali vi razumete angleško? Vidim, da imate angleški časopis. 5 Zanimivo. Ali ima veliko dela? 6 Če potrebuje pomoč ... moja telefonska številka v Sloveniji je nič enainšestdeset petsto šestinsedemdeset osemsto štiriindvajset.

10 (examples)

1 Študent sem. 2 Študiram slovenščino. 3 Kaj ona študira? 4 Kje študira? 5 V Angliji.

11

1 igralka; 2 novinar; 3 pisateljica; 4 frizerka; 5 if you are a male, študent; if you are a female, študentka.

12

(a) Moj oče ni učitelj. Moj oče ni profesor. Moj oče ni zdravnik. Moj oče ni novinar. Moj oče ni študent.

(b) Ali je tvoja mama študentka? Ali je tvoja mama prevajalka? Ali je tvoja mama novinarka? Ali je tvoja mama gospodinja? Ali je tvoja mama tajnica?

13 (examples)

1 To je John. Anglež je. Govori angleško in razume tudi malo slovensko. 2 To je Pauline. Američanka je. Govori angleško in razume tudi že malo slovensko. 3 To je Maria. Ona je Španka. Govori špansko in razume tudi malo slovensko. 4 To je Laura. Italijanka je. Govori italijansko in razume tudi malo slovensko. 5 To je Angela. Angležinja je. Govori angleško in razume tudi malo slovensko. 6 To je Darja. Slovenka je. Govori slovensko.

14

Telefonska številka. Časopis. Koliko je ura? Samo trenutek, prosim. Po poklicu sem študent. Ali ste vi Slovenec?

Translation of the dialogue for comprehension

ROBERT: Jane, hello, how are you? You look well.
JANE: I'm sorry I'm late. It's already 6 o'clock.
ROBERT: Don't worry. Are you tired?
JANE: Yes, very. I'm not coming by train ever again. Have you been waiting long?

ROBERT: Yes, since three. But I'm not bored. I know a few people here.

JANE: Do you often come here?

ROBERT: Yes, two or three times a week, usually in the afternoon. Sometimes I have lunch here. Are you hungry?

JANE: No, I'm only thirsty. And sleepy. You've been here for three months now. Do you speak Slovene well?

ROBERT: Yes, reasonably. I have problems sometimes. But many people here speak English.

JANE: You always write that you have a lot of work.

ROBERT: Yes, I'm always very busy. But tonight I'm free!

Lesson 4

1

1 Robert se nikoli ne uči slovensko. 2 Danes ni nikogar doma. 3 Jaz se nikoli ne počutim dobro. 4 Moj prijatelj se nikoli ne smeji. 5 Sabina nikoli nič ne ve.

2

1 Ime mi je (your name). 2 Pišem se (your surname). 3 V Ljubljani, to je moj naslov. 4 Ja, moja telefonska številka je nič enainšestdeset tristo petinsedemdeset tristo štiriinpetdeset. 5 Ne, tretjič. 6 Ne, delam tukaj. 7 Ja, zmeraj pomaga, če govoriš jezik.

3

1 slabe volje; 2 star slovar; 3 lahek jezik; 4 majhna knjigarna; 5 grdo mesto.

4

1 Kolikokrat na teden ima Robert slovenski tečaj? 2 Kdo je Jane? 3 Koliko je ura? 4 Čigava je ta knjiga? 5 Oprostite, kje je knjigarna?

5

(a) 1 pet; 2 mesto; 3 hiša; 4 avto; 5 slovar. Down you get **pošta**.

(b) 1 gospod; 2 učitelj; 3 osem; 4 pomoč; 5 prosim. Across you get **pismo**.

6

(a) 1 Ali nameravaš iti letos na dopust? 2 Ali želiš priti v kino danes zvečer? 3 Ali moraš začeti delati zgodaj jutri zjutraj?

(b) 1 Jaz ti lahko pomagam. 2 Trenutno se ne morem odločiti. 3 V petek zvečer ne morem iti na zabavo.

7

(a) 1 Zato, ker sem dobre volje. 2 Zato, ker se učim slovensko. 3 Zato, ker ima moj avtobus vsak dan zamudo.

(b). 1 Zakaj si slabe volje? 2 Zakaj greš na pošto? 3 Zakaj greš peš?

8

1 Ali lahko tukaj kadim? 2 Ali želiš iti danes v kino? 3 Ali lahko prideš danes zvečer? 4 Ali lahko kupim slovar v kiosku? 5 Ali grem lahko peš?

9

1 Ne skrbi! 2 Pohiti! 3 Oprostite! 4 Pridi sem! 5 Verjemi mi! 6 Počakaj!

10

1 Oprostite, kje je hotel Slon? 2 Oprostite, ali mi lahko poveste, kje je pošta? 3 Ali je avtobusna postaja kje blizu? 4 Ali je avtobus po navadi točen? 5 Ali veste, koliko je ura?

11

1 Hotel ni daleč. Lahko greste peš. 2 Trgovina je blizu. Tukaj za hotelom. 3 Avtobusna postaja ni daleč. Sto metrov na ravnost. 4 Žal mi je, ampak ne vem, kje je poštni nabiralnik. 5 Znamke lahko kupite v kiosku.

12

Oprostite, ali veste, kje je pošta? Prva ulica na levo. Tista pošta je zaprta. Ali želite kupiti znamke? Ja, in razglednice. Tukaj za vogalom je kiosk. Tam lahko kupite znamke. Ali grem lahko peš? Ja, ni daleč. Pet minut peš.

13

1 Kje je pošta? 2 Kje je poštni nabiralnik? 3 Kje je telefonska govorilnica? 4 Kje lahko kupim znamke? 5 Kje lahko telefoniram?

14

1 **četrtek** is the odd one (it is a day of the week). The other words are professions. 2 **Američan** is the odd one (it is in the masculine form). The others are all feminine. 3 **prideš** is the odd one (it is in the second person singular). The other verbs are in the first person singular. 4 **prevajalec** is the odd one (it is a profession). The other words are days of the week. 5 **velika** is the odd one (it is in the feminine form). The other adjectives are all in the masculine.

Translation of the dialogue for comprehension

MAN: Excuse me, do you know where the hotel Lev is?
ROBERT: Yes, I know. I live near there. In another hotel.
MAN: Is it far?
ROBERT: Hmm. . . . Are you walking?
MAN: Yes. But I can take a bus.
ROBERT: I am going in that direction. You can come with me. It's twenty minutes' walk.
MAN: Oh, thank you. I must reserve rooms in the hotel. I'm expecting a visit over the weekend.
ROBERT: Are you a tourist?
MAN: No, I'm here for a year's work. I teach English at the university.
ROBERT: Are you English?
MAN: No, I'm American.
ROBERT: Oh, so we can speak English!

Lesson 5

1

1 tukaj; 2 tja; 3 sem; 4 tukaj; 5 tam.

2

govorite; ste vi; stanujete; vi; imate; vam; vam; imate.

3

1 Midva delava od devetih do petih. 2 Po navadi imava kosilo ob enih. 3 Ob sobotah in nedeljah ne delava. 4 Domov prideva okoli sedmih. 5 Vsako leto greva avgusta na dopust.

4

2 Prvi vlak v Ljubljano pelje ob sedmih zjutraj. 3 Prvi vlak v Pariz pelje ob osmih zjutraj. 4 Prvi vlak v Amsterdam pelje ob petih zjutraj. 5 Prvi vlak v Ženevo pelje ob devetih zjutraj. 6 Prvi vlak v Prago pelje ob štirih zjutraj.

5

2 Zadnji avtobus v Ljubljano pelje ob sedmih zvečer. 3 Zadnji avtobus v Pariz pelje ob osmih zvečer. 4 Zadnji avtobus v Amsterdam pelje ob petih popoldne. 5 Zadnji avtobus v Ženevo pelje ob devetih zvečer. 6 Zadnji avtobus v Prago pelje ob štirih popoldne.

6

1 b; 2 b; 3 you are supposed to choose what you like best.

7

1 ju; 2 nas; 3 jo; 4 ga; 5 jih.

8

1 Ta kjiga je temno modra. 2 Njen slovar je rdeč. 3 Ta hotel je siv. 4 Njegov novi avto je svetlo rjav. 5 Moje staro vozniško dovoljenje je roza.

9

1 mleko; 2 čaj; 3 kava; 4 sreda; 5 denar; 6 limona; 7 banka; 8 kavarna.

10

1 V sredo moram iti na banko in zamenjati denar. 2 Avgusta grem v Italijo. 3 V četrtek imam sestanek v Ljubljani. 4 Vprašati moram, kdaj pelje zadnji vlak v Milano. 5 Moja tajnica je decembra v Nemčiji.

11

1 Angleži radi igrajo nogomet. 2 Ann rada plava. 3 Tomaž rad igra tenis. 4 Jaz rad igram badminton. 5 Moja sestra rada smuča.

12

1 znamka za pismo; 2 potni list; 3 dežnik. 4 športno igrišče; 5 jesen.

13

1 official document; 2 ID; 3 postcard; 4 driving licence; 5 church.

14 (examples)

1 dober, zanimiv, slab; 2 lepo, slabo, grdo; 3 težko, zanimivo, pomembno; 4 težek, tuj, lep; 5 črna, bela, sladka; 6 dobra, stara, bogata.

Translation of the dialogue for comprehension

BARBARA: Waitress, can I order please?
WAITRESS: Yes, of course. What would you like?
BARBARA: A white coffee, a black coffee, a juice and a tea with lemon.

NICK: Tomaž, do you often go to the leisure centre?
TOMAŽ: Yes, I often go there in the winter. Now in spring I spend
          more time outside. Nick, do you play cricket? I don't
          know anything about this game.
NICK: I don't play cricket but a lot of my friends play this game.
TOMAŽ: I can't understand. . . . It seems to me to be so boring . . .
NICK: If you think about it, tennis is also a boring game.
TOMAŽ: Oh, no, if you want we can go and play it tomorrow.
NICK: Yes, and Barbara and Ann can go swimming.

Lesson 6

1

1 Tomaž išče dežnik. 2 Njegov plašč je v dnevni sobi na stolu.
3 Njegov dežnik je v kopalnici. 4 Njegov ključ je v kuhinji na mizi.
5 Hrana za psa je v hladilniku.

2

1 Monika, ali greš na pošto? 2 Petra, ali greš na banko? 3 Oto,
ali greš na sestanek? 4 Nadja, ali greš k prijatelju? 5 Sebastjan, ali
greš k zdravniku? 6 Anja, ali greš v trgovino? 7 Sergej, ali greš po
časopis?

3 (examples)

1 Kaj iščeš? 2 Mislim, da je tvoj plašč v dnevni sobi. 3 Mrzlo je.
Temperatura je minus dve stopinji celzija in vetrovno je. 4 Ja. Ali
veš, kje je ključ od avta? 5 Ali si pripravljen? Mudi se nama. Ura
je že sedem!

4

1 že; 2 še; 3 še; 4 že, še; 5 šele.

5

1 Ali mi lahko pomagaš jutri popoldne? 2 Ali lahko pridem danes
zvečer k tebi? Nekaj ti moram povedati. 3 Ali mi lahko svetuješ,
kaj naj naredim? 4 Pokaži mi tvoj novi plašč! 5 Ali se ti mudi?

6

1 Tomaž in Barbara sta na avtobusni postaji. 2 Avtobus številka pet pelje na letališče. 3 Zato ker je petek in gredo vsi iz mesta. 4 Ne, Tomaž in Barbara gresta na obisk v Anglijo. Tam imata prijatelje. 5 Taksist jima zaželi prijeten dopust in srečo pot.

7

(a) Čakam na avtobus. Čakam na vlak. Čakam mojo prijateljico.
(b) Matic čaka svojo punco. Matic čaka Sonjo. Matic čaka na letalo.

8

1 V torem moram iti k zdravniku. 2 Jutri zjutraj moram iti po časopis. 3 Silva mora iti popoldne na pošto. 4 Danes zvečer grem na obisk k prijatelju. 5 V soboto moram iti po kruh in mleko.

9

1 Ta kozarec je prazen. 2 Na jugu je po navadi toplo. 3 Ta ulica je ozka. 4 Moja soseda Larisa je zelo prijazna. 5 London je veliko mesto.

10

2 V Parizu je danes toplo. Temperatura je sedemnajst stopinj celzija. 3 V Berlinu danes dežuje. Temperatura je dvanajst stopinj celzija. 4 V Moskvi je danes mrzlo. Temperatura je minus dvaindvajset stopinj celzija. 5 V Lizboni je danes sončno. Temperatura je devetnajst stopinj celzija. 6 V Rimu je danes vroče. Temperatura je osemindvajset stopinj celzija.

11

Dober dan, kako si?
Dobro, hvala, in ti?
Ne počutim se dobro. Vse me boli.
Pojdi k zdravniku!
Ja, nameravam iti jutri popoldne.
Mimogrede, Alenka te lepo pozdravlja.
Hvala enako!

12

(a) 1 igrati; 2 morati; 3 svetovati; 4 pomagati; 5 priti; 6 misliti; 7 stati; 8 imeti; 9 govoriti.

(b) 1 Kaditi prepovedano; 2 Parkiranje prepovedano; 3 Nehaj govoriti; 4 Oprostite, vstop prepovedan; 5 Srečno pot in prijeten dopust.

13

1 Mudi se nam. 2 Mudi se ti. 3 Mudi se mu. 4 Mudi se ji. 5 Mudi se vam.

14

1 **Dežnik** is the odd one out. The other words are rooms of a house or flat. 2 **Radio** is the odd one out. The other words are all food items. 3 **Sporočilo** is the odd one out. The other words describe the weather. 4 **Sosed** is the odd one out. The other words are verbs. 5 **Osmi** is the odd one out. It is an ordinal number.

Translation of the dialogue for comprehension

BARBARA: I'm going to the opera in London for the first time.
ANN: Do you go in Ljubljana often?
BARBARA: No, Tomaž doesn't like opera. But we go to the cinema often. Are we going by bus now?
ANN: No, we're going by train. I have a car but the traffic here is terrible. My car is almost always in the garage.
BARBARA: Yes, the traffic here is really very heavy. And all these cars on the left side of the road. It always seems to me there will be an accident any minute.
ANN: You're not used to it. Do you drive a lot?
BARBARA: No, hardly every. Tomaž has the car all the time. He drives to work. And when we go somewhere together he drives. Are we in a hurry?
ANN: No, the performance starts at eight, now it's only 6 o'clock.
BARBARA: Do we have time for another coffee?
ANN: Yes, if you want we can have a coffee somewhere in town.

Lesson 7

1 (examples)

1 Kako je bilo? 2 Ali je deževalo? 3 Junija? 4 Ampak na severu je po navadi tako. 5 Jaz grem tudi na jug oktobra. 6 V Grčijo.

2

1 Zgodaj zjutraj, ob šestih. 2 Ne, popoldne sem bil pri prijatelju. 3 Pozno zvečer. 4 Ne, na žalost nimam časa. Danes popoldne ob štirih imam sestanek. 5 Ne, jutri zvečer grem v kino.

3

1 Ne, danes dopoldne sem imel sestanek. 2 Ne, prejšnji teden sem bil na dopustu. 3 Zelo lepo vreme smo imeli. 4 Ja, zelo nam je bilo všeč. 5 Ja, zgodaj zjutraj je prišla domov.

4

1 Sonja bere počasi in razločno. 2 Pavarotti poje glasno. 3 V gledališču je bilo zanimivo. 4 Na dopustu sem se imela zelo dobro. 5 Ta vaja je bila lahka.

5

1 Avstrija; 2 Hrvaška; 3 Italija; 4 Madžarska.

6

1 d; 2 e; 3 b; 4 a; 5 c.

7

1 slabo; 2 ozka; 3 nezanimiv; 4 prepričana; 5 lačen, žejen.

8

1 Ali je Gregor vaš brat? 2 Ne on je moj bratracec. Ampak že zelo dolgo ga nisem videl. 3 Jaz ga poznam. V šolo je hodil z mojim sinom. Ali vi poznate Ireno? 4 Ja, ona je šla za eno leto v Anglijo.

5 Prišla je že nazaj. 6 Zakaj ni ostala za eno leto? 7 Oh, jaz vem, ampak vam ne morem povedati.

9

1 Vreme je bilo zelo slabo, ampak imeli smo se lepo. 2 Bilo je zelo mrzlo, ampak na severu je zmeraj tako. 3 Moj prijatelj je že doma, ampak nisem ga še videl. 4 Avgusta grem na dopust, ampak ne vem še kam. 5 Ves dan sem delal, ampak nisem utrujen.

10

1 sem se poročil; 2 moje staro stanovanje, majhno hišo; 3 Moji starši; 4 so nama ga ukradli; 5 Letos, noseča.

11

1 Kaj te boli? 2 Pokliči me jutri! 3 Kaj se ji je zgodilo? 4 Kje si jo spoznal? 5 Iz kod je?

12

A: Ali si že videla ta film?
B: Ja, ali ti nisem povedala?
A: Mogoče, ampak ne spomnim se. Pozabila sem. Ali ti je bil všeč?
B: Ne, ni mi bil všeč.
A: Zakaj ne?
B: Zdel se mi je dolgočasen.

13

1 semafor; 2 grlo; 3 teta; 4 zob; 5 vaja; 6 pes; 7 zahod; 8 hčerka; 9 plaža; 10 kitara. At 11 across you get **fotoaparat**.

14

(a) 1 malo; 2 visok, suh; 3 slabo; 4 ozka; 5 težka.

(b) 1 Eno *veliko* pivo, prosim. 2 Njen fant je zelo *majhen* in *debel*. 3 Imeli smo *lepo* vreme. 4 Ta ulica je zelo *široka*. 5 Ta vaja ni bila *lahka*.

Translation of the dialogue for comprehension

BARBARA: Anita, hello. I must tell you something, that is to say, I must ask you something.

ANITA: Yes, what?

BARBARA: Yesterday on the way home Tomaž met Sandra, quite by chance. Did Sandra tell Sabina anything about the trip?

ANITA: Do you mean Emilio?

BARBARA: Oh, is his name Emilio?

ANITA: Yes, Sandra says that he has long hair. She saw the photographs. He apparently writes poetry and plays the guitar.

BARBARA: Does Eva knows anything about this?

ANITA: I doubt it. But Sandra wants to go back to Italy.

BARBARA: Poor Eva. I'm sure she doesn't know anything. She only told me how they stole her camera.

ANITA: It wasn't stolen. She gave it to him on the last day, as a memento.

Lesson 8

1

1 Soba v hotelu je za Roberta premajhna. 2 Matej je včeraj zvečer srečal Sabino. 3 V Sloveniji je poleti za Roberta prevroče. 4 Sabinina teta oddaja sobe. 5 Robert ni našel plana mesta.

2

1 Moj avto je prestar za na cesto. 2 Moje stanovanje je pozimi premrzlo. 3 Ekspresso kava je zame premočna. 4 Jaz nikoli ne vozim prehitro. 5 Tista restavracija je bila predraga.

3

1 Ali si kupil hišo ali stanovanje? 2 Ali je bilo drago? 3 Prepričan sem, da imaš sedaj veliko dela. 4 Kdaj se seliš? 5 Hmm ... ne zavidam ti!

4

1 stanovanje; 2 pisalno mizo; 3 teta; 4 razpolago; 5 pekarno.

5

1 kuhinja; 2 elementi; 3 sesalec; 4 štedilnik; 5 miza; 6 stol; 7 spalnica; 8 pohištvo; 9 kavč; 10 hladilnik.

6

1 Kupil si bom tri knjige. 2 Ob desetih dopoldne bom šel v kavarno. 3 Ves popoldan se bom učil slovenščino. 4 V mesto se bom peljal z avtobusom. 5 Od sedmih do osmih zjutraj bom igral tenis.

7

Davor: Kje je stanovanje?
Sergej: Blizu centra. Ali ga hočeš priti pogledat?
Davor: Ali si danes zvečer prost?
Sergej: Ja, če želiš, se lahko dobiva v centru.
Davor: Ja, kje?
Sergej: V kavarni 'Marija'.
Davor: Koliko stane najemnina?
Sergej: Zvečer ti bom vse povedal.

8 (translation of the sentences)

1 I live in a block of flats. 2 I have a two-room flat. 3 My flat is in the centre of the town. 4 I live on my own. 5 I don't have the kitchen.

9

1 bo; 2 deževalo; 3 od; 4 do; 5 V četrtek; 6 popoldne; 7 Temperature; 8 okoli; 9 Dopoldne; 10 sonce.

10

2 Ali bo Davor naslednje leto šel na dopust? 3 Ali bo Sabina jutri zvečer šla v gledališče? 4 Ali bo Sergej danes zvečer šel v kino? 5 Ali bo Davor jutri zjutraj šel k zdravniku? 6 Ali bosta Barbara in Tomaž septembra šla v Španijo?

11

1 Lahko se dobiva v kavarni, če je to bolje zate. 2 Stanovanje je bilo veliko, ampak ni bilo opremljeno. 3 Robert ima vse svoje knjige in papirje na tleh, zato ker je soba v hotelu za njega premajhna. 4 Povedal sem ji, da nisem imel časa. 5 Pridi z nami v kino, če imaš čas.

12

1 e; 2 d; 3 f; 4 g; 5 a; 6 h; 7 b; 8 c.

13

1 Kaditi prepovedano! 2 Parkiranje prepovedano! 3 Nehaj govoriti! 4 Vstop prepovedan! 5 Srečno pot in prijeten dopust!

14

1 prehitro; 2 predaleč; 3 predraga; 4 premrzlo; 5 prevroče.

Translation of the dialogue for comprehension

JANE: Hello?
ROBERT: Jane, it's me.
JANE: Oh, how are you?
ROBERT: I'm in a good mood. I'm finally moving!
JANE: Where? When?
ROBERT: I think I'll be there next week. Matej helped me. His friend, actually his aunt, lets flats. Last week someone moved out and she has a three-bedroom flat available at the moment.
JANE: Do you like it? Is it in the centre?
ROBERT: Yes, it's quite large and furnished. I'll have a kitchen, very small bathroom and three rooms. I need a desk.
JANE: Oh, I'm pleased.
ROBERT: By the way, apparently it always smells nicely of bread. Underneath is a bakery.
JANE: So when I come next you'll prepare me a fresh breakfast.
ROBERT: Of course!

Lesson 9

1

2 Ali si zapeljal avto v garažo? 3 Ali si dal mleko v hladilnik?
4 Ali si odnesel dežnik v kopalnico? 5 Ali si dal časopis na mizo?
6 Ali si postavil rože v vazo?

2

2 Avto je v garaži. 3 Mleko je v hladilniku. 4 Dežnik je v kopalnici. 5 Časopis je na mizi. 6 Rože so v vazi.

3 (examples)

SERGEJ: Ali si bil v turistični agenciji?
DAVOR: Ja, bil sem. Vprašal sem, koliko stane letalska vozovnica.
SERGEJ: Ali je poceni ali draga?
DAVOR: Zelo draga. Mislim, da je predraga.
SERGEJ: Ali nimajo čarterskih poletov?
DAVOR: Ne, poleti jih nimajo.

4

2 Ali ti je treba kaditi? 3 Ali ti je treba rezervirati karte en mesec
v naprej? 4 Ali ti je treba iti v kino dvakrat na teden? 5 Ali ti je
treba delati vsak večer? 6 Ali ti je treba poslušati glasbo ves dan?

5

2 Ne, ni mi treba kaditi, ampak jaz rad kadim. 3 Ne, ni mi jih treba
rezervirati en mesec v naprej, ampak jaz jih rad v naprej
rezerviram. 4 Ne, ni mi treba iti v kino dvakrat na teden, ampak
jaz rad hodim v kino. 5 Ne, ni mi treba delati vsak večer, ampak
jaz rad delam ob večerih. 6 Ne, ni mi treba poslušati glasbe ves
dan, ampak jaz rad poslušam glasbo.

6

1 veš; 2 poznaš, poznam; 3 znaš, znam; 4 vedel; 5 vem, vem.

7

1 odločiti; 2 prodal; 3 plačal; 4 posoditi; 5 kupim.

8

1 Sabina študira ekonomijo. 2 Tanja študira pravo. 3 Milena študira zgodovino. 4 Ana študira matematiko. 5 Janez študira biologijo.

9 (translation of what you are supposed to fill in)

1 Your surname; 2 Your name; 3 Your sex (m., f.); 4 Your nationality; 5 Your date of birth; 6 The place of your birth; 7 Your permanent address; 8 Your signature; 9 The date.

10

1 b; 2 c; 3 a; 4 b; 5 a.

11

1 Ura je tri četrt na eno. 2 Ura je četrt na deset. 3 Ura je pol osmih. 4 Ura je tri četrt na štiri. 5 Ura je tri četrt na šest. 6 Ura je pol petih.

12

kava – coffee; **kruh** – bread; **čaj** – tea; **mleko** – milk; **jajca** – eggs; **krompir** – potatoes; **sir** – cheese.

13

Ali lahko dobim:
1 en kilogram kruha; 2 dva litra mleka; 3 en jogurt; 4 deset dekagramov sira; 5 pol kilograma jabolk.

14 (examples)

1 težek kovček, težka lekcija, težko delo; 2 lep dan, lepa hiša, lepo vreme; 3 dober krompir, dobra zelenjava, dobro jabolko; 4 nezanimiv film, nezanimiva knjiga, nezanimivo delo; 5 majhen radio, majhna restavracija, majhno darilo.

Translation of the dialogue for comprehension

SERGEJ: Good evening, Come in!

ROBERT: No, unfortunately I can't. I only came to tell you that I can't stop today. I'm going to supper. Do you know Sabina and her aunt?

SERGEJ: No, I don't know her. I only moved in last month. But Boštjan and Davor know them. Sabina studies law.

ROBERT: Yes, Matej mentioned that she was a student. Apparently she has been in the first year for three years already. But this doesn't matter. I wanted to ask you if you'd like to go out to supper on Friday evening. I'm inviting you.

SERGEJ: Yes, but on Fridays we usually go to a café where they play jazz. If you wish you can come too.

ROBERT: Yes, we can first go and have something to eat.

SERGEJ: Come in for five minutes! Let's ask Boštjan and Davor!

ROBERT: I really can't. I'm late already!

Lesson 10

1

jabolka – apples; **hruške** – pears; **marelice** – apricots; **slive** – plums; **borovnice** – bilberries; **jagode** – strawberries.

2

Dobro jutro, ali lahko dobim:
1 en kilogram jabolk; 2 pol kilograma marelic; 3 štiri hruške; 4 dve breskvi; 5 en ananas.

3 (examples)

1 Dober dan, mizo za dva, prosim. 2 Ali je tista miza pri oknu prosta? 3 Ja, ali lahko dobiva jedilni list? 4 Ali nama lahko kaj priporočate? 5 Jaz bi rad nekaj malega. Pogledal bom, kaj imate. Ali lahko naročim pijačo?

4 (examples)

1 Kaj boste pili? 2 Ali imaš rad testenine? 3 Ali lahko dobim jedilni list? 4 Ali si lačen? 5 Ali bi kavo?

5

1 ampak; 2 niti, niti; 3 zato ker; 4 da; 5 zato; 6 če.

6 (example)

Gospod natakar, jaz bi rad naročil:
eno zelenjavno juho; en dunajski zrezek, krompir in zeleno solato;
eno sadno kupo; in kozarec rdečega vina.

7

1 sol in poper; 2 malo kruha; 3 še eno zeleno solato; 4 nož in vilico;
5 servijeto.

8

1 ... bi gledal televizijo. 2 ... bi ti povedala. 3 ... bi ti priporočal,
da greš v kino. 4 ... bi ga poklical. 5 ... bi mi lahko prinesel tisto
knjigo.

9

1 c; 2 e; 3 f; 4 a; 5 b; 6 d.

10

1 jedilni list; 2 zelje; 3 zrezek; 4 sladoled; 5 žlica; 6 vilica; 7 nož;
8 sir; 9 mleko; 10 riž; 11 solata; 12 torta.

11

1 Če bi poslušala, bi slišala. 2 Če bi vedel, bi ti povedal. 3 Če bi
jo videl, bi jo pozdravil. 4 Če okno ne bi bilo odprto, ne bi bilo
tako mrzlo. 5 Če bi imel tvojo telefonsko številko, bi te poklical.

12

1 He recommends him their fish because it is always fresh. 2 Oto
had fish for lunch every day that week and he wanted to order
something else. 3 He eventually orders a salad, some bread and a
fruit juice.

13

1 Oprostite, natakar, ta juha je neslana. 2 Oprostite, natakar, ta solata je prekisla. 3 Oprostite, natakar, ta zrezek ni dovolj pečen. 4 Oprostite, natakar, ta riž je preslan. 5 Oprostite, natakar, ta zelenjava sploh ni kuhana.

14

1 **Jabolko** is the odd word out. The other words are pieces of cutlery. 2 **Malica** is the odd word out. The other words are pieces of furniture. 3 **Večer** is the odd word out. The other words are meals. 4 **Kosilo** is the odd word out. The other words are courses. 5 **Kruh** is the odd word out. The other words are adjectives describing food.

Translation of the dialogue for comprehension

DAVOR: Robert, did you like it?

ROBERT: I liked the fish very much. I'm not really used to having it prepared in this way. In England you get it fried in breadcrumbs with chips. The one here was definitely better. But I thought the wine was rather acidic.

DAVOR: Yes, we usually drink this sort of wine with a bit of mineral water.

ROBERT: You mean you mix it?

DAVOR: Yes, this is called 'špricer'.
Robert, when will you cook a typical English dish for us?

ROBERT: If I'd had more time I would've done it a long time ago. One evening next week!

DAVOR: Do you enjoy cooking?

ROBERT: Yes, I enjoy making sweets most. I'll make a bread pudding.

DAVOR: What?

ROBERT: You'll see!

Lesson 11

1

(a) 1 Komu sem jaz podoben-bna? 2 Komu si ti podoben-bna?
3 Komu je podobna Ana?

(b) 1 Moj brat je podoben mami. 2 Moja sestrična je podobna moji
teti.

2

1 lekarno; 2 počutil; 3 si; 4 tablete; 5 ga; 6 mu; 7 videl.

3

1 kupimo; 2 odločiti; 3 govorim; 4 lahko; 5 ne morejo.

4

usta – mouth; **zob** – tooth; **lasje** – hair; **hrbet** – back; **obraz** – face;
vrat – neck; **oko** – eye; **telo** – body.

5

1 Zob me boli. 2 Želodec me boli. 3 Ušesa me bolijo. 4 Hrbet me
boli. 5 Vse me boli.

6

1 berem; 2 igram; 3 poslušam; 4 gledam; 5 učim se; 6 kuham.

7

1 V kolikor jaz vem, je bolan. 2 V kolikor jaz vem, ima gripo.
3 V kolikor jaz vem, bo še enkrat telefoniral. 4 V kolikor jaz vem,
bo šel k zdravniku. 5 V kolikor jaz vem, bo jutri tukaj.

8

(a) 1 Zato, ker sem bil bolan ... 2 Zato, ker so bile cene visoke
...

(b) 1 Komaj čakam, da bo jutri. 2 Komaj čakam, da pride pomlad.

9

1 d; 2 e; 3 c; 4 b; 5 a.

10 (examples)

1 Žal mi je, nimam časa. V službi imam veliko dela in konec tedna dobim obisk. 2 Na žalost ne morem. Že ves teden se slabo počutim. Prehlajen/-a sem. Glava me boli in grlo.

11

N	O	G	A	A	T	N	O	S	L
P	R	S	T	V	Č	O	V	Z	K
U	T	Š	R	Z	A	U	I	O	O
S	I	Ž	E	L	O	D	E	C	B
T	E	Z	B	L	K	B	R	M	R
A	P	O	U	H	O	D	D	M	A
N	T	B	H	K	R	I	Ž	A	Z

12 (examples)

1 Danes ga ni v pisarni. 2 Bolje je, če pokličete naslednji teden. Bolan je. 3 Gripo ima. 4 Žal mi je, nimam je. Danes zjutraj je telefoniral in rekel je, da bo nazaj v ponedeljek. 5 Bom, hvala. Zapisala si bom. Oprostite, povejte mi še enkrat, kdo kliče?

13

(a) 1 (i); 2 (iii); 3 (iv); 4 (v); 5 (ii).

(b) 1 Na trgu lahko kupiš zelenjavo. 2 V lekarni dobiš zdravila. 3 V trgovini lahko kupiš kruh in mleko. 4 Na pošti dobiš znamke in pisma. 5 Na banki lahko zamenjaš denar.

14

1 konec filma; 2 konec tedna; 3 predsednik države; 4 člani družine; 5 center mesta; 6 začetek predstave.

Translation of the dialogue for comprehension

ROBERT: Excuse me, will they call me?
WOMAN: Yes, haven't you been here before?
ROBERT: No, the doctor came to my house last week.
WOMAN: Did anything terrible happen to you?
ROBERT: No, I had flu. But I could hardly move. Everything hurt and I was feeling dizzy. My neighbour called the doctor.
WOMAN: Yes, yes, I know that flu. A colleague of mine has already been at home for two weeks. She is sneezing, coughing and apparently all her bones hurt. Do you also feel like that?
ROBERT: No, I've already recovered. I'm feeling much better. I only came for a check-up.
WOMAN: You were lucky. You're still young! That helps!

Lesson 12

1

1 V sredo popoldne sem na sestanku. 2 Za v petek imam nekaj v planu. 3 Naslednji teden nisem v mestu. 4 V četrtek zvečer grem v kino. 5 Ob ponedeljkih po navadi igram košarko.

2 (examples)

1 Sabine ni doma. Kdo kliče? 2 Ne, Sabina ima začasno službo na Bledu. 3 Dela v hotelu ob jezeru, v recepciji. 4 Dva meseca, do oktobra. 5 Pravi, da, ampak ima veliko dela. Sedaj je turistična sezona.

3

1 začasno; 2 v enem hotelu; 3 v recepciji; 4 zasedene; 5 Sergej.

4 (examples)

1 Ali vas lahko nekaj vprašam po angleško? 2 Ali mi lahko poveste, kdaj je tukaj turistična sezona? 3 Ali mislite, da boste imeli kakšno prosto sobo avgusta? 4 Ali mi lahko poveste, kakšne so cene? 5 Ali lahko sedaj rezerviram sobo?

5

(a) 1 Jaz bi rad imel hišo ob jezeru. 2 Jaz bi rad imel hišo ob glavni cesti. 3 Jaz bi rad imel hišo ob reki.

(b) 1 Včeraj sem bil pri zdravniku. 2 Včeraj sem bil pri frizerju. 3 Včeraj sem bil pri moji mami.

6 (examples)

1 Dober večer, ali imate kakšno prosto sobo? 2 Za eno noč. Kakšna je cena? Ali želite moj potni list? 3 Ja, seveda. Kdaj je zajtrk? 4 Ali veste morda, kje bi lahko dobil kaj malega za pojest? 5 Mimogrede, ali je v moji sobi telefon?

7

1 Luč v kopalnici ne dela. 2 Televizija je pokvarjena. 3 Okno v sobi se ne odpre. 4 Vrata v kopalnici se ne zaklenejo. 5 V moji sobi ni telefona.

8

1 Kdo je to? 2 Kdaj greste k zdravniku? 3 Kako vam je ime? 4 Kje je avtobusna postaja? 5 Zakaj je Nadja ostala doma?

9

Prosim?
Dobro jutro, ali je to hotel 'Lev'?
Ja, je. Želite, prosim?
Rad bi rezerviral sobo za naslednji konec tedna.
Za koliko oseb?
Za dve osebi.
Trenutek, prosim. Žal mi je, ampak naslednji konec tedna je vse zasedeno. Poizkusite hotel 'Slon'.

Tja sem že poklical in tudi oni imajo vse zasedeno. Ali imate morda informacije o privatnih sobah?
Ne, pokličite turistične informacije. Njihovo številko imam, če želite.
Tisto številko imam sam. Hvala, nasvidenje.

10 (examples)

1

Oprostite, ali veste kje je restavracija 'Kaj'?
Ne, na žalost ne vem.

2

Kaj iščeš?
Iščem moj dežnik.
Jaz sem ga videla v kopalnici.

3

Katero restavracijo mi priporočate?
Za vogalom je ena nova, znana po ribah.
Ali je draga ali poceni?

11

(a) 1 Vprašal sem, če imajo prosto dvoposteljno sobo za eno noč. 2 Vprašal sem, kakšna je cena. 3 Vprašal sem, kdaj je zajtrk.

(b) 1 Rekel je, da imajo dve enoposteljni sobi. 2 Rekel je, da je cena enaka. 3 Rekel je, da sta sobi veliki in lepo opremljeni.

12

1 Sergej ji je rekel, naj več študira. 2 Boštjan ji je rekel, naj ne dela to poletje. 3 Davor ji je rekel, naj se ne druži s Sandro. 4 Sabina je rekla Sergeju, naj se briga za sebe. 5 Sabina je rekla Boštjanu, naj si poišče punco.

13 (example)

Dobro jutro gospod direktor. Monika Černe je telefonirala. Danes je ne bo v službo. Bolna je. Že od včeraj se zelo slabo počuti. Kašlja, kiha in glava jo boli. Ponoči je bruhala. Dopoldne bo šla k zdravniku in popoldne bo še enkrat poklicala.

14

avto – garaža; omara – hiša; receptor – hotel; pivo – gostilna; zrezek
– restavracija; znamka – pošta; knjiga – knjigarna.

Translation of the dialogue for comprehension

ROBERT: I hope this private house will be better than the one
where I stayed the night last year.
SERGEJ: What was wrong?
ROBERT: Everything was wrong. It was in the winter, it was very
cold and the heating didn't work. The window in my
room didn't close. The light in the bathroom was broken
and I had a shower in the dark. The shower worked but
as soon as someone above us had a shower the water
stopped running. Something was also wrong with the
lavatory: the bathroom smelt. And around the corner
there was a pub, open all night. The music was very loud.
No one could sleep.
SERGEJ: Why didn't you all go to that pub?
ROBERT: I had worked all day and I was tired in the evening.
I wanted to have a rest. My friends were also tired.
SERGEJ: I'll be looking after the music tonight. You aren't tired
and we shall all have a party.
ROBERT: Aren't we going to the lake tomorrow early in the morning?
SERGEJ: Yes, don't you know that every lake looks best from the
terrace of some café?

Lesson 13

1

1 Sandra bo zavila darilo za Roberta. 2 Zato, ker jih ni našla. 3
Ne vem. 4 Kozarci bi morali biti v eni škatli v dnevni sobi. 5 Če
se bodo spomnili.

2

1 Ne spomnim se, koliko sem plačal za to knjigo. 2 Ne spomnim
se, kako se piše moja tajnica. 3 Spomni me, telefonirati moram
mami! 4 Spomni me, iti moram na banko! 5 Ne spomnim se, kako
se to reče po slovensko.

3

1 Avto sem parkiral pred hišo. 2 V službo sem šel z vlakom. 3 Ja. Med malico sem šel na banko. 4 Jutri ne pridem domov pred šesto. 5 Prišel bom s tabo.

4

They bought him a cookery book because he once mentioned to them that he liked cooking. The book is a vegetarian cookery book because Sabina knows that Robert is a vegetarian.

5

Sok je v hladilniku. Pivo je v hladilniku. Mineralna voda je na mizi. Belo vino je v kleti. Rdeče vino je v eni škatli v kuhinji.

6

hlače – trousers; **bluza** – blouse; **kravata** – tie; **krilo** – skirt; **čevlji** – shoes; **rokavice** – gloves; **šal** – scarf.

7

1 Kaj raje nosiš, čevlje ali sandale? 2 Kaj raje nosiš, bluze ali puloverje? 3 Kaj raje nosiš, krila ali hlače? 4 Kaj raje nosiš, obleke ali kostime? 5 Kaj raje nosiš, očala ali leče?

8 (examples)

1 Samo gledam, hvala. 2 Iščem pulover za mojega brata. 3 Ne vem. Ali mi lahko pokažete nekaj moških puloverjev? 4 Modrega ali rjavega. 5 Najlepša hvala, pogledala bom še kje drugje.

9

1 manjše, večje; 2 bliže, dlje; 3 boljša, slabša; 4 cenejša, dražja; 5 bogatejši, revnejši.

10

1 Ali je Bled največje jezero v Sloveniji? 2 Ali je najlepše? 3 Če ni daleč, bi lahko šli tja en dan. Meni so všeč jezera. Vedno sem si želel videti Baikal. To je najglobje jezero. In tudi najbolj mrzlo. 4 Ne, Loch Ness je najglobje in najdaljše jezero na Škotskem, ampak ne na svetu.

11

Danes smo: šestnajstega petega; štiriindvajsetega tretjega; devetega sedmega; enaintridesetega šestega; četrtega prvega.

12 (examples)

1 bere; 2 Uči; 3 kupiti; 4 nosiš/nosite; 5 grem *or* moram iti, oblečem.

13

1 jo; 2 ga; 3 je; 4 mu; 5 ga; 6 jo, je.

14

1 slabe; 2 ugasni; 3 odprta; 4 blizu, poceni; 5 dobro; 6 počasi, vedno ima zamudo.

Translation of the dialogue for comprehension

ROBERT: Do you celebrate all birthdays like this?
SERGEJ: No, your birthday was special.
ROBERT: Why?
SERGEJ: Because you'll soon go back to England. We can't wait for your fiftieth birthday or engagement or wedding or christening . . .
ROBERT: Do you celebrate national holidays in Slovenia?
SERGEJ: Yes, but if there isn't one. . . Your birthday came really at the right time.
ROBERT: And what if no one has a birthday?
SERGEJ: Oh, we always find a reason to celebrate.

Slovene–English glossary

adijo	bye	**biti**	to be
ali	or, indicates a question	**blagajna (f.)**	till
		blizu	close by
Amerika	America	**bluza (f.)**	blouse
ampak	but	**bogat/-a/-o**	rich
ananas (m.)	pineapple	**boleti (bolim)**	to hurt, to ache
Anglija	England	**borovnica (f.)**	bilberry
avto (m.)	car	**branjevka (f.)**	greengrocer
avtobus (m.)	bus	**brat**	brother
badminton (m.)	badminton	**bratranec**	cousin (male)
baje	supposedly	**breskev (f.)**	peach
banka (f.)	bank	**bruhati (bruham)**	to vomit
bel/-a/-o	white	**cena (f.)**	price

cerkev (f.)	church	frizer/-ka	barber/
čaj (m.)	tea		hairdresser
čakati (čakam)	to wait	garaža (f.)	garage
četrt	quarter	garsonjera (f.)	studio flat
četrtek (m.)	Thursday	gasilci (pl.)	fire brigade
črn/-a/-o	black	gimnastika (f.)	gymnastics
čuden/-dna/-o	strange	glasba (f.)	music
da	that	glava (f.)	head
dan (m.)	day	glavna cesta (f.)	main road
danes	today	glavna jed (f.)	main meal
dati (dam)	to give	globok/-a/-o	deep
datum (m.)	date	gospa	Mrs
delati (delam)	to work	gospod	Mr
denar (m.)	money	gospodinja	housewife
dež (m.)	rain	gost (m.)	guest
deževati (dežuje)	to rain (it rains)	gost/-a/-o	heavy (traffic),
dežnik (m.)	umbrella		thick, dense
dežurni/-a/-o	on duty	gostilna (f.)	pub
dihati (diham)	to breathe	govoriti	to speak
dišati (dišim)	to smell nice	(govorim)	
dnevna soba (f.)	living-room	grd/-a/-o	ugly
dober/-bro/-bra	good, well, fine,	gripa (f.)	flu
dokument (m.)	document	grlo (n.)	throat
dolg/-a/-o	long	harmonika (f.)	accordion
doma	at home	hčerka	daughter
domov	to go home	hiša (f.)	house
dopoldan	morning	hlače (pl.)	trousers
dopoldne	in the morning	hladilnik (m.)	fridge
dopust (m.)	holiday	hoditi (hodim)	to walk, to
dovolj	enough		attend
driska	diarrhoea	hokej (m.)	hockey
drsališče (n.)	skating rink	hotel (m.)	hotel
družina (f.)	family	hoteti (hočem)	to want
družiti se z	to mix with	hrana (f.)	food
(družim se z)		hruška (f.)	pear
država (f.)	country	hvala	thank you
državljanstvo (n.)	nationality	igralec/-lka	actor
dvigalo (n.)	lift	igrati (igram)	to play
dvomiti	to doubt	imeti	to have
(dvomim)		imeti na	to have available
fižol (m.)	bean	razpolago	
Francija	France	in	and

iskati (iščem)	to look for		**kavč (m.)**	couch
Italija	Italy		**kihati (kiham)**	to sneeze
iti (grem)	to go		**kisel/-sla/-o**	sour
izbira (f.)	choice		**kitara (f.)**	guitar
izbrati (izberem)	to choose		**klavir (m.)**	piano
izmeriti (si) (izmerim)	to measure		**klet (f.)**	cellar
izplačati se (izplačam se)	to be worth while		**kljub temu**	in spite of this
izposoditi si (izposodim si)	to borrow		**ključ (m.)**	key
			knjiga (f.)	book
izstopiti (izstopim)	to exit		**knjigarna (f.)**	book shop
			koliko	how much, how many
izvolite	here you are		**kolikokrat**	how often, how many times
ja	yes			
jabolčni zavitek (m.)	apple strudel		**kolo (n.)**	bicycle
			kompas (m.)	compass
jabolko (n.)	apple		**kopalnica (f.)**	bathroom
jagoda (f.)	strawberry		**kos (m.)**	piece, slice
jahati (jaham)	to ride		**košarka (f.)**	basketball
jajce (n.)	egg		**kosilo (n.)**	lunch
jaz	I		**kostim (m.)**	suit (for a woman)
jed (f.)	meal		**kozarec (m.)**	glass
jedilni list (m.)	menu		**kratek/-tka/-o**	short
jedilni pribor (m.)	cutlery		**kravata (f.)**	tie
			kredit (m.)	loan
jesen (f.)	autumn		**krilo (n.)**	skirt
jesti (jem)	to eat		**križ (m.)**	cross, back (coll.)
jetra (pl.)	liver		**križanka (f.)**	crossword puzzle
jezero (n.)	lake		**krompir (m.)**	potato
jezik (m.)	tongue, language		**krožnik (m.)**	plate
jogurt (m.)	yoghurt		**kruh (m.)**	bread
jug	south		**kuhan/-a/-o**	cooked
juha (f.)	soup		**kuhinja (f.)**	kitchen
jutro (n.)	morning		**kupiti (kupim)**	to buy
kako	how		**kurjava (f.)**	heating
kakor hitro	as soon as		**(biti) lačen/-čna/-o**	(to be) hungry
kakorkoli	anyway, anyhow			
kašljati (kašljam)	to cough		**ladja (f.)**	ship
kateri	which one		**lahek/-hka/-o**	easy, light
kava (f.)	coffee		**lahko noč**	good night
kavarna (f.)	café		**lani**	last year

las (m.)/lasje (pl.)	hair	moder/-dra/-o	blue
lastnik/-ica	owner	mogoče	maybe, possibly
leče (pl.)	contact lenses	morati (moram)	must
led (m.)	ice	morda	maybe
lekcija (f.)	lesson	motiti (motim)	to disturb
lep/-a/-o	beautiful	mrzel/-zla/-o	cold
letališče (n.)	airport	muzej (m.)	museum
letalo (n.)	plane	na zdravje	cheers
leto (n.)	year	načrt (m.)	plan
letos	this year	najemnina (f.)	rent
likalnik (m.)	iron	najti (najdem)	to find
limona (f.)	lemon	naključje (n.)	chance
ljubezen (f.)	love	nalezljiv/-a/-o	contagious
ločen/-a	divorced	nameravati (nameravam)	to intend
luč (f.)	light	namizni tenis (m.)	table tennis
mačeha	stepmother		
majhen/-hna/-o	small	napisati (napišem)	to write
malenkost (f.)	trifle, small thing	napitnina (f.)	tip
malica (f.)	snack	napolniti (napolnim)	to fill up
malina (f.)	raspberry	napraviti (napravim)	to do, to make
malo	little		
malokrat	rarely	narediti (naredim)	to do, to make
mama	mother		
manjkati (manjkam)	to be missing	naročiti (naročim)	to order
marelica (f.)	apricot	naslov (m.)	address, title
med (m.)	honey	na svidenje	goodbye
meglen/-a/-o	foggy, hazy	natakar/-ica	waiter, waitress
menza (f.)	canteen	navadno, po navadi	usually
mešati (mešam)	to mix		
mesec (m.)	month	(biti) navajen/-a/-o	(to be) used to
mesnica (f.)	butcher's		
mesto (n.)	town	nazaj	back(wards)
mi	we	nečak	nephew
mimogrede	by the way	nečakinja	niece
mineralna voda (f.)	mineral water	nedelja (f.)	Sunday
misliti (mislim)	to think	nekaj	some, something
miza (f.)	table	Nemčija	Germany
mleko (n.)	milk	nemogoče	impossible
močen/-čna/-čno	strong		

neprijazen/-zna/-o	unfriendly	**odločiti se (odločim se)**	to decide
neslan/-a/-o	unsalted	**odpovedati (odpovem)**	to cancel, to give notice
nesrečen/-čna/-o	unhappy		
nesti (nesem)	to carry	**odpreti (odprem)**	to open
neudoben/-bna/-o	uncomfortable	**oglasiti se (oglasim se)**	to come round
neumen/-mna/-o	stupid	**oko (n.)**	eye
nevaren/-rna/-o	dangerous	**okus (m.)**	taste
nezanimiv/-a/-o	uninteresting	**okusen/-sna/-o**	tasty
nihče	no one, nobody	**omaka (f.)**	gravy
nikoli	never	**omara (f.)**	wardrobe
nobenkrat	never	**on**	he
noč	night	**ona**	she
noga (f.)	leg	**oni**	they
nogavice (pl.)	socks, tides	**ono**	it
nogomet (m.)	football	**opoldan**	noon
nos (m.)	nose	**opoldne**	at noon
nositi (nosim)	to carry, to wear	**oprostiti (oprostim)**	to excuse
nov/-a/-o	new		
novinar/-ka	journalist	**oseba (f.)**	person
nož (m.)	knife	**osebna izkaznica (f.)**	identification card
o	about		
obdržati (obdržim)	to keep	**ostati (ostanem)**	to stay
obisk (m.)	a visit	**otrok (m.)**	child
obleči (oblečem)	to wear	**ozdravljiv/-a/-o**	curable
obleka (f.)	dress, suit	**ozek/-zka/-o**	narrow
obljubiti (obljubim)	to promise	**pameten/-tna/-o**	clever
		papir (m.)	paper
obraz (m.)	face	**paradižnik (m.)**	tomato
obrok (m.)	meal course	**pečen/-a/-o**	fried, baked
očala (pl.)	spectacles	**pekarna (f.)**	bakery
oče, ata	father	**pes (m.)**	dog
očim	stepfather	**pešec**	pedestrian
oddahniti se (oddahnim se)	to rest, to recover breath	**petek (m.)**	Friday
		peti (pojem)	to sing
oddaja (f.)	broadcasting	**pijača (f.)**	drink, beverage
oddati (oddam)	to give in, away	**pisalna miza (f.)**	desk
oddelek (m.)	department	**pisatelj/-ica**	writer
odličen/-čna/-o	very good, superb	**pisati (pišem)**	to write
		pismo (n.)	letter
		pismonoša (m.)	postman

piti (pijem)	to drink	ponedeljek (m.)	Monday
pivo (n.)	beer	ponoči	at night, during
plašč (m.)	coat		the night
plavati (plavam)	to swim	ponuditi	to offer
plaža (f.)	beach	(ponudim)	
pljuča (pl.)	lungs	pooblastilo (n.)	authorization
počutiti se	to feel	pooblastiti	to authorize
(počutim se)		(pooblastim)	
podariti	to give as a	poper (m.)	pepper
(podarim)	present, to	popoldan	afternoon
	donate	popoldne	in the afternoon
podoben/-bna/-o	similar, alike	popraviti	to repair
podstrešje (n.)	attic	(popravim)	
pogovarjati se	to converse	poročen/-a	married
(pogovarjam se)		poročiti se	to get married
pogreb (m.)	funeral	(poročim se)	
pogrešati	to miss	poslati (pošljem)	to send
(pogrešam)		posoditi	to lend
pohištvo (n.)	furniture	(posodim)	
pohiteti	to hurry	pošta (f.)	post office
(pohitim)		postajati	to become
poizkusiti	to try	(postajam)	
(poizkusim)		postava (f.)	figure
pojutrišnjem	day after	postaviti	to put, to place
	tomorrow	(postavim)	
pokazati	to show	postelja (f.)	bed
(pokažem)		pošten/-a/-o	honest
poklic (m.)	profession,	poštni nabiralnik	letter box
	occupation	(m.)	
pol	half	potiti se	to sweat
poletje (n.)	summer	(potim se)	
polica (f.)	shelf	potni list (m.)	passport
policija (f.)	police	potovati	to travel
policist	policeman	(potujem)	
poln/-a/-o	full	potrebovati	to need
polt (f.)	complexion	(potrebujem)	
pomagati	to help	povabiti	to invite
(pomagam)		(povabim)	
pomemben/	important	povedati	to tell
-bna/-o		(povem)	
pomlad (f.)	spring	pozabiti	to forget
pomoč (f.)	help	(pozabim)	

pozanimati se	to find out	**približno**	approximately
(pozanimam se)		**prihodnje, drugo leto**	next year
pralni stroj (m.)	washing machine	**priimek (m.)**	surname
prav	correct, alright, OK	**prijatelj**	friend (male)
		prijateljica	friend (female)
pravo (n.)	law	**prijava (f.)**	declaration
pravzaprav	actually	**prijaviti**	to declare
prazen/-zna/-o	empty	**(prijavim)**	
predpisati	to prescribe	**prijazen/-zna/-o**	friendly
(predpišem)		**prikuha (f.)**	side dish
predsednik	president	**primer (m.)**	example
predvčerajšnjim	day before yesterday	**prinesti**	to bring
		(prinesem)	
pregled	check-up, medical examination	**pripraviti**	to prepare
		(pripravim)	
pregledati	to examine	**pristen/-tna/-o**	genuine, authentic, typical
(pregledam)			
prehitevati	to be fast	**priti (pridem)**	to come
(biti)	(to have a) cold	**prodajalec/-lka**	shop assistant
prehlajen/-a/-o		**profesor/-ica**	lecturer
prehod za pešce (m.)	zebra crossing	**promet (m.)**	traffic
		prositi (prosim)	to ask, to request
premikati	to move		
(premikam)		**prošnja (f.)**	application, request
prenočišče z zajtrkom	bed and breakfast		
		prostor (m.)	space
prenočiti	to stay overnight	**pulover (m.)**	pullover
(prenočim)		**pustiti (pustim)**	to leave
(biti) prepričan/-a/-o	(to be) sure	**radio (m.)**	radio
		ravno	just
presenečenje (n.)	surprise	**ravnokar**	just
presenetiti	to surprise	**razglednica (f.)**	postcard
(presenetim)		**razmišljati**	to think about
prevajalec/-lka	interpreter	**(razmišljam)**	
prevesti	to translate	**razočaran/-a/-o**	disappointed
(prevedem)		**razprodaja (f.)**	sale
previden/-dna/-o	careful	**razstava (f.)**	exhibition
preživeti	to survive	**rdeč/-a/-e**	red
(preživim)		**rebra (pl.)**	ribs
prha (f.)	shower	**reči (rečem)**	to say

red (m.)	order	**sin**	son
redko	rarely	**sir (m.)**	cheese
reka (f.)	river	**sit/-a**	full
rekreacijski center (m.)	leisure centre	**siv/-a/-o**	grey
		skrbeti (skrbim)	to worry
reportaža (f.)	report	**skromen/ -mna/-o**	modest
res	true		
resen/-sna/-o	serious	**slab/-a/-o**	bad
restavracija (f.)	restaurant	**sladek/-dka/-o**	sweet
reven/-vna/-o	poor	**sladica (f.)**	dessert
rezervacija (f.)	reservation	**sladoled (m.)**	ice-cream
riba (f.)	fish	**slan/-a/-o**	salty
riž (m.)	rice	**slika (f.)**	picture, photo-
rjav/-a/-o	brown		graph, painting
rojstni dan (m.)	birthday	**slikati (slikam)**	to take
roka (f.)	hand, arm		photographs
rokavice (pl.)	gloves	**sliva (f.)**	plum
rokomet (m.)	volleyball	**slovar (m.)**	dictionary
roža (f.)	flower	**Slovenija**	Slovenia
rumen/-a/-o	yellow	**slučaj (m.)**	chance
Rusija	Russia	**službeno potovanje (n.)**	business trip
sadje (n.)	fruit		
sadna kupa (f.)	fruit salad	**smejati se (smejim se)**	to smile, to laugh at
sam/-a	alone, on one's own		
		smeti (smem)	to be allowed
samopostrežna (f.)	supermarket	**smola (f.)**	bad luck
		smrdeti (smrdim)	to smell bad
sandali (pl.)	sandals		
sedaj	now	**smučati (smučam)**	to ski
sedeti (sedim)	to sit		
semafor (m.)	traffic light	**snaha**	daughter-in-law
servijeta (f.)	napkin, serviette	**sneg (m.)**	snow
sesalec (m.)	vacuum cleaner	**sobota (f.)**	Saturday
sestanek (m.)	meeting	**sodelavec/-vka**	colleague
sestra	sister	**sok (m.)**	juice
sestrična	cousin (female)	**sol (f.)**	salt
sever	north	**solata (f.)**	salad
shujšati (shujšam)	to lose weight	**sonce (n.)**	sun
		sosed/-eda	neighbour
sicer	namely	**spalnica (f.)**	bedroom
sigurno	certainly, definitely	**spodnje perilo (n.)**	underwear

spol (m.)	sex (m., f.)	**škornji (pl.)**	boots
(moški, ženski)		**Španija**	Spain
spomin (m.)	memory	**špinača (f.)**	spinach
za spomin	as a souvenir, memento	**športni park (m.)**	sports park
spomniti se (spomnim se)	to remember	**športno igrišče (n.)**	playground
sporočilo (n.)	message	**štedilnik (m.)**	cooker, stove
spoznati (spoznam)	to meet	**študent/-ka**	student
		tajnik/-ica	secretary
sprehod (m.)	walk	**tašča**	mother-in-law
srce (n.)	heart	**tast**	father-in-law
sreča (f.)	luck	**teči (tečem)**	to run
srečati (srečam)	to meet	**teden (m.)**	week
srečen/-čna/-o	happy	**telefon (m.)**	telephone
sreda (f.)	Wednesday	**telefonirati (telefoniram)**	to telephone
sredi	in the middle		
stanovanje (n.)	flat	**telefonska številka (f.)**	telephone number
star/-a/-o	old		
stara mama, babica	grandmother	**telo (n.)**	body
		temperatura (f.)	temperature
stari starši	grandparents	**tenis (m.)**	tennis
stari ata, dedek	grandfather	**termometer (m.)**	thermometer
starši	parents	**testenine (pl.)**	pasta
stati (stojim)	to stand	**teta**	aunt
steklenica (f.)	bottle	**težek/-žka/-o**	difficult, heavy
stol (m.)	chair	**ti**	you
stopnice (pl.)	stairs	**točen/-čna/-o**	exact, punctual, accurate
storiti (storim)	to do		
stranišče	lavatory	**toda**	but
stric	uncle	**topel**	warm
svak	brother-in-law	**torek (m.)**	Tuesday
svakinja	sister-in-law	**torta (f.)**	cake
svet (m.)	world	**tovornjak (m.)**	lorry
svetovati (svetujem)	to advise, to suggest	**trebuh (m.)**	belly
		trenutek (m.)	moment
svež/-a/-e	fresh	**trenutno**	at the moment
svinčnik (m.)	pencil	**trg, tržnica (f.)**	market
svoj/-a/-e	one's own	**trgovina (f.)**	shop
šal (m.)	scarf	**tri četrt**	three quarters
širok/-a/-o	wide	**trim steza (f.)**	running track
škatla (f.)	box	**tudi**	also

tukaj	here
tuš (m.)	shower
tuširati se	to have a
(tuširam se)	shower
učitelj/-ica	teacher
učiti se	to learn, to
(učim se)	study
učiti (učim)	to teach
udoben/-bna/-o	comfortable
uho (n.)	ear
ukrasti (ukradem)	to steal
ulica (m.)	street
drsanje (n.)	ice-skating
umreti (umrem)	to die
ura (f.)	time, watch, clock
uradni/-dna/-o	official
usta (pl.)	mouth
ustaviti (ustavim)	to stop
utrujen/-a/-o	tired
v kolikor	as far as
vaza (f.)	vase
važen/-žna/-o	important
včasih	sometimes
včeraj	yesterday
večer	evening
večerja (f.)	supper
večkrat, velikokrat	often
vedenje (n.)	behaviour
vedeti (vem)	to know
vedno, zmeraj	always
velik/-a/-o	big
veter (m.)	wind
vi	you (plural)
videti (vidim)	to see
vilica (f.)	fork
vino (n.)	wine
vlak (m.)	train
vnuk	grandson
vnukinja	granddaughter
voda (f.)	water

vogal (m.)	corner
vozniško dovoljenje (n.)	driving licence
vozovnica (f.)	ticket (bus, train)
vrat (m.)	neck
vreme (n.)	weather
vrniti se (vrnem se)	to get back
vrt (m.)	garden
vsekakor	by all means
biti všeč (with dative)	to like (something)
vzhod	east
vživeti se v (vživim se)	to get used to
vzrok (m.)	reason
vstopiti (vstopim)	to enter
WC (m.)	lavatory
zabava (f.)	party
začasen/-sna/-o	temporary
začeti (začnem)	to start, to begin
zadovoljen/ -ljna/-ljno	satisfied
zahod	west
zahvaliti se (zahvalim se)	to thank oneself
zajtrk (m.)	breakfast
zakaj	why
zaljubiti se (zaljubim se)	to fall in love
zamenjati (zamenjam)	to change
zanimiv/-a/-o	interesting
zaostajati	to be late
zapreti (zaprem)	close
zaradi	because of
zaročenec	fiancé
zaročenka	fiancée
zaslužiti (zaslužim)	to earn

zaspan/-a/-o	sleepy	zgodovina (f.)	history
zastonj	in vain, free	zima (f.)	winter
zato da	so that	zjutraj	in the morning
zato ker	because	zmrzovalnik	freezer
zavidati	to envy	(m.)	
(zavidam)		značaj (m.)	character
zaviti (zavijem)	to turn, to wrap	znamka (f.)	stamp
zboleti (zbolim)	to become ill	znan/-a/-o	to be famous,
zdavnaj	long ago		noted for
zdi se	it seems	zob (m.)	teeth
zdravilo (n.)	medicine	zrediti se	to put on weight
zdravje (n.)	health	(zredim se)	
zdravnik/-ica	doctor	že	already
zelen/-a/-o	green	žejen/-jna/-o	thirsty
zelenjava (f.)	vegetables	želeti (želim)	to wish, to
zelje (n.)	cabbage		desire
zelo	very	želodec (m.)	stomach
zet	son-in-law	živio	hello
zgodaj	early	žlica (f.)	spoon
zgoditi se	to happen	žlička (f.)	teaspoon
(zgodim se)			

English–Slovene glossary

about	**o**	always	**vedno, zmeraj**
accordion	**harmonika (f.)**	America	**Amerika**
actor	**igralec/-lka**	and	**in**
address, title	**naslov (m.)**	anyway, anyhow	**kakorkoli**
to advise, to	**svetovati**	apple	**jabolko (n.)**
suggest	**(svetujem)**	apple strudle	**jabolčni zavitek**
afternoon	**popoldan**		**(m.)**
in the afternoon	**popoldne**	application,	**prošnja (f.)**
airport	**letališče (n.)**	request	
to be allowed	**smeti (smem)**	approximately	**približno**
alone	**sam**	apricot	**marelica (f.)**
already	**že**	as soon as	**kakor hitro**
also	**tudi**	as far as	**v kolikor**

to ask	prositi (prosim)	body	telo (n.)
at the moment	trenutno	book	knjiga (f.)
attic	podstrešje (n.)	bookshop	knjigarna (f.)
aunt	teta	boots	škornji (pl.)
authorization	pooblastilo (n.)	to borrow	izposoditi si
to authorize	pooblastiti		(izposodim si)
	(pooblastim)	bottle	steklenica (f.)
autumn	jesen (f.)	box	škatla (f.)
to have	imeti na	bread	kruh (m.)
available	razpolago	breakfast	zajtrk (m.)
back (one's back)	hrbet (m.), (coll.)	to breathe	dihati (diham)
	križ (m.)	to bring	prinesti
backwards	nazaj		(prinesem)
bad	slab/-a/-o	broadcasting	oddaja (f.)
bad luck	smola (f.)	brother	brat
badminton	badminton (m.)	brother-in-law	svak
bakery	pekarna (f.)	brown	rjav/-a/-o
bank	banka (f.)	bus	avtobus (m.)
basketball	košarka (f.)	business trip	službeno
bathroom	kopalnica (f.)		potovanje (n.)
beach	plaža (f.)	but	ampak, toda
bean	fižol (m.)	butcher	mesnica (f.)
beautiful	lep/-a/-o	to buy	kupiti (kupim)
because	zato ker	by all means	vsekakor
because of	zaradi	by the way	mimogrede
to become	postajati	bye	adijo
	(postajam)	cabbage	zelje (n.)
to become ill	zboleti (zbolim)	café	kavarna (f.)
bed	postelja (f.)	cake	torta (f.)
bed and	prenočišče z	to cancel, to	odpovedati
breakfast	zajtrkom	give notice	(odpovem)
bedroom	spalnica (f.)	canteen	menza (f.)
beer	pivo (n.)	car	avto (m.)
behaviour	vedenje (n.)	careful	previden/-dna/-o
belly	trebuh (m.)	carry, to wear	nositi (nosim)
bicycle	kolo (n.)	cellar	klet (f.)
big	velik/-a/-o	certainly,	sigurno
bilberry	borovnica (f.)	definitely	
birthday	rojstni dan (m.)	chair	stol (m.)
black	črn/-a/-o	chance	naključje (n.),
blouse	bluza (f.)		slučaj (m.)
blue	moder/-a/-o	to change	zamenjati

	(zamenjam)	cousin (male)	**bratranec**
character	**značaj (m.)**	crossword puzzle	**križanka (f.)**
check-up,	**pregled**	curable	**ozdravljiv/-a/-o**
medical		cutlery	**jedilni pribor**
examination			**(m.)**
cheers	**na zdravje**	dangerous	**nevaren/-rna/-o**
cheese	**sir (m.)**	date	**datum (m.)**
child	**otrok (m.)**	daughter	**hčerka**
choice	**izbira (f.)**	daughter-in-law	**snaha**
to choose	**izbrati (izberem)**	day	**dan (m.)**
church	**cerkev (f.)**	day after	**pojutrišnjem**
clever	**pameten/-tna/-o**	tomorrow	
to close	**zapreti (zaprem)**	day before	**predvčerajšnjim**
close by	**blizu**	yesterday	
coat	**plašč (m.)**	to decide	**odločiti se**
coffee	**kava (f.)**		**(odločim se)**
cold	**mrzel/-zla/-o**	declaration	**prijava (f.)**
to be cold	**biti prehlajen**	to declare	**prijaviti**
	/-a/-o		**(prijavim)**
colleague	**sodelavec/-vka**	deep	**globok/-a/-o**
to come	**priti (pridem)**	department	**oddelek (m.)**
to come round	**oglasiti se**	dessert	**sladica (f.)**
	(oglasim se)	desk	**pisalna miza (f.)**
comfortable	**udoben/-bna/-o**	dictionary	**slovar (m.)**
compass	**kompas (m.)**	to die	**umreti (umrem)**
complexion	**polt (f.)**	difficult, heavy	**težek/-žka/-o**
contact lenses	**leče (pl.)**	disappointed	**razočaran/-a/-o**
contagious	**nalezljiv/-a/-o**	to disturb	**motiti (motim)**
to converse	**pogovarjati se**	divorced	**ločen/-a**
	(pogovarjam	to do	**napraviti**
	se)		**(napravim),**
cooked	**kuhan/-a/-o**		**narediti**
cooker, stove	**štedilnik (m.)**		**(naredim),**
corner	**vogal (m.)**		**storiti (storim)**
correct, alright,	**prav**	doctor	**zdravnik/-ica**
OK		document	**dokument (m.)**
couch	**kavč (m.)**	dog	**pes (m.)**
to cough	**kašljati**	doubt	**dvomiti**
	(kašljam)		**(dvomim)**
country	**država (f.)**	dress, suit	**obleka (f.)**
course	**obrok (m.)**	to drink	**piti (pijem)**
cousin (female)	**sestrična**	drink, beverage	**pijača (f.)**

driving licence	**vozniško dovoljenje (n.)**	to find	**najti (najdem)**
ear	**uho (n.)**	fire brigade	**gasilci (pl.)**
early	**zgodaj**	fish	**riba (f.)**
to earn	**zaslužiti (zaslužim)**	flat	**stanovanje (n.)**
		flower	**roža (f.)**
east	**vzhod**	foggy, hazy	**meglen/-a/-o**
easy, light	**lahek/-hka/-o**	food	**hrana (f.)**
to eat	**jesti (jem)**	football	**nogomet (m.)**
egg	**jajce (n.)**	to forget	**pozabiti**
empty	**prazen/-zna/-o**		**(pozabim)**
England	**Anglija**	fork	**vilica (f.)**
enough	**dovolj**	France	**Francija**
to enter	**vstopiti (vstopim)**	freezer	**zmrzovalnik (m.)**
		fresh	**svež/-a/-e**
evening	**večer (m.)**	Friday	**petek (m.)**
in the evening	**zvečer**	fridge	**hladilnik (m.)**
exact, punctual, accurate	**točen/-čna/-o**	fried, baked	**pečen/-a/-o**
		friend (female)	**prijateljica**
to examine	**pregledati (pregledam)**	friend (male)	**prijatelj**
		friendly	**prijazen/-zna/-o**
example	**primer (m.)**	fruit	**sadje (n.)**
exhibition	**razstava (f.)**	fruit salad	**sadna kupa (f.)**
to exit	**izstopiti (izstopim)**	full (not empty)	**poln/-a/-o**
		to be full up	**sit/-a**
to excuse	**oprostiti (oprostim)**	funeral	**pogreb (m.)**
		furniture	**pohištvo (n.)**
eye	**oko (n.)**	garage	**garaža (f.)**
face	**obraz (m.)**	garden	**vrt (m.)**
family	**družina (f.)**	genuine, authentic, typical	**pristen/-tna/-o**
(to be) famous, noted for	**znan/-a/-o**		
		Germany	**Nemčija**
to be fast	**prehitevati**	to get back	**vrniti se (vrnem se)**
father	**oče, ata**		
father-in-law	**tast**	to get used to	**vživeti se v (vživim)**
to feel	**počutiti se (počutim se)**	to give	**dati (dam)**
fiancé	**zaročenec**	to give as a present, to donate	**podariti (podarim)**
fiancée	**zaročenka**		
figure	**postava (f.)**	to give in, away	**oddati (oddam)**
to fill up	**napolniti (napolnim)**	glass	**kozarec (m.)**

gloves	rokavice (pl.)	to be at home	doma
to go	iti (grem)	honest	pošten/-a/-o
good night	lahko noč	honey	med (m.)
good, well, fine,	dober/-bro/-bra	hotel	hotel (m.)
goodbye	na svidenje	house	hiša (f.)
granddaughter	vnukinja	housewife	gospodinja
grandfather	stari ata, dedek	how	kako
grandmother	stara mama, babica	how much, how many	koliko
grandparents	stari starši	how often, how many times	kolikokrat
grandson	vnuk		
gravy	omaka (f.)	hungry	lačen/-čna/-o
green	zelen/-a/-o	to hurry	pohiteti (pohitim)
grey	siv/-a/-o		
guest	gost (m.)	to hurt, ache	boleti (bolim)
guitar	kitara (f.)	I	jaz
gymnastics	gimnastika (f.)	ice	led (m.)
hair	las (m.)	ice-cream	sladoled (m.)
hairdresser	frizer/-ka	ice-skating	umetnostno drsanje (n.)
half	pol		
hand, arm	roka (f.)	identification	osebna izkaznica (f.)
to happen	zgoditi se (zgodim se)	important	pomemben/-bna/-o, važen/-žna/-o
happy	srečen/-čna/-o		
to have	imeti (imam)		
he	on	impossible	nemogoče
head	glava (f.)	in the middle	sredi
health	zdravje (n.)	in spite of this	kljub temu
heart	srce (n.)	in vain, free	zastonj
heating	kurjava (f.)	to inform oneself	pozanimati se (pozanimam se)
heavy (traffic), thick, dense	gost/-a/-o		
hello	živio	to intend	nameravati (nameravam)
to help	pomagati (pomagam)	interesting	zanimiv/-a/-o
help	pomoč (f.)	interpreter	prevajalec/-lka
here you are	izvolite	to invite	povabiti (povabim)
here	tukaj		
history	zgodovina (f.)	it	ono
hockey	hokej (m.)	Italy	Italija
holiday	dopust (m.)	journalist	novinar/-ka
to go home	domov	juice	sok (m.)

just	**ravnokar, ravno**	to fall in love	**zaljubiti se (zaljubim se)**
to keep	**obdržati (obdržim)**	luck	**sreča (f.)**
		lunch	**kosilo (n.)**
key	**ključ (m.)**	lungs	**pljuča (pl.)**
kitchen	**kuhinja (f.)**	main meal	**glavna jed (f.)**
knife	**nož (m.)**	main road	**glavna cesta (f.)**
to know	**vedeti (vem)**	market	**trg (m.), tržnica (f.)**
lake	**jezero (n.)**		
last year	**lani**	to be married	**poročen/-a**
to be late	**zaostajati**	to get married	**poročiti se (poročim se)**
to laugh (see smile)		maybe, possibly	**mogoče, morda**
lavatory	**WC (m.)**	meal	**jed (f.)**
law	**pravo (n.)**	measure	**izmeriti (izmerim)**
to learn, study	**učiti se (učim se)**	medicine	**zdravilo (n.)**
to leave	**pustiti (pustim)**	to meet	**spoznati (spoznam), srečati (srečam)**
lecturer	**profesor/-ica**		
leg	**noga (f.)**		
leisure centre	**rekreacijski center (m.)**	meeting	**sestanek (m.)**
lemon	**limona (f.)**	memory	**spomin (m.)**
to lend	**posoditi (posodim)**	menu	**jedilni list (m.)**
		message	**sporočilo (n.)**
lesson	**lekcija (f.)**	milk	**mleko (n.)**
letter	**pismo (n.)**	mineral water	**mineralna voda (f.)**
letter-box	**poštni nabiralnik (m.)**	to miss	**manjkati (manjkam), pogrešati (pogrešam)**
lift	**dvigalo (n.)**		
light	**luč (f.)**		
to like	**biti všeč**		
little	**malo**	to mix	**mešati (mešam)**
liver	**jetra (pl.)**	to mix with a person	**družiti se z (družim se z)**
living-room	**dnevna soba (f.)**		
long	**dolg/-a/-o**	modest	**skromen/-mna/-o**
long ago	**zdavnaj**	moment	**trenutek (m.)**
to look for	**iskati (iščem)**	Monday	**ponedeljek (m.)**
to lose weight	**shujšati (shujšam)**	money	**denar (m.)**
		month	**mesec (m.)**
lorry	**tovornjak (m.)**	morning	**jutro**
love	**ljubezen (f.)**	mortgage	**kredit (m.)**

mother	**mama**	question	
mother-in-law	**tašča**	order	**red (m.)**
mouth	**usta (pl.)**	to order	**naročiti**
to move	**premikati**		**(naročim)**
	(premikam)	owner	**lastnik/-ica**
Mr	**gospod**	paper	**papir (m.)**
Mrs	**gospa**	parents	**starši**
museum	**muzej (m.)**	party	**zabava (f.)**
music	**glasba (f.)**	passport	**potni list (m.)**
must	**morati (moram)**	pasta	**testenine (pl.)**
namely	**sicer**	peach	**breskev (f.)**
napkin, serviette	**servijeta (f.)**	pear	**hruška (f.)**
narrow	**ozek/-zka/-o**	pedestrian	**pešec**
nationality	**državljanstvo**	pencil	**svinčnik (m.)**
	(n.)	pepper	**poper (m.)**
neck	**vrat (m.)**	person	**oseba (f.)**
to need	**potrbovati**	photograph	**slika (f.)**
	(potrebujem)	(picture,	
neighbour	**sosed/-a**	painting)	
nephew	**nečak**	piano	**klavir (m.)**
never	**nikoli, nobenkrat**	piece, slice	**kos (m.)**
new	**nov/-a/-o**	pineapple	**ananas (m.)**
next year	**prihodnje,drugo**	plan	**načrt (m.)**
	leto	plane	**letalo (n.)**
niece	**nečakinja**	plate	**krožnik (m.)**
night	**ponoči**	to play	**igrati (igram)**
nobody, no one	**nihče**	playground	**športno igrišče**
noon	**opoldan**		**(n.)**
at noon	**opoldne**	plum	**sliva (f.)**
north	**sever**	police	**policija (f.)**
nose	**nos (m.)**	policeman	**policist**
now	**sedaj**	poor	**reven/-vna/-o**
to offer	**ponuditi**	postcard	**razglednica (f.)**
	(ponudim)	post office	**pošta (f.)**
official	**uradni/-dna/-o**	potato	**krompir (m.)**
often	**večkrat,**	to prepare	**pripraviti**
	velikokrat		**(pripravim)**
old	**star/-a/-o**	to prescribe	**predpisati**
on duty	**dežurni/-a/-o**		**(predpišem)**
one's own	**svoj/-a/-e**	president	**predsednik**
to open	**odpreti (odprem)**	price	**cena (f.)**
or, indicates a	**ali**	profession,	**poklic (m.)**

occupation		Saturday	sobota (f.)
to promise	obljubiti	to say	reči (rečem)
	(obljubim)	scarf	šal (m.)
pub	gostilna (f.)	secretary	tajnik/-ica
pullover	pulover (m.)	to see	videti (vidim)
to put, to place	postaviti	to seem (it seems)	zdeti se (zdi se)
	(postavim)	to send	poslati (pošljem)
to put on	zrediti se	serious	resen/-sna/-o
weight	(zredim se)	she	ona
quarter	četrt	shelf	polica (f.)
radio	radio (m.)	ship	ladja (f.)
rain	dež (m.)	shop	trgovina (f.)
to rain	deževati	shop-assistant	prodajalec/-lka
rarely	malokrat, redko	short	kratek/-tka/-o
raspberry	malina	to show	pokazati
to read	brati (berem)		(pokažem)
reason	vzrok (m.)	shower	prha (f.), tuš
red	rdeč/-a/-e		(m.)
to remember	spomniti se	side dish	prikuha (f.)
	(spomnim se)	similar, alike	podoben/-bna/-o
rent	najemnina (f.)	to sing	peti (pojem)
to repair	popraviti	sister	sestra
	(popravim)	sister-in-law	svakinja
report	reportaža (f.)	to sit	sedeti (sedim)
reservation	rezervacija (f.)	skating rink	drsališče (n.)
rest, recover	oddahniti se	to ski	smučati
breath	(oddahnim se)		(smučam)
restaurant	restavracija (f.)	skirt	krilo (n.)
ribs	rebra (pl.)	sleepy	zaspan/-a/-o
rice	riž (m.)	Slovenia	Slovenija
rich	bogat/-a/-o	small	majhen/-hna/-o
to ride	jahati (jaham)	to smell bad	smrdeti
river	reka (f.)		(smrdim)
running track	trim steza (f.)	to smell nice	dišati (dišim)
Russia	Rusija	to smile, laugh	smejati se
salad	solata (f.)	at	(smejim se)
sale	razprodaja (f.)	snack	malica (f.)
salt	sol (f.)	to sneeze	kihati (kiham)
salted	slan/-a/-o	snow	sneg (m.)
sandals	sandali (pl.)	so that	zato da
satisfied	zadovoljen/	socks	nogavice (pl.)
	-ljna/-ljno	some	nekaj

something	**nekaj**	Sunday	**nedelja (f.)**
sometimes	**včasih**	supermarket	**sampostrežna**
son	**sin**		**(f.)**
son-in-law	**zet**	supper	**večerja (f.)**
soup	**juha (f.)**	supposedly	**baje**
sour	**kisel/-sla/-o**	sure	**prepričan/-a/-o**
south	**jug**	surname	**priimek (m.)**
space	**prostor (m.)**	to survive	**preživeti**
Spain	**Španija**		**(preživim)**
to speak	**govoriti**	to sweat	**potiti se (potim**
	(govorim)		**se)**
spectacles	**očala (pl.)**	sweet	**sladek/-dka/-o**
spinach	**špinača (f.)**	to swim	**plavati (plavam)**
spoon	**žlica (f.)**	table	**miza (f.)**
sports park	**športni park**	table tennis	**namizni tenis**
	(m.)		**(m.)**
spring	**pomlad (f.)**	to take	**slikati (slikam)**
stairs	**stopnice (pl.)**	photographs	
stamp	**znamka (f.)**	taste	**okus (m.)**
to stand	**ostati (stojim)**	tasty	**okusen/-sna/-o**
to start, begin	**začeti (začnem)**	tea	**čaj (m.)**
to stay	**stati (ostanem)**	to teach	**učiti (učim)**
to stay	**prenočiti**	teacher	**učitelj/-ica**
overnight	**(prenočim)**	teaspoon	**žlička (f.)**
to steal	**ukrasti**	teeth	**zobje (pl.)**
	(ukradem)	telephone	**telefon (m.)**
stepfather	**očim**	to telephone	**telefonirati**
stepmother	**mačeha**		**(telefoniram)**
stomach	**želodec (m.)**	telephone	**telefonska**
to stop	**ustaviti**	number	**številka (f.)**
	(ustavim)	to tell	**povedati**
strange	**čuden/-dna/-o**		**(povem)**
strawberry	**jagoda (f.)**	temperature	**temperatura (f.)**
street	**ulica (m.)**	temporary	**začasen/-sna/-o**
strong	**močen/-čna/-čno**	tennis	**tenis (m.)**
student	**študent/-ka**	terminal (illness)	**neozdravljiv/-a/-o**
studio flat	**garsonjera (f.)**	to thank oneself	**zahvaliti se**
stupid	**neumen/-mna/-o**		**(zahvalim se)**
suit (for a	**kostim (m.)**	thank you	**hvala**
woman)		that	**da**
summer	**poletje (n.)**	thermometer	**termometer (m.)**
sun	**sonce (n.)**	they	**oni**

to think	**misliti (mislim)**	unfriendly	**neprijazen/**
to think about	**razmišljati**		**-zna/-o**
	(razmišljam)	unhappy	**nesrečen/-čna/-o**
thirsty	**žejen/-jna/-o**	uninteresting	**nezanimiv/-a/-o**
this year	**letos**	unsalted	**neslan/-a/-o**
three quarters	**tri četrt**	to be used to	**navajen/-a/-o**
throat	**grlo (n.)**	usually	**navadno, po**
Thursday	**četrtek (m.)**		**navadi**
tie	**kravata (f.)**	vacuum cleaner	**sesalec (m.)**
ticket	**vozovnica (f.)**	vase	**vaza (f.)**
till	**blagajna (f.)**	vegetables	**zelenjava (f.)**
time, watch,	**ura (f.)**	very	**zelo**
clock		very well	**odličen/-čna/-o**
tip	**napitnina (f.)**	visit	**obisk (m.)**
tired	**utrujen/-a/-o**	volleyball	**rokomet (m.)**
today	**danes**	to vomit	**bruhati**
tomato	**paradižnik (m.)**		**(bruham)**
tongue, language	**jezik (m.)**	to wait	**čakati (čakam)**
tooth	**zob (m.)**	waiter	**natakar/-ica**
town	**mesto (n.)**	walk	**sprehod (m.)**
traffic	**promet (m.)**	to walk, attend	**hoditi (hodim)**
traffic light	**semafor (m.)**	to want	**hoteti (hočem)**
train	**vlak (m.)**	wardrobe	**omara (f.)**
to translate	**prevesti**	warm	**topel/-pla/-o**
	(prevedem)	washing	**pralni stroj (m.)**
to travel	**potovati**	machine	
	(potujem)	water	**voda (f.)**
trifle, small thing	**malenkost (f.)**	we	**mi**
trousers	**hlače (pl.)**	weather	**vreme (n.)**
true	**res**	Wednesday	**sreda (f.)**
to try	**poizkusiti**	week	**teden (m.)**
	(poizkusim)	west	**zahod**
Tuesday	**torek (m.)**	which one	**kateri**
to turn (left,		white	**bel/-a/-o**
right)	**zaviti (zavijem),**	why	**zakaj**
to turn (around)	**vrteti (vrtim)**	wide	**širok/-a/-o**
ugly	**grd/-a/-o**	wind	**veter (m.)**
umbrella	**dežnik (m.)**	wine	**vino (n.)**
uncle	**stric**	winter	**zima (f.)**
uncomfortable	**neudoben/-bna/-o**	to wish, to	**želeti (želim)**
underwear	**spodnje perilo**	desire	
	(n.)	to work	**delati (delam)**

world	**svet (m.)**	year	**leto (n.)**
to worry	**skrbeti (skrbim)**	yellow	**rumen/-a/-o**
to be worth	**izplačati se**	yes	**ja**
while	**(izplačam se)**	yesterday	**včeraj**
to wrap	**zaviti (zavijem)**	you	**ti**
to write	**pisati (pišem),**	you (plural)	**vi**
	napisati	yoghurt	**jogurt (m.)**
	(napisem)	zebra crossing	**prehod za pešce**
writer	**pisatelj/-ica**		**(m.)**

Grammatical index

The numbers below refer to the lessons in the book.